Growing Wisdom,
Growing Wonder

Growing Wisdom,

Helping Your Child Learn

BY ELIZABETH M. GREGG

ILLUSTRATIONS BY *Sally Reynolds Motley*

Growing Wonder

from Birth Through Five Years

AND JUDITH D. KNOTTS

PREFACE BY *Dr. T. Berry Brazelton*

MACMILLAN PUBLISHING CO., INC.

NEW YORK

Macmillan Publishing Co., Inc.
866 Third Avenue, New York, N.Y. 10022
Collier Macmillan Canada, Ltd.

Library of Congress Cataloging in Publication Data

Gregg, Elizabeth M
    Growing wisdom, growing wonder.

    Includes index.
    1. Cognition in children—Problems, exercises, etc.
2. Concept learning—Problems, exercises, etc.
I. Knotts, Judith D., joint author.   II.   Title.
BF723.C5G73 1980   155.4'13   80–13456
ISBN 0–02–545580–X

---

10   9   8   7   6   5   4   3   2   1

Printed in the United States of America

*We dedicate this book
to our husbands, Joe and Charlie;
to our children,
Dan, Laura, Sam, Joby, Charlie, Chris, and Liz;
and to all the children
who have touched our lives,
causing us to grow in wisdom
and in wonder.*

Contents

Preface

*W*HEN MRS. GREGG ASKED ME to contribute an introduction to a book she and Judith Knotts were writing, I felt it a fair trade for all she had taught me in the past. She is the mother of three of my first patients—Dan, Laura, and Sam. When I was first beginning to realize the need that new parents have for the support that books can give them, I asked my patients to bring me anecdotes and experiences they were having in day-to-day living at home. These "gifts" formed the base for my *Infants and Mothers* and *Toddlers and Parents*. Betty was a "new" mother but one who had had professional experience in some of the top-notch nursery schools in Boston. She had learned how to work with children, how to play with them, and how to learn with them. She was an expert teacher and observer who had learned how to "get inside" the children she knew. They adored her, and they quickly learned how to "get inside" her. Her capacity to relate to them and to feel life the way they did seemed to me to be a prerequisite for working with small children, for they *know* when you are on their wavelength—and when you're not.

When her own children came along, she went through the same kind of adjustment that I have seen in many, many intelligent, talented, trained young women when they must trade their satisfying careers for the relative isolation of a new, demanding family. Wanting desperately to feel committed to and rewarded by her new family, such a woman may feel at sea and even "empty," despite very satisfying times with her children. This will certainly reflect on the child's experience and will give them all—mother, father, and child—a less rewarding, less fulfilling time than they could have.

Since I saw this as a rather common experience for young mothers, fathers, and their babies, I have been looking for ways to fill that gap, to back them up at such a time, intellectually as well as emotionally. That was the reason I wrote my books, and I think it is the purpose of this one. It seems to me that this book is the thoughtful and rewarding effort of two mothers who have lived through times when they could have used just such a "cookbook." For this is, indeed, a book of ideas that lead to rewarding interactions—interactions between a wondering child and a somewhat distracted, overwhelmed mother who wants to get on the child's wavelength in ways that matter.

Books can't be of much help, but they can surely offer caring parents the rewards of an understanding of common experiences, of ideas, of reinforcement for all the things a parent wants so desperately to do for his or her children. This book is full of ideas that will help them to do what they may do anyway. But having it to refer to, to back one up, to give one a richer matrix of ideas is confirming. Being a parent no longer feels so lonely. For the child himself becomes the parent's companion, a rewarding, responsive "person."

This book does *not* say it is necessary for parents to *teach* a child all the time, for that can make for a somewhat pressured parent–infant relationship. It does say that learning together can be fun, and if it is, the child's experience in growing up will be richer. I feel strongly that what children learn is relatively unimportant compared to *how* they learn it. If they learn in a climate of rewarding interactions with the adults around them, if they learn by testing things out and mastering them for themselves, they will not only love learning but they will learn to value themselves. And that's surely the most important lesson. This book can lead parents on many different and rewarding paths for learning with and about their small children.

T. Berry Brazelton
Children's Hospital Medical Center
Harvard Medical School

This Introduction was written while the author was supported by the Robert Wood Johnson Foundation, The Carnegie Corporation, and the National Institute of Mental Health.

If a child is to keep alive his inborn sense of wonder,
he needs the companionship of at least one adult who
can share it, rediscovering with him the joy, excitement,
and mystery of the world we live in.

from *The Sense of Wonder*
by Rachel Carson

Growing Wisdom,
Growing Wonder

Chapter 1

A Message to Parents

THE LATEST WORD from the experts is that what happens to a child before he* gets to school is all important for his future emotional, social, and intellectual development. Their message seems to be that diapers and discipline are no longer enough. This puts you as parents in a muddle if you are supposed to create security, educate, and live a little yourselves too! If learning really begins at birth, what is it children learn? Can parents help or does it just happen? We know parents can help and have their own lives too, but how do the experts' findings translate to your kitchens and living rooms, your busy lives?

As parents and professionals we found the experts' research exciting because it confirmed our everyday experiences with young children. Jean Piaget, the French psychologist, has written many volumes describing children's thinking. His research explains how sensory explorations are the basis for concepts and abstract thought. He shows that children, as they lick, sniff, and touch, are performing activities of the mind! T. Berry Brazelton, the Boston pediatrician, emphasizes in his research and writing parent-child relationships and individual styles. His work confirms our feeling that a caring relationship is all important and sets the stage for intellectual growth. Maria Montessori, the Italian physician and educator, is known for developing play materials which lead children to discovery through using all their senses. At home we watch our own children make discoveries through everyday materials,

---

* In this book we have consistently referred to your child as "he" as a matter of convenience. If you have a girl, read "she" for "he." You can rest assured that every activity is equally suitable for either sex.

just as children do in Montessori classes with special equipment. The studies of Harvard professor Burton White describe the home environment and the parent-child interaction which produce capable and independent children. His research confirms our mothering style—being available to our children but not overwhelming them. M.I.T. linguist Noam Chomsky has written about the complexity of language development and turned our attention to the importance of language and its place in the thought process.

We think *Growing Wisdom, Growing Wonder* can help you by putting these research theories into practice, by showing how your child learns and how his mind works. We think understanding how a child learns can make parenthood more exciting. Daily life with a preschooler is very physical for parents, lots of laundry and mess, lots of wearying caretaking. Some days it's hard to remember that a child's preschool years are basic and vital to his emotional, social, and intellectual growth: most days you wonder what happened to your own emotional, social, and intellectual growth! With diapering, feeding, and following the trail of an incredibly restless explorer who crawls, totters, or climbs through your once-neat and attractive home, you lose your grip on the important stages he's galloping through. By knowing these stages and understanding your part in them, life is bound to be more interesting for you too!

As professionals, we have seen this emphasis on the early years make parents anxious. Parents know these years are very important, but parents often do not know what they should and should not do. We see parents who care trying to find time and space to "educate" their children. They buy expensive "toys that teach," and plunk their toddlers religiously in front of "Sesame Street." They take time to sit down with their children, going over letters, shapes, and numbers. These parents have books full of ideas and activities, but no organized picture of the sequence and overall framework of their child's learning. Yet they spend time, money, and emotional energy trying to be teachers. Children learn best not by being "taught" by parents, but by "doing" and by discovering as they bump through life day in and day out. They learn best with the approval of a caring adult who talks to them about what they are doing.

We have guided our own seven children through the preschool years, even to college, and have seen the results of what we did and *did not* do with our children. We did not sit down and teach our own children. We mixed it all into the days full of shopping trips, laundry sorting, and meal making. We enjoyed our children and they have prospered. By knowing what was best to do for our children we had time for our own lives too.

If you as a parent can understand how a child learns through daily activities you can create an environment where you and your child are free to be independent yet know when and how to interact. You can enjoy your child free of the over-serious instructor-pupil role. We think parents need to know what the best activities are—activities that are normal and possible in an ordinary household. We'll show you how your child learns by "doing" during his daily eating, playing, and exploring. Many of the activities we have picked are what any child may do anyway, but we'll show you how your child's mind works and grows when he does these things. We added some of our zany ideas that you might not think of. These ideas will spark ideas of your own. Our book should brighten the day for you and your child. We offer a fresh perspective on everyday tasks and everyday objects. We know young parents have limited time and money, so we won't send you to the store with a list of necessary materials to buy or to the workshop to saw and sand. Special toys and equipment are not needed.

It's hard to believe that your child's simple daily explorations could lead to later high-level thinking. Adults remember learning beginning in school, a dimly recalled blur of flash cards, numbers, and letters leading up to the all important reading of that first "Dick and Jane" book. *Growing Wisdom, Growing Wonder* will show you that learnings precede letters and numbers, clocks and calendars. There are many experiences between crib and classroom. Lying in the crib your infant receives impressions without form or meaning. Gradually, bit by bit, the passing sensations take on meaning. By the time your child is two he can name a running whir of fur "dog" or "cat," can tell an apple from an orange, a cookie from a cracker.

What learnings create order out of chaos and ideas from sensations? During the first two years your child's interactions with the world bring knowledge in every area of learning: texture, size, shape, color, sound, position in space, temperature, taste and smell, weight, speed, time, number, volume, feelings, and relationships. In each of these areas your child acquires basic concepts, the tools he needs to sort out his world. Knowledge about shape and size and texture help him tell the dog from the cat, the apple from the orange, the cookie from the cracker. Concepts in each area of learning are the clues to likenesses and differences, the tools of classification and abstraction. Without these tools the dog and cat, apple and orange, cookie and cracker cannot be differentiated. Layer by layer, experiences change your child's perspective. As he grows older, this dynamic process leads to thinking with greater and greater complexity. The body of knowledge in each concept area becomes more sophisticated with every year. The toddler may call all four-legged creatures "doggie," but the five-year-old can distinguish a St. Bernard from a Shetland pony because of his experiences with color and shape, size and texture.

What about all these different concepts of size, shape, color, and texture? You may accept the fact that a child must learn each of them to know what the world is about, but does the *way* that he learns make any difference? Isn't a book's color picture just as good as playing with an orange? No, it isn't.

Concepts cannot be fully understood by looking at pictures or by memorizing the word. They have to be experienced. Concepts are not learned overnight: they must be met in a variety of settings over a long period of time. You can't teach your child "round" (or "orange" or "soft" or "big") by finding one "round" in the world and pointing it out. The round of the cookie is different from the round of the orange. The child who has munched a round cookie, rolled a round orange, curled his body up round, been around the block, felt and seen a ball as round, danced "Ring Around the Rosie," and put a bracelet around his arm has a much more developed concept of round than a child who has learned "round" in a two-dimensional picture book. When all the pieces of the abstract concept "round" (or "orange" or "soft" or "big") fit together, this concept experienced many ways becomes a word, a thought, an idea. This idea is something to talk about with family and friends. The concepts in this book are basic to your child's knowledge of the world and his readiness for first grade and life. Tests of school readiness and language development examine these same areas.

Language development is a complex and sophisticated process. In this book language development is described in relation to the concept areas. As your child acquires the understanding of concept words, he can use the concepts to identify and classify the dog and cat, the cookie and cracker, the apple and orange. The richer the child's experience, the richer will be his language and abstract thought.

Children who have mastered the concepts of color, size, shape, and so forth have an order to their world. They can use these concepts as tools to approach any new experience. Once these concepts are fully understood children have the freedom to communicate and to use their minds flexibly. A child who learns this way has powers of reasoning well beyond the child who has memorized the ABCs. Much of a child's later school learning will be from books, reading the words that describe the world. The child who has not only memorized the names of shapes, but run his fingers around the edges feeling what happens to form in curves and corners, who has combined and recombined shapes in designs, will marvel at the design of a flower and the shape of a bird's beak. The child who has stood close to an elephant and looked up at its great size, who has carried a heavy weight and imitated the elephant's lumbering walk and trumpeting sound, will have rich images far more evocative than the child who identifies the elephant by its distinctive shape in a picture book. When he reads Kipling, the child's mind will be filled with the weight and size and even the smell of the beast.

In schools the new curriculums emphasize this same conceptual approach. Active learning has replaced memorization. Two generations ago history was names, places, and dates, not cause and effect relationships; science was facts and formulas, not the process of scientific reasoning; math was chanting times tables, not the "new math" of theoretical understandings. The world's knowledge can no longer be reduced to simple charts and chants, studied and recited. A child with lively curiosity who has the tools to approach any new subject is ready for the knowledge explosion. Each enthusiastic learning begins in the crib and goes well beyond college.

There are a number of intellectual tasks which cut across all areas of learning. They can be found in each chapter. Children must learn to group objects and ideas in classifications and to order them in sequence. They must grasp the notions of cause and effect, and change. They must understand the use and function of things. Each chapter will contribute to your understanding of your child's growth in these general areas.

There are many different ways to learn and many kinds of learners. There are the touchers and lookers and the movers and shakers. It's fun to discover your own and your child's special style. In *Growing Wisdom, Growing Wonder* there are more activities than any one parent or child would ever undertake. The wealth of suggestions is not meant to overwhelm you or to overstimulate your child. You want your child to be an eager learner interested in the world, all senses alert, tingling and ready to use. You want your child to like himself for the particular kind of child he is. Respect his interest and pace. If you try to rush your child to activities or through stages, you get only a sense of his gaps, rather than a view of his strengths. If you reduce the concepts in this book to three-by-five file cards and follow your child around checking off his knowledge, you will produce a child who tunes out and turns away. If your six-month-old is enjoying the feel of an orange, that's not your cue to dump the fruit bowl in his lap. Children do not need a concept a minute. Learning takes place slowly and repetitively for young children. If your toddler masters one four-year-old task, that does not mean he's as mature as a four-year-old across the board. Overexpectations alert a child to unreachable goals that may cause him to stop trying.*

The relationship between you and your child is what determines his attitude toward learning. You have plenty of time together to work out your interests and the pace that is best for you both. You can't be something you're not or make your child be something he isn't. There's no perfect formula that fits every child and parent. Trust yourself to work out the one that fits you both. You'll have a sense of when your child is eager for new experiences or happy with repetition of old ones. Accepting yourself and your child with your particular strengths, talents, and interests will make you eager learners together. First you learn about each other, then you teach each other about the world.

Children's physical, social, and emotional development are all a part of the growing intellectual process and part of this book. Children's physical capabilities and drives are what get them into a relationship with an ever-widening circle of people and things. Children's social growth can be encouraged if you know what to expect of each age and stage. Children's emotional development is dependent upon happy capable parents. We think the more you know about children and the more you are able to enjoy your child's growth, the better you'll feel about each other. The format of our book will let you know what concepts are learned at what age. Some are more important, some are more complicated. Some are barely grasped in preschool, but together they make the whole, your child's world.

We think a little practice in looking at the world the way your child looks at it will be exciting for you. Watching your child make discoveries will sharpen your senses too. In this book the joy of watching a child learn is woven through the whole day in the shape of a leaf, the feel of cat's fur, the sound of the wind, the taste of honey, and the texture of toast. Messes there will be, effort there will be, but we think some of your tears of frustration will give way to laughter if you know the what's and why's of your child's explorations. It all goes round in a circle: when you and your child share day by day feeling, smelling, tasting, looking, listening, and talking, you enjoy each other—and the trust and the communication grow. It's a good beginning!

* The ages in this book are for your convenient referral. Children are far too complex to fit any fixed norm. Expect your individual child to have a great deal of variation from the average child described in this book, and read about the ages both above and below your child's age.

Chapter 2

"Little Drops of Water,
Little Grains of Sand"
How a Child Learns
About Texture

SHOULD A PARENT CARE if his child is knowledgeable about texture? Would experiences with textures train your child for anything but fashion design? Every child must have experiences with touch and textures for normal intellectual and emotional development. Piaget, the French psychologist, has discovered that children learn by doing; they mouth, grasp, and handle everything in reach. Reaching out for food or comfort and finding pleasant and rewarding experiences is the beginning of the infant's intellectual, social, and emotional growth. If interaction with the world is stimulating and interesting, an infant will learn to reach again, and engage in a reciprocal relationship with his environment.

Touch is not only a way of learning about the world, but a way of enjoying it. Museums in major cities are establishing "please touch" exhibits for children, an acknowledgment of the importance of touch in children's learning. The bygone era of the English prammed or play-penned toddler isolated from his surroundings is being replaced by the carrier-toted and tag-along toddler exploring the world about him, free to touch and be touched. Schools are filled with textured numbers and letters to handle as well as observe. Art and carpentry areas invite children to explore and create with textures. For all ages texture provides an avenue for learning and pleasure.

The suggestions in each age section are to get you thinking; to have ideas of your own, to see things in your house which would comfort or stimulate your child. Our ideas are not a laundry list of "must do's." If you don't have a chenille bedspread, don't buy one. If your husband doesn't have a hairy chest, don't turn him in! Let your own good sense and creativity take over. Develop your own and your child's style.

TEXTURE CONCEPT WORDS

Least Difficult	*More Difficult*	*Most Difficult*
soft—hard	smooth—rough	stiff
wet—dry	sharp	firm
		slick
		dull

Many texture words, such as those listed below, are determined from experiences with objects: furry, stringy, sticky, bumpy, prickly, spongy, creamy, sandy, and rubbery.

The Infant: Birth to Eight Months or Crawling Age *You Bring the World to Your Infant*

Touch speaks to the infant first. The world is known through touch long before your child has words to describe his experiences. Recent research has shown that a newborn is more affected by his surroundings than was previously thought. Before birth, babies live in a warm protective environment. The contrast between this environment and the world of light, noise, and confusion after birth is great. Dr. Leboyer, the pioneer in the handling of babies just after birth, advocates soft light, warm water, and comfortable swaddling to lessen the shock from womb to world. The ancient art of infant body massage as practiced in many primitive cultures is being tried by our own more urbane society.

Parents can create an environment which will be comfortable and secure if they are aware of the importance of texture in a baby's life. Lying in crib with vision and hearing barely developed, an infant first learns about the world by touch. Through touch his earliest movements find the breast or bottle. Babies feel with their whole body, from head to toe. Even at a few weeks, contrasts of texture can begin to stimulate an infant's skin and arouse his awareness of the world. You can stimulate his earliest curiosity by providing variety when your baby is ready for it. Watch your child: get to know his special pace and interests. The first textures a baby will experience are his clothes, his bedding, his food, and you!

PEOPLE

Infants notice the textures of skin and clothes as you hold them. They feel textures in their mouths, on their cheeks, on their feet. Infants are quick to associate certain textures with comfort. The mother who simply cannot quiet her wailing infant to get back downstairs to her dinner party may be dealing with the baby's reaction to her prickly lamé dress instead of the feel of the old furry bathrobe he associates with nighttime comforting. Be aware of what your baby is held against and his reaction

to it. Mommy's soft breast feels very different from Daddy's hairy chest; Daddy's shaved cheek in the morning feels different from bristle at night. Infants need the experience of change, but they may react to it by restlessness or surprise.

At about three or four months of age infants begin to be less frantic about their needs. They start to notice and interact with the world around them. They are actively touching those things that touch them, at first accidentally, then purposefully as hand and foot coordination develop. As you care for your infant, lifting and carrying him from bed to bath, watch his reactions. Is he a "snuggler" who cradles in your arms or a "struggler" who is aching to be free? The "snuggler" may enjoy being held cheek to cheek, while the "struggler" may be tugging at your hair, experiencing texture in his own way. At changing time the "snuggler" may like being stroked gently on his back or tummy while the "struggler" may need a more vigorous rubdown. We know there are as many different kinds of parents as there are babies. Our advice is to be yourself. If you favor the papoose style and carry your infant in a carrier sling or resting on one hip while you move through the day, fine. If you prefer a one-session frolic on the rug, fine. The important thing is to expose your baby to texture in the world in a way you both enjoy. An infant will be surprised and interested in the feel of your wool sweater, tweed jacket, fur collar, corduroy jacket or jumper, slick raincoat, starched shirt, or velour sweater. Exposing your baby to such things will start him learning the difference between "smooth" and "rough."

CLOTHING AND COVERINGS

Infants react not only to your clothing, but also to their own. Infants' clothing comes in a variety of fabrics from cool stiff "wash and wear" to fuzzy acrylic jump suits. The season, be it hot or cold, the efficiency of your furnace or air conditioner, or the body temperature of your infant will determine to some extent what you put on him. One infant may burble contentedly swaddled in layers; another may fight and struggle if hemmed in. When you are dressing your infant let his hands and feet be free to feel and explore. (The thumb sucker will fret if he gets a terry-cloth-covered fist instead.) Let his whole body wiggle and roll on different surfaces (sometimes with no clothes on). At a few months of age infants begin to establish preferences for certain kinds of textures. One infant may lie happily with an angora bonnet tucked around his head, while another may fret at anything with more tickle than corduroy. Hardened plastic pants or stiff disposable diapers may keep some babies from settling to sleep, while others will wear these without fuss.

After a few months, infants discover their feet and enjoying pulling and tugging at foot coverings; they should be allowed to experience the victory of pulling off a bootie. When you find yourself annoyed or angry at that little foot waving in a cool breeze, haul out his footed stretch suit and you are the victor. For days when he's in charge, try these:

- Smooth socks (watch that your infant doesn't stuff them in his mouth and choke)

- Ribbed corduroy booties
- Knitted bumpy booties from Great Aunt Sally

Changes in blankets and sheets can stimulate too. Sometimes your infant will like to be swaddled or snuggled tightly in soft fabric; at other times he will want to squirm on a rougher surface. Your infant may enjoy rolling from one texture to another. For variety in swaddling, snuggling, and rolling try a smooth cool sheet, a fuzzy wool or orlon blanket, a waffle-weave diaper or honeycombed woven blanket, or the slippery satins of nylon. Some textures not manufactured for babies can be included: a terry-cloth towel, a square of wide- or narrow-wale corduroy, a piece of velour. Just pink the edges of any nice cloth you have and save the price of a receiving blanket.

Parents vary in their willingness to put a baby anywhere besides a crib or carriage. Perhaps it should depend on the state of your housekeeping and the number of people or pets that might step on your floor-based baby. If you dare put your infant on the floor, choose a floor covering from the suggestions above. The contrasting textures will stimulate a wiggling, thumping baby.

Don't always put your infant in the middle of the floor or the crib. Instead give him something he can kick against—a chair, a wall, or the sofa—so his feet can discover the textures. Put a living room bolster or a big firm cardboard box (a liquor store box is very sturdy) at the foot of the crib and cover it with a bath towel or beach towel, a tufted bed-spread, or any other textured blankets noted above.

FOOD

Infants experience texture as well as taste in their food. The breast-fed baby may reject the bottle nipple because the texture is unfamiliar. All young babies' swallowing reflexes are immature, so they cannot handle lumps or solids. Even so, babies vary greatly in their preferences for texture, such as in the thickness of cereal or strained fruits and vegetables. Advice differs on when to introduce cereals, fruits, and vegetables to a baby and when to move to firmer textures. Within the framework of your pediatrician's advice, experiment with a variety of textures to find out what your baby prefers.

A teething baby who can hold a cookie, cracker, or biscuit in his hand will enjoy this new texture even though he still prefers smooth pureed foods for his meals. Some interesting teething textures:

- Hard pretzels (sold with or without salt)
- Twice-toasted bread
- Whole peeled raw carrot. Stay near if he has real teeth and could chew off a bit of it.
- Whole raw celery stalk (peel the "strings" off)
- Fruit juice Popsicle
- Bagels

BATH

Bath time is a fine time to give infants whole-body experiences with textures. If your newborn screams and goes rigid at bath time, try easing him into the warm water slowly with comforting words and gentle rubs. See Chapter 8 for further suggestions. If all this fails, avoid experimenting any further and get the job done quickly. Both you and the baby will be grateful. For the more relaxed bather who is beginning to enjoy the water and the gentle rubs and pats, try the following:

- Soft cotton baby washcloths and those of rougher terry
- Different textures on different parts of baby (feet, hands, or scalp can tolerate rougher textures than cheek or tummy)
- An after-bath nude frolic on terry cloth, cotton jersey, or cotton flannel in a warm room

After the bath see what makes your baby purr—powder pat-down, lotion rubdown, or baby oil massage.

Older infants (four to eight months) use bath time as playtime. By now they have probably outgrown the baby bathtubs. For an easy transition to the regular bathtub, use only a few inches of water and a sponge mat or towel in the bottom of the tub. The texture of a hard enamel tub is different from the soft, yielding plastic of the baby bath. Once the baby has grown accustomed to the new, big tub he will enjoy his freedom to kick and splash with abandon. He will seem very small in that big tub and be as slippery as an eel for you to handle, but he will take his cues from you. If you are enjoying the bath (yes, you can . . . forget that you're on your knees in that awkward position being drenched from head to toe) he will enjoy it too. Some textures for the bath:

- Two sponges or washcloths for bath time (one for each of you)
- Textured plastic bottles with tops on to float in the bath. (These bottles will bounce and bobble and scoot away as the baby tries to catch them.)
- Prickly brushes—baby hairbrushes and nail-and-complexion brushes are

good sizes for tiny hands (watch out for stiff bristles near baby's eyes).
· Nylon pot scrubbers in bright colors

After the bath have a clean, textured bath mat on the floor to lay your baby on for drying and dressing. This is easier than a hurried, cold trip back to the bedroom and your baby will enjoy being dried and dressed on a new texture. Your baby is beginning his learning about "wet" and "dry."

TOYS AND ACTIVITIES

Infants' first "toys" are not conventional toys—they are his hands, your hands, your face, and your hair. Even a baby a few hours old will find his fist and suck it, but until he is older he cannot get hand to mouth at will. Some other texture "toys" which will comfort an infant are a pacifier and a knuckle or a finger on a parent's well-washed hand. It will just fit into a baby's mouth when nothing else is handy. Did you ever notice how babies suck at your collar bone when you hold them on your shoulder?

You have a captive audience in your precreeping crawling child. His exploration of objects is limited to what is brought to him. Make his "feeling" discoveries interesting for both him and you. As soon as your infant's hands or feet begin to move purposefully, take down from the shelf the decorative stuffed animals he got as presents. Put the furry lambs or slick oilcloth elephants where his hands or feet can brush the textures. Also put balls of many textures where baby's feet or hands can touch them. These may include:

· A big slick beach ball
· Furry tennis ball
· A football or basketball with a pebbly surface
· Spongy foam balls
· Smooth rubber balls

Beware of small-sized balls—Ping-Pong, golf, or jacks balls—that may end up wedged in a mouth, and balloons which could pop and frighten your baby or leave dangerous pieces that could suffocate him.

An older baby will find it interesting to play with an adult's hand. Your ring, bracelet, or watchband will add interest. When you are desperate to finish that chapter of a book you are reading or the thank-you note to your mother-in-law, dangle one hand over baby's crib to amuse him while you get your task done. This sometimes takes practice but it does work.

Teething babies enjoy biting many other things besides store-bought texture teethers. Look around your house and see what would be good to bite on. Try offering sponges, nylon pot scrubbers, or a netting ball made by a creative mother (sold at church fairs as tub and sink scrubbers). All these "toys" can go in your mesh laundry bag and cycle through with your wash load if baby burps on them. Other household items will supplement your baby's bought toys:

- Spoons made of wood, plastic, or metal
- Bowls or cups made of wood, plastic, or metal
- Plastic bottles with textured outsides (ridged, bumpy)
- New powder puffs
- Clean plastic flyswatter

Playing with items such as these will help your baby distinguish between "soft" and "hard," and "stiff" and "firm."

LANGUAGE

Though your under-a-year-old can't "talk" to you, he will respond to the sound of your voice. Many texture words have sound quality somewhat like the word meaning. Your baby will hear "soft" blanket, "sharp" pin, or "smooth" lotion in the tone of your voice.

The Baby on the Move: Crawling Age to Twenty-Four Months Your Crawler/Toddler Goes to the World

You are reminded of the immortal words of Bell Telephone, "Let your fingers do the walking." Your child's fingers as well as his hands, mouth, knees, and feet seem to go exploring everywhere. The baby who used to be content to lie on his back with his two hands feeling each other now squishes a banana through his fingers and massages it into the carpet tufts with the serious preoccupation of a chemist. Piaget tells us the focus has shifted from self to the objects in the world.

This "on the move" age is vitally important for a child's growth and the toughest age for a parent with any housekeeping standards at all. Take your lead from the new museums for children by putting imaginary "Please Touch" signs all over your house, knowing that your child's feel of "curves" and "corners," of "soft" and "hard" is the beginning of his intellectual grasp of these concepts. While you're making signs, post one in the front hall for office-weary father or nosy sister-in-law. This sign reads: "Burton White of Harvard University says, 'Babies reate clutter. It is as natural as breathing. A cluttered house with a ten-month-old baby is, all other things being equal, a good sign. In fact an immaculately picked up house and a ten-month-old baby who is developing well are, in my opinion, usually incompatible.' "* Anyone who can keep a child's hands clean will be producing a child *not* free to touch

and "know" the properties of all about him. The temptation is to move a child this age from crib to stroller, to playpen, to car seat, selecting for him the objects he can touch. This is not best for the child. Instead you can keep him safe by moving big chairs in front of outlets, bracing tippy tables, and moving kitchen poisons. You are creating an environment in which he can move freely for the next several years. The homework of moving the furniture and breakables will save you hundreds of "no's."

As your sitting baby becomes a creeper or crawler, your puller-upper becomes a walker and climber, your dropper and thrower becomes a carrier, he will develop judgment. He will learn what falls over and what stays up.

Children vary greatly in their drive at this age. Some are motor-minded, veritable "bulldozers" moving from room to room. Others are gentler souls needing encouragement to touch and wiggle. Sometimes gentle parents have "bulldozer" babies. Get to know your baby and

* Burton White, *The First Three Years of Life* (Englewood Cliffs, N.J.: Prentice-Hall Publishing Co., Inc., 1975).

your own limits. If your baby's activity level is beyond your capacities, hire the local high school fullback or cheerleader to spell you some days!

Don't worry if you feel ready to send up flags of surrender (and are too tired to raise them) when your eight- to twenty-four-month-old is finally in bed. Many parents feel this way. This age is one of the most physically and emotionally challenging for parents and one of the most important intellectually for young children.

PEOPLE

Your crawler/toddler is an explorer and if you can stand it, he'll explore you too. He'll find the rough spot on your elbow you forgot to soothe with cold cream and the furry place the barber didn't trim on your neck. At about eight months, a baby often becomes shy with strangers, recognizing and preferring the familiarity of his parents. But as soon as your baby passes that developmental hump you'll find him stroking Uncle Louis' bald head in the same way he strokes the top of a waffle. It's texture to him!

He'll be developing favorites among the clothes in your wardrobe: the tweed that is good to hang onto as he walks; the soft corduroy to snuggle up to when the wind blows. You'll be in for an education and so will he when he tries to hang onto your slippery panty hose knees to steady his pace!

CLOTHING AND COVERINGS

You'll begin to know your child's clothing preferences. You may have a baby who is bothered by wet or messy diapers and will be content only if dry and clean, or your baby may resist the easily cleaned plastic bib because the plastic ties around his neck scratch and bother him. The child who has been swaddled in soft blankets and cosy stretch suits as an infant may suddenly be subjected to lace collar and cuffs or binding "dress-up" outfits with buttons, ties, and elastics. If your baby reacts to these new textures you will know soon enough. He will protest while being dressed or later become fussy when wearing his new outfit at grandmother's family dinner. He is feeling much the same as adults who, after an evening of starched collars and prickly brocade, quickly strip as they walk in the front door heading for the comfortable old flannel or terry robe. Remember that a baby's skin is more sensitive than an adult's, so respect his wishes. His comfort is more important than showing off the new knit dress or scratchy wool imported suit.

If your baby is "on the move" creeping, crawling, or walking, make sure his clothes do not hamper his movements. Be aware that slippery nylon snowsuits are great for sliding like a baby seal but frustrating for the crawling baby. Put away all slippery booties when your baby makes the grand leap from moving on all fours to tottering on two feet. The socks that kept his crawling feet warm are no help now. He needs to feel the texture he is walking on, and for the beginning, staggering walker nothing is better than bare feet. When you feel he needs shoes (the season should guide you), put strips of adhesive tape on the new soles to reduce the shoes' slick texture that makes walking difficult. Even a baby who has toddled easily on floors and grass with bare feet will walk as gingerly as an ice skater on his first skates in the unaccustomed stiff texture of his first real shoes.

A restless baby may settle and relax with the comforting texture of a familiar bed covering. He will probably have shown a preference for one "security" blanket, quilt, or diaper with a texture that pleases him. A baby of this age often goes to sleep while rubbing a furry blanket on his cheek, moving the smooth satin binding back and forth under his nose, or fingering his waffly acrylic crib blanket. Texture is soothing and comforting as well as stimulating.

FOOD

At this age food is a big focus. Babies not only eat food but play with it. Pureed baby foods are replaced by junior foods, "finger" foods, and "table" foods. At about nine or ten months most children move easily to commercial junior foods or mashed "table food" (what you eat rendered in smaller form by fork, grinder, or food processor). Children vary in their readiness to experience new textures in food. Some plunge in (literally up to the eyeballs), while others gingerly probe and prod a new food with finger or tongue. Like it or not, most babies this age like to explore the texture of food with more than their mouths. Pediatricians will tell you this phase is important for the child's mastery of his world. The mother who keeps hold of the spoon herself with washcloth nearby may have a cleaner kitchen and baby but she'll also have a child dependent on her for "spoon to mouth" well beyond the age when "hand to mouth" serves nicely for the baby. Your child will smile as the carrots squeeze through his fingers, grin as he batters a teething biscuit to a pulp, and chortle as he strokes spinach through his hair. This mess drives any mother up the wall but provides your baby with varied food textures to explore and this phase too will pass. Some suggestions to save your sanity:

- Putting high chair or feeding table outdoors in good weather
- Scheduling bath time just after feeding time. You can't bathe him three times a day! Let the bath follow the meal when you allow him the longest time to explore.
- Using a bib on baby, an apron on you, a shower curtain on the floor (if you'd rather wash plastic than linoleum!)
- Keeping lots of sponges handy. Since you run washer loads all the time anyway you can run the sponges through (in a zipper laundry bag or they'll float) and into the drier and they'll stay "fresh" for months.
- Saving the chocolate pudding for the day you feel strong of spirit and full of resolve

When your child begins to pick up small things with his thumb and forefinger he will enjoy finger foods with different textures, such as dry cereals. Make a little row or put them out two or three at a time. The picking up will be entertainment. He will also enjoy soft cubes of cheese, stiff gelatin cubes (make them with less water than the recipe), bits of bananas, little bits of cooked hamburger or hot dog, small cubes of cooked but still firm carrots or potatoes, and bits of graham crackers. For a texture surprise give your toddler a taste of honey or peanut butter when you're around the kitchen to watch out for choking.

When you are cooking your own dinner let him feel some things he is not ready to eat. Let him feel the skin of a smooth eggplant, a rough pineapple, a pebbly orange, a ribbed celery stalk, or porous mushroom caps. Just think as you barely survive all this awful mess that your baby has begun to learn the concepts of "soft" and "hard," "wet" and "dry," "smooth" and "rough," "stiff" and "firm," and "sticky" and "creamy."

BATH

Bath time may be a relatively restful time for your mobile baby. At least for a few moments he is happily contained in one area, making it a relaxing time for you. Make your daily spinach-and-mud-removal ritual also a playtime for both of you. If your baby will sit happily in the tub, take the newspaper into the bathroom with you. You will soon learn to read with one eye and watch your splashing baby with the other. To keep your bather playing happily—and to let you finish at least one editorial—add these interesting texture "toys" to the bath:

- A new kitchen dish mop with floppy fuzzy strings for washing tummy or tub
- A bar of soap that floats for easy finding and squishing
- Natural sponges with wonderfully strange textures full of holes, hills, and valleys to rub on knees and head or poke with fingers and toes
- Any of his "found" toys that are suitable for the bath—spatula, strainer, wisk, mesh bags, plastic berry baskets, and so forth

Before or after the bath let your child stay naked for a bit, enjoying the textures of his world. The bumpy tile bath floor and fuzzy bath mat will feel very different to a bare bottom.

TOYS AND ACTIVITIES

Your baby "on the move" considers everything he comes in contact with to be a toy, something to explore. The carefully selected and purchased jack-in-the-box, Busy Box, or plastic nesting blocks may sit idle after a brief examination at playtime. Why? The toy manufacturer's suggested age was right for your child and you find these toys colorful, safe, and attractive. Our experience with babies between eight and twenty-four months has been that children of this age want to explore their whole world, creeping, crawling, and tottering about from room to room, object to object, not spending much time with any one thing. Their attention span is still quite short. They finger and mouth everything. The screened door and venetian blinds are as interesting as blocks and pull toys. To satisfy your child's incredible curiosity and to avoid the frustration of buying an expensive educational toy that just sits in crib or playpen, begin collecting an interesting group of "found" texture toys.

With a baby this age you're not going to have much spare energy to play games, make pastry, polish your shoes, or style your hair. So prop your most glamorous photograph in front of your mirror, smile at your growing baby, and recycle your sport, cooking, and cosmetic gadgets as toys. Your baby will enjoy:

- Balls—tennis, Ping-Pong, and smooth rubber. Watch that small balls don't get stuck in his mouth.
- Brushes—vegetable, pastry, or a new shoe brush. That scalp massager you got from your Avon lady in a weak moment is a dandy too.
- Kitchen utensils with interesting textures—spatula, slotted spoon, bulb baster, and colander
- Empty plastic and paper cartons from milk, cottage cheese, and yogurt

- Plastic or paper cookie trays and meat trays with ridges for fingers to follow
- Pot holders—quilted puffy ones, terry ones, grandmother's crocheted ones that let your fingers burn anyway. They are great for finger poking.

All of these "toys" can be stored in a special low kitchen drawer or cabinet, just for your baby to explore, or in a special wastebasket, laundry basket, or grocery carton. Change the variety for your child, keeping your eyes open for good "recycled" texture toys.

Besides constant exploration of the world around him, your child may begin to favor a special stuffed toy. He will enjoy carting about this new friend and sleeping with it, the texture having a special meaning to him.

At about eighteen months, in addition to purchased toys and found toys, sand, water, and mud become excellent texture toys. If you can bear the muddy overalls or occasional "tastes," these are some of the best toys your child can have.

INDOORS AND OUTDOORS

Indoors and outdoors, hands, feet, and mouth check out everything by feel. Early in this stage texture is very important because the slickness or roughness of a surface can make a big difference in whether or not a baby can get the traction to creep or crawl. A bare crawler on a linoleum floor can move quickly; a corduroyed baby on a shag rug has drag that slows him down. You'll be amazed at the textures your baby will explore that you never knew existed, bits of decor on chair feet or table legs you long ago stopped looking at. If you have a shy, quiet baby, encourage him to touch. Some things your crawler/toddler will discover and feel indoors:

- The dog and the cat
- Caned chair seats
- Carved designs in wood
- Louvers on cabinet doors
- Flocked wallpaper
- The textural difference between wet and dry spots on your kitchen floor
- Ridges in woodwork, baseboard, or chair rails

Some things to discover and feel outdoors:

- Sand
- Grass. Long, tickly grass blades bother some children and they won't crawl on grass. Others won't walk barefoot on short-cut prickles of grass.

- Tree bark. Even if you've never been a nature buff, you and your child will begin to notice the contrasting smoothness and coarseness of bark on different trees.
- Brick and gravel
- Wet and dry leaves
- Sharp pine needle ends

Feeling texture takes time. A toddler's trip through one room or down one block may take an hour. Let him set the pace for discovery. Take your knitting along on the walk and stitch as he runs his hands back and forth along the neighbor's fence and the worn place in the sidewalk. If your goal is a quick trip to the grocery, then it isn't a walk for him. That's a time to let him explore the food you are buying as he rides in the cart. All the objects in his world don't have much meaning to a child, but he touches everything and his touching is the beginning of understanding.

LANGUAGE

The "on the move" baby is beginning to repeat the names of the objects he touches if you first name them for him. Texture words being adjectives, they are refinements of speech that most under-two-year-olds are not ready to utter. They are into nouns, the names of things, and verbs, the actions. Although your child won't use your texture words he will understand many of them as you talk with him. The danger word "sharp" or the cozy word "soft," and definitely "wet" will be parts of his receptive vocabulary. Be of good cheer. "Dry" will be a big feature in the second year!

Two- and Three-Year-Olds: Your Child Finds Words for the World

The rough and stormy seas of age two become the smooth calm sailing of age three. Two is a growing time, growing of personality and of language. Your child's motor skills are practiced, practiced, and practiced. Two-year-olds need room to run in. Three-year-olds begin to have a lengthened attention span and can sit and play for ten minutes at a stretch. The sign of a developing personality is seen as a two-year-old says "I, me, and mine" and "No," seeing himself as someone separate from his parents. He practices being separate and assertive, and certainly enjoys his new identity. Three can be the most reasonable of ages, a household helper. Giant steps toward independence must be mastered during these two years: he learns to dress, toilet, and feed himself.

Sometimes parent and child move with the same pace and sometimes the motion is a deadlock of opposing energies as the growing two-year-old pushes an exasperated parent to his limits. At those moments the "texture" the parent feels like introducing is the texture of palm to britches!

For the two- and three-year-old, language is no longer just the naming of what is right at hand, the "cookie," "doggie," and "milk" talk of the "on the move" child. It is beginning to be real sentences and communication, a satisfaction to both parent and child. The motor maniac roaring through your home is on his way to becoming a civilized human being.

PEOPLE

The nine-month-old who was shy with "strangers" may now be the two-year-old master of ceremonies of the local grocery store, amusing strangers with his chatter and antics.

Two- and three-year-olds are still very physical people; they like the touch and texture of hugs, kisses, and pats. Boisterous or gentle cheek to cheek encounters express interest in you, the baby, or the dog next door. Your child will like to feel these textures:

- His hand in your hand
- His cheek on your cheek
- His bare foot touching your bare foot
- Your casual pat of his hair
- Your soothing touch on his often wounded knees, hands, and forehead (his motor drive exceeds his maneuvering skills)

BODY

With your child's emerging sense of identity comes a renewed interest in his own body. Like Buddha reflecting upon his navel, he will study tiny toes and spreading palm with the concentration of a mystic. Once toilet trained, two- and three-year-olds will no longer be bulkily diapered. They can feel themselves all over. This is a big age for "discovery" of the anatomy. Don't get upset, it's normal in two- and three-year-olds to "discover" genitals along with all their other body parts.

Two- and three-year-olds are the last of the big-time cuddlers. (Four- and five-year-olds will be much more fidgety and self-conscious.) You are discovering your child's touch style and your own. You know whether the soft hug or the brusque back rub, the passing peck on the forehead or the cheek-to-cheek story hour, is his style. Enjoy the quick pats and strokings your two- or three-year-old will give you as he passes. These growing years have their calm moments.

CLOTHING AND COVERINGS

Nap time sometimes disappears in the second and third year, and three-year-olds go through a phase of liking to sleep anywhere but their beds. Texture can encourage a balky child to nap, rest, or sleep. Try a furry rug *under* the crib for nap, his familiar blanket in the corner of the playroom for rest, or a special new surface (old velvet evening cape) to rest on.

FOOD

Your independent thinker, aged two or three, may suddenly exercise great control over what he eats. The favorite hot cereal he has liked most of his life for breakfast may be suddenly rejected. Some of his violent likes and dislikes are caused by boredom (he may have had it with lumpy oatmeal every day) and some are caused by fear of the unknown (he may push away the new rough-textured granola). But most of your child's rejections are caused by his new-found identity "I am and I decide what I eat." You can engage in a head-to-head confrontation and insist he eat his oatmeal, in fact saying "You'll eat what I say you'll eat," or take our advice and give in, give up, ignore. Your child will win the battle (not the war) because he needs to feel he has some control over what happens to him, more than he needs to eat his oatmeal. What he learns by making his own decisions is more important than one hundred calories. You can also scurry about, shopping and preparing a tempting "dish to set before the king" only to have him push it off his high-chair tray without a taste. Probably the sanest approach is to offer some foods he has eaten in the past and slowly introduce new foods with interesting textures. Your child will enjoy using his new teeth to chomp on crunchy carrots, crisp celery, hard apples, and wrinkled raisins. Noticing likenesses and differences is an important intellectual task. Your two- or three-year-old can contrast two kinds of peanut butter, creamy and crunchy; pudding, creamy or lumpy (add rice, raisins, or tapioca); eggs, soft and hard boiled; scrambled eggs, soft and dry; crackers, smooth "white biscuits" and rough Triscuits. To encourage an interest in foods (and eating) let your child "cook"—another experience of learning by doing. Let him prepare:

- Instant mashed potatoes. They will be creamy or lumpy depending on "the cook's design" but will most likely be tasted because "he did it!"
- Peanut butter spread on crackers, toast, or celery for lunch. Let him use a spatula or broad-bladed table knife for spreading. The texture surprise of spreading peanut butter can be frustrating or challenging for your child. Let him try. If he succeeds, he'll enjoy his lunch more than a ready-made sandwich.
- A dessert treat. He can "ice" cupcakes or stiff cookies with very spreadable frosting.

With all of this crunching, comparing, and cooking, your two- or three year-old will probably still prefer foods in their virgin state. Children of this age are suspicious of any combination, concoction, or casserole. They will eat the cheese, pasta, and tomatoes separately but balk at the textural combination of lasagna. Two- and three-year-olds are food purists and must investigate the texture of foods one by one before they are ready for Aunt Violet's beef casserole or coq au vin.

TOYS AND ACTIVITIES

The messiness of some texture play materials may be unacceptable to some children who are feeling ambivalent about their own bodies and toilet training. If your child refuses to touch squishy mud, sticky play dough, or messy sand, respect his wishes and simply offer these "toys" at another time.

Your child is becoming adept at using his hands to examine, compare, and create with objects. He is not merely stroking or patting things along the way but is beginning to distinguish likeness and differences. As parents you can encourage your child to "think" about concepts of likeness and difference in textures:

- Use your texture collection of earlier months to compare: "put all the prickly brushes in this box," "put all of the smooth spoons in this box." Children of this age like to put in and pull out anything so why not make it challenging!
- Let your child make collections of texture treasures gathered lovingly— smooth and rough pebbles, strings, acorns, sticks, and so forth.
- Make a "texture book" (book is rather a grand term for shirt cardboard glued with interesting fabric scraps). These cardboard pages could be hole-punched and tied with yarn. The effect may not be elegant, but your child will enjoy feeling the textures and talking about them with you.
- Buy a bag of mixed nuts (recycle later into cookies or nutbread) and let your child sort the nuts by the textures he sees and feels—the smooth pecans into one bowl, the rough walnuts into another bowl. Besides the sorting, your child will just plain relish the feel of nuts in the shell.
- Put familiar objects with great textural differences into a bag (hairbrush, mitten, comb, sneaker, teddy bear, and so on) for feeling. Let your two- and three-year-old feel the objects and try to imagine what he is touching. He will probably peek more than guess. Let him. The important thing is that he is beginning to notice textural differences in his world and you are encouraging him to think and talk about them.

Your child has probably mastered a kiddie car or mini-trike. For a change let him try different textured surfaces to move on: the smooth tile of the basement/playroom floor; an old rug with a firm surface; rough or slick driveway surface, cement or blacktop; or textured sidewalk with cracks and bumps.

INDOORS AND OUTDOORS

Two- and three-year-olds need room to move. They are no longer content with a snuggled stroller ride. If you confine your child to tiny spaces the frustration escalates. He enjoys motion for the sheer pleasure of feeling his own body running through space. Pick an open space (park, field, yard, a big local building) and take a "walk" with texture interests along the way. Your child will walk on, roll on, and run through everything in sight. Textures along the way will fascinate him, giving you a needed pause to catch your breath. He will be the first to find the dog or bird dropping, or the oil slick in a puddle. Try some more wholesome texture activities:

• A jog on bumpy hummocks or a rough piece of turf
• A jog on the smooth polished floor of the local auditorium or the shopping mall. Feed your child early and go at 5 or 6 o'clock when no one will notice your jog; they're home cooking dinner!
• A trot in the slick mud after a rain (have a hose handy)
• A slide on an icy pond (hold your child's hand)

On your walks find some textures to feel besides the bark, leaves, and grass he enjoyed as a toddler:

• Mosses
• Soft rose petals (children often put soft things on their cheeks to feel them)
• Sharp holly prickles or rose thorns (he'll use a tentative touch, but he'll learn sharp)
• Rain on ground and grass
• Wet worms (do you dare!) or fuzzy caterpillars

While you're out, have your jog at the zoo and visit the "touchable" animals (looking isn't as interesting at this age): pat a soft lamb, a rough elephant baby, or a slick snake's back. If the zoo doesn't have a "touch" section, try a farm, a pet shop, or a nature center. Closer to home you can try "water play" by washing the car (he'll get one spot gleaming while you do the rest) or sloshing in the rain.

There will be times when there's no way to get out to the open spaces that two- and three-year-olds crave, so use their interest in touch and texture as an indoor amusement by taking a texture walk through your closet, feeling stiff, slick, soft, and furry clothes; shoes of rough suede and smooth patent; satin evening slippers and furry bedroom slippers. Put your wooly socks on your child's feet and let him "skate" on your best polished floor (wood or linoleum). Point out buttons and let your child feel the differences in texture. Let your child play with bumpy zippers and fuzzy Velcro fasteners.

In the kitchen keep an eye on those texture-happy fingers. A two-year-old's birthday cake left out may be explored beyond recognition. For some acceptable activities encourage your child to feel the texture of these:

- All the fruits and vegetables you have (naming the smooth, cool cucumber and the rough, bumpy pineapple are fun too)
- Paper napkins, towels, woven and vinyl table mats
- Dishes, china, silver, glassware
- A smooth ice cube to "drive" with a finger around a metal pan or a slick plate

If you are "lucky" enough to have pets, the texture of kitty's or doggy's fur will occupy your child for long periods (if you can get the wary pet to cooperate as he is used as a security blanket). If you don't have pets try the neighbor's friendly dog, cat, iguana, or hamster.

LANGUAGE

Some two-year-olds are full-fledged talkers. Others are primarily doers. Words are best learned while the child is interacting with the object, the "soft" of the kitty, the "sharp" of a gingerly touched needle-point, the "wet" of a soggy towel. You will provide this beginning richness of language as your child repeats your words to describe his experiences. Variety in texture experiences, and repetition of your language will lead a child to the generalization necessary for the abstraction of the textural qualities of "soft," "hard," or "stiff."

The great variety of experiences is necessary in part because textural qualities are not only abstract but relative. "Smooth" to one person may be "rough" to another. Your child will first learn the more obvious extremes (very "soft," very "smooth"), and not until school age will he be able to wrestle with the subtle gradations. Mysteriously (probably it's all clear to the linguistics experts), children will learn one quality long before its opposite: "wet" before "dry" has any meaning; "soft," though "hard" is not of interest; "smooth," while "rough" remains an unknown. All will come in time and with experience and the urge to communicate.

Four- and Five-Year-Olds: Your Child Begins to Order His World

Four- and five-year olds are ready to move out into the world beyond family and home, developing relationships with friends, neighbors, teachers. Experimentation with words and actions is the keynote at four, an "out of bounds" age when your child is full of "silly" behavior and talk, never knowing quite when to stop. You will wish your four-year-old hadn't learned texture words when he rattles off that the pudding is "mushy, gushy, and ushy" or worse. Fortunately, age five follows, an age of equilibrium, developed patterns of behavior, and a sense of reasonable limits. Five-year-olds are getting things into categories, sorting leaves, rocks, and bark bits into "smooth" or "rough." Like two-year-olds, four-year-olds are creative, a trial to harassed parents, but four is an exciting "growing" year. Like three-year-olds, five-year-olds are more peaceful; parents can sit back and beam a bit. "Fours" and "fives" need variety—a variety of people, a variety of places to go, a variety of things to do. Four and five are great ages for the consolidation of old knowledge and the acquisition of new.

By four your child will have had many experiences of texture: "stiff" and "firm," "fine" and "coarse." At this age children are ready to use their understanding of texture to help organize the world. Texture is one identifier, one of the clues children use for classifying the animals, vegetables, and minerals around them. The rock collector will ask you to notice the texture in the grain of the rock. The heroine of the kindergarten play may have a strong feeling about the appropriate fabric for her costume—it has to feel and look right.

Your child who once touched and felt his way through the world can now tell texture by looking. You will notice a great decrease in the finger marks on your furniture. Your child not only looks but tells you about what he sees and understands, and you have the pleasure of communication with him. This enthusiastic engagement with objects and words, with people and space, brings your child a sense of mastery, a competence, and for the first time some real independence.

BODY

Preschoolers find their own bodies of endless interest, seeing what they can do, how high they can climb, how long they can hang on, what they feel like. Your child will be fascinated by feeling body textures:

- Goose bumps
- Chapped lips and hands
- Calloused feet
- Rough outer elbows and smooth inner elbows
- Soft spots with hard bones underneath
- Bare feet. Depending on your hang-ups, let your child go barefoot indoors and outdoors to feel the changes of texture as he walks.
- Slippery soapy skin—you may even get his hands clean while he enjoys the lather.
- A baby's furry hair and soft skin
- Pictures drawn with your finger (or letters when he has learned them) on his back. Get him to guess what you draw. Have him do it to you. This is a very difficult way of "seeing" things and hard for some people.

FOOD

Your food purist of age two has suddenly grown into a social butter-fly with a more adventuresome attitude toward food. He is attending birthday parties, having a friend over for lunch, and going to a restaurant with Grandmother. Suddenly he is asking you why you always serve peanut butter and jelly sandwiches for lunch (forgetting momentarily that in the past that is all he ate) and suggesting you try the peanut butter and banana sandwich he had at his friend's house. This is a time to swallow your pride and not be offended. Take advantage of your four- or five-year-old's new interest in food and offer him new foods with interesting textures as well as tastes. Some suggestions to get you thinking:

- Sponge cake and angel cake
- Waffles

- Shredded wheat
- Pomegranate. Beware of your child's enthusiastic exploration of fruits: either feed him nude or send for the U.S. government pamphlet on food stains.
- Poppy and sesame seeds on bread and in noodles
- Regular and super-fine sugar
- Cheeses (hard, soft, creamy, lumpy)
- Avocado
- Cotton candy (a new texture in food)

Play a game with any food that has an interesting texture. Have your child eat the first bite with eyes closed and try to guess what he is eating. The textural clues as well as the taste will make him a detective. Try "cooking" activities that include a textural change. These include things a child can see as well as feel in his hands or mouth: toasting marshmallows (firm to oozy); whipping cream (liquid to solid); making butter (liquid to solid); making bread (soft to hard); and making applesauce (hard to soft).

Many four- and five-year-olds tend to balk at the soft texture of cooked vegetables, and prefer the texture of raw vegetables (carrots, celery, cucumber, green pepper, cauliflower, mushrooms, green peas, green beans, broccoli, and even parsnips). Explore together the textural differences of some foods that are different on the outside from the inside:

- Pineapples and coconuts
- Pumpkins (the outside texture of the pumpkin is firm and slick, or firm and bumpy, and the inside is, in the words of a four-year-old, "yucky")
- Peas (velvet pods and smooth peas)
- Onions
- Corn on the cob (rough husk and smooth silk)

These activities are only suggestions to make life more interesting (and possibly messier) for you and your child. You will both learn from new foods and from each other. The adventurer who has enjoyed different foods will do you proud in later years when he manages not to gag on scalloped oysters or boiled okra.

TOYS AND ACTIVITIES

Four- and five-year-olds enjoy doing things with others. Many of their toys or play activities are "more fun" done with a friend. There is something very satisfying about unstructured play materials that free a child to create. Many an early Saturday morning or a week with the flu can be happily spent cutting, pasting, or constructing. We suggest the following texturally interesting materials for four- and five-year-olds:

- Clay (water base and oil base, each have a different textural quality)
- Play dough (make or buy, you can never have enough!)
- Sand—have a sandbox or sandpile outside. If you need new sand in the spring try buying a bag of super-fine grained sand and a bag of coarser-grained sand for each side of the sandpit. The hardware store clerk will think you wacky and in one week you will have all "medium" grained sand, but your child will have had the brief opportunity to explore sand textures.
- Rope, string, telephone wire, yarn, ribbon, and so forth, for twisting, tying, winding, and "creating"
- Pencils, crayons, and chalk for drawing on all textural surfaces; slick typing paper, coarse manila paper, bumpy napkins and paper towels, ridged paper plates, and corrugated papers
- Scissors—give your child his own pair of high-quality, blunt-end scissors and a wide variety of paper with varying textures. Developing cutting skill with all textures requires time and practice. Your child will enjoy cutting just to master cutting, not necessarily to make anything. Thin and stiff textures are easier for first cutting experiences. Save floppy paper and fabrics for later. (For a sequence of cutting skill see Chapter 3.)
- Erasers—four- and five-year-olds will feel very "grown up" with an eraser or two of their own. They have a "paper and pencil complex" anyway, wanting to play at real schoolwork. A soft gum or hard rubber eraser will give them an interesting textural experience.
- Fabric—ask Grandmother or a neighbor who sews to help you collect interesting fabric scraps or remnants. These are great for "feeling," classifying (sorting), talking about, or playing with. They are also great to have on hand for impromptu costumes.
- Fur—any kind, fake or real; children love to stroke and feel it. One child we know sleeps with a rabbit skin on her pillow to touch while drifting off to sleep. Look for the old coat lining or the trim on a collar or hat. One of our neighbors remembers how her preschooler stroked her raccoon coat and upholstered his bedroom chair with it when it wore out. Zany lady, happy child!
- Felt—men's hats
- Feathers—found on walks in the woods or on a great aunt's old hats
- Velvet—save your old holiday dresses
- Cotton flannel—"tired" baby blankets can be a treat even when your "baby" is five
- Satin—scraps of blanket binding
- Lace or crocheted pieces—the texture of the thread is appealing to little fingers
- Corduroy—everyone has outgrown overalls

- Straw place mats—the last one of the worn-out set
- Rug samples—loved by all four- and five-year-olds to touch and compare
- Terry cloth
- Cheesecloth—your child can feel the weave and actually see through it
- Chiffon—scarves are great. Look through your drawers for the ones from high school; remember, some were even accordion pleated! Your child will love this texture.

Four- and five-year-olds like special projects. Use many of the textural materials listed above to satisfy their urge to "create." Your child will enjoy practicing these skills:

- Drawing with pencils. Let your energetic four- or five-year-old sharpen his pencil with an emory board.
- Working with wood. Give your woodworking enthusiast several different grades of sandpaper to smooth rough wood. Let him discover which paper works best for what wood.
- Making a collage (a pasting masterpiece). Use many different paper or fabric textures for pasting.
- Doing rubbings on a large sheet of paper. Inside the house try cut-glass cake plates with wonderful textures, bathroom tile walls or floors, screenings, and so forth. Look at your house with a critical eye: finding a good rubbing surface is half the fun. For the more adventuresome souls outside try manhole covers or tombstones. The method is easy. Use a sturdy but not too heavy weight paper (standard typing paper is great) and pencils or crayons. Place the paper on top of the surface and rub your pencil/crayon back and forth. You and your child will love your results.
- Sorting fabric, paper, and sandpaper as smooth or rough, bumpy or slick. Classifying is an important intellectual skill.

INDOORS AND OUTDOORS

Four- and five-year-olds love to make choices. They will have opinions about the texture of their clothes, their bedspreads, even the towels you give them to use. They begin to have collections of objects that interest them, often the outdoors brought indoors. One of these objects may become a special favorite, a stroking stone or a worry bead always found in a pants pocket.

Indoors you can capitalize on your child's sociability and growing capabilities for texture experiences. He will love to polish furniture, silver, shoes, mirrors, and windows. Don't be fussy about the finished job but express appreciation and complete the job if you must when your child is out playing. As he grows in capability you will have some real help if you have encouraged it.

He can also straighten up your closet, putting pairs of shoes together by texture: the slick, the furry, and the firm. Test your communication abilities and his by asking him to bring you your shoes by texture names rather than color or purpose names.

Let him verbally classify the contents of your kitchen cabinets by texture: smooth or bumpy glasses, sharp or dull knives. Play a word game five different ways if your four- or five-year-old gets restless and you have your hands full:

- Ask your child to find something rough, smooth, and so forth.
- Hand your child an object and ask him to describe what it feels like. You don't have to correct a child's categories; what's slick to him may be sticky to you. It's the sorting into classes or categories that's the important mental task.
- If he's good at the game ask him to find something the opposite of what you point out, for example, dull, not sharp; hard, not soft.
- If he's underfoot move the game to the living room and you stay in the kitchen. Ask him to call back what he's found describing it without your seeing it.
- Try one of the home or outdoor magazines if your child is full up on experiences and ready for abstraction. "Find the firm and bumpy, the sharp or rough" in a picture and talk about why.

The outdoors is brim full of texture. Fours and fives will open your eyes to the exciting variety any short walk will bring. Your child will find petals of flowers (velvet pansy, satin tulip petal); a cactus, a magnolia leaf, evergreen branches; bird feathers and nests; seeds and pods; beach glass (worn) and shells; seaweed; pine resin; rocks; and butterfly wings and bugs' backs. Bring these found objects indoors. Suggest that your child make a design with his collection. Four- and five-year-olds are ready to pattern, following directions you give them. This structured approach is a good preparation for the patterns of numbers and letters he will need to follow and understand in school. Try suggesting collecting "pictures" or designs on your coffee table of "soft, hard" or "rough, smooth" objects. If you have a whole sackful of leaves or rocks start a design and ask your child if he can continue it, detecting the pattern you planned. Make two repeats of your pattern if you expect a child to follow, for example, smooth, rough, rough; smooth, rough, rough. Copying your pattern by looking at it is very different from copying it by having you say the words. Try both; the auditory and visual are both ways children need to learn.

This is a great age to take a trip to farm and zoo. If your child has felt worms and kittens, even the neighbor's cat's tongue, and if he's had a trip to the "touch it" zoo for bunnies, snakes, and goats, he's ready for a visual tour of the animals you can't touch. It's amazing to think that as adults all our texture feedback is usually visual. We don't have to touch the icy road to know when we'll skid. Even four- and five-year-olds are often overwhelmed by the many animals they see at the farm or zoo, and texture can be one handle on comprehending all the varieties. A super nursery teacher of our acquaintance assigned each member of her class to a group, the "texture" group, the "tails" group, the "ears" group, and so forth. The "texture" group noticed fur, feathers, and fins, with skin slick, rough, or smooth. When they came back to school and joined the "tails" and "ears" groups, these children were getting a picture of the whole by taking a long look at one of the parts at a time. That's the way children learn

LANGUAGE

Four- and five-year-olds are bursting with ideas and opinions which they want to share with everyone. For the child of this age communication is everything. The four-year-old who states at the dinner table that the pot roast is "stringy" is as interested in sharing his opinion as he is in finding an excuse for hurrying on to dessert. The four- and five-year-old, unlike the one- through three-year-old, can also talk about things in their absence; he is not completely tied down to the concrete world. He will venture opinions of the prickly cactus he saw in the plant store and the furry gerbil classroom pet. His language will become richer as it includes more and more adjectives. Many texture words that were experienced and understood as a toddler are now part of your child's speaking vocabulary. If they are encouraged, children of this age will be able to use opposite analogies. A great car game or waiting game in a restaurant is "complete the sentence please." The floor is hard, the bed is (soft). Four- and five-year-olds are able to re-experience textures in pictures, nursery rhymes, and stories. If they have stroked your velvet skirt they will understand the nursery rhyme line that says "some in rags and some in velvet gowns." Visiting the National Gallery in Washington with a group of nine-year-olds we again became aware of how important early experiences are. The guide showed the class a group oil portrait picturing many different textures of clothing. The children were asked to name the velvets, silks, and satins pictured. They were unfamiliar with these textures and their fabric names. As a result their art appreciation was limited by their early experiences. They could not marvel that the painter had made smooth and soft, slick and silky, all come alive with brush strokes.

Language is a tool for the imagination. Ideas and feelings can be expressed through the written and spoken word. Young children who have crawled over fuzzy rugs and touched slick wallpapers, and have these words in their vocabulary, can use language in a creative way.

A child learns language in his own way at his own pace. Most young children are fascinated by words, and their language seems to grow by leaps and bounds if they have things to talk about and someone to listen. A four- or five-year-old child who speaks of the smooth stone or the rough road is ready for enrichment games. If he knows what a rough road is, he may be ready for the expression "rough time." Using texture words in this way requires real understanding and a high level of abstract thinking. Watch for these uses in your child. It's an exciting moment.

Great fun for four- or five-year-olds is an imagination game. Ask your child how it would feel to lay on a cloud, walk on gelatin, sleep on a bed of nails, take a mud bath, and swim in a pot of honey. Four-year-olds are beginning to define words. Other word games for car trips and waits in the dentist's office are: "What is 'stringy?', 'lumpy?', 'prickly?'" Make it harder: "What is 'sandy' and 'fine'—can you guess?" "Sandpaper!" "What is 'soft' and 'sticky' and 'furry'?" Have fun, put some humor in: "A kitten jumping out of a jam pot is sticky and soft and furry!" Remember, four-year-olds like to be silly, so join 'em—you can't beat 'em.

Chapter 3

"How Big Is Little Anne?"
How a Child Learns
About Size

A MITE OF A CHILD of our acquaintance always acted "big." His teacher couldn't understand how a child so little thought of himself as "big." When his teacher found out that at three and one-half years old he was the oldest in a family of three children, she knew the reason. Compared to the children at home, he was "big." Most adults have had the experience of returning to a house or school remembered from childhood; everything looked so small because your perspective had changed.

Size is relative and full of emotional connotations too. There's the burly football player daddy with the tiny premature baby, and all the emotions that brings forth. There's the two-year-old newly into "big boy" underpants with a mother hopeful that that badge will encourage quick toilet training. There's the tall three-year-old who's always treated like a five-year-old because he is the size of one. Through many encounters your child will begin to learn about different sizes and their many connotations.

For measurement adults have some "handles" to peg the width, length, and height of things. Adults can use inches, and feet and yards. If you've tried to "move to metric" you know how a child feels. A child has a grasp of only gross comparative measure, big or little, large or small. He knows he's bigger than a baby and smaller than his daddy but memorizing that he is thirty-six inches tall has no meaning. That number is beyond his mathematical comprehension. You'd feel the same way if someone said your new office was three meters long. Is it a ballroom or a phone booth in size? Children need to establish the feel of "big" and "little," "tall" or "short," in terms of things or people in their environment, before they can move to abstract numbers.

Children learn not only to compare objects of two sizes (hills, trucks, apples, people), but eventually to line up whole series larger to smaller or smaller to larger. Like Goldilocks the child must try many bowls, chairs, and beds to know what is "big" and what is "small" and what "just fits." These experiences lead to the comprehension necessary in handling the abstractions of math or science. Size comparisons provide a basis for later numerical comparisons. The concrete precedes the abstract. A first grader who has had many experiences with objects can grasp eight as a larger quantity than four, can see ten as part of a continuing sequence. The basic grasp of the concept of size will prepare not only the first grade mathematician but your future microbiologist, cartographer, or carpenter.

SIZE CONCEPT WORDS

Least Difficult	More Difficult	Most Difficult
big—little	large—small	long
	tall—short	wide—narrow
	fat—thin	thick—thin

Comparative words (for example, bigger, biggest) are introduced when the child is ready to compare two or more objects. Standard units of measure (cups, inches, rulers, yards) are introduced at the kindergarten level after the child understands objects in terms of measurement relative to other objects.

The Infant: Birth to Eight Months or Crawling Age
You Bring the World to Your Infant

Much of the fear and anxiety in handling a newborn is related to an infant's size. You as parents will view your infant as a five-pound "China doll" or a ten-pound "bruiser." This view of your baby is subjective but will affect the way you treat him and the way he responds. To new parents even a ten-pound wonder baby is a startling size experience. No amount of practice with baby dolls in the parent education class prepares you for the task of diapering a week-old bottom. Many a new daddy has become weak in the knees with the first plunk of that tiny bundle in his arms. Life coming in that small size is awesome. One advantage of the rooming-in scheme in many maternity wings is that mothers and fathers can become comfortable with their baby and accustomed to his size within the "S.O.S." range of an experienced nurse.

As parental confidence grows day by day, the carrying, feeding, diapering, and bathing become second nature.

As your child's first months go by, size becomes an important measure of progress before the physical feats of sitting, standing, and walking. Each baby checkup is highlighted by how much he has grown, how big he is compared to the other three-month-old in the doctor's office or his cousin in Cleveland.

BODY

An infant does not know where his body begins or ends, or even that he is a separate person. Before birth his one experience of size is being snug in a just-fitting space. We as adults are amazed at how one could manage in such a space. Yet watching a newborn in crib or carriage, we see him wiggle himself into the tiniest, coziest corner available. As new mothers, we were surprised to find our newborns always snuggling in the bumpers at the crib corners, regardless of where they were placed. Older and hopefully wiser now (the child being the teacher), we know that newborns seem to yearn for the confined spaces of the womb. To help your newborn adjust to the world slowly try these techniques:

- Swaddling (an old-fashioned technique that really works sometimes)
- Using bassinets, cradles, or carriages for the first few months
- Dividing your big crib in half by horizontally using a big blanket rolled up as a bolster until your "little one" begins to demand more open spaces
- Using an infant seat or baby carrier for those awake moments

At about four months your baby will begin to enjoy experiencing bigger spaces. Try a playpen, a standard-sized crib, your double bed (this is a fine big place for your infant to kick, stretch, and practice turning over while you fold laundry nearby), or a blanket on the floor.

TOYS AND ACTIVITIES

Your infant's interest in the world around him can be heightened by letting him see things of various sizes (as well as colors and shapes). When choosing objects for your infant to look at make sure the objects are not so small that he can't focus on them or so large that his eyes are lost on their surface. Research has shown that a baby can focus best on objects roughly the size of a tennis ball at about a foot away from his face. When he is lying in a crib, playpen, or carriage, hang things of varying sizes for him to enjoy looking at, such as a mobile of fancy bows from party packages, strips of fabrics or yarn with some difference in size: long/short, big/little, wide/narrow, or small individual cereal or gelatin boxes. These "mobiles" need not be fancy or permanent; they are size toys for seeing, not for batting and gumming. If your infant is in the swatting stage, check the safety and security of your mobile. Changing your baby's environment is the important thing. The same kiddie mobile, even to an infant, gets boring after a while. Remember, you bring the world to your infant; he can't get about. When your baby is ready for an infant seat or feeding table there are new size experiences for him to enjoy:

- The patterns on wallpaper. Does your dining room have lovely flower bouquets for your infant to examine while you set the dinner table?
- The pattern on a quilt or blanket thrown over the end of crib or playpen near his infant seat
- A bright picture torn from an old magazine and taped to your refrigerator, down low for an infant-seat art gallery. An older preschooler would love being in charge of the changing art display.

At about four months your baby is ready for a whole new range of size experiences. The infant who has experienced size with his whole body and looked at size with his eyes is ready to get the feel of size with his hands and mouth. Between four- and five-and-one-half months of age, a baby can gradually coordinate hand and eye to reach purposefully. As your baby begins to grasp objects and get things from hand to mouth at will (a big step!), it's time for toys that will fit into hand and mouth nicely. You have the tough task of finding "toys" that are little enough to fit into tiny hands, but not so little that your baby will choke on them. These direct interactions with his environment develop his concept of size. Some ideas for infant size toys:

- Standard rattles and teethers
- Small plastic measuring cups
- Plastic ribbon or adhesive tape spools
- Melamine bowl scraper
- Plastic bracelets
- Anything of smooth plastic, rubber, or metal which could be threaded on a stout key chain or cord, for example, plastic tea strainer, large beads, rubber sink stopper, clear plastic tubing from the hardware store. By stringing items together you prevent your baby from swallowing them. Think of the size of your baby's open mouth and never leave him alone with small toys even on a cord.

LANGUAGE

This fingering and mouthing of objects advances your baby's learning about size. He does not know yet what the words "big and little," "wide and narrow" mean, but he is beginning to experience size through his whole body, his sight, and his touch.

The Baby on the Move: Crawling Age to Twenty-Four Months Your Crawler/Toddler Goes to the World

By eight months or so your baby won't be content to lie on his back staring with interest at his own hands and feet; he'll want food, toys,

objects, and people to interact with. Soon he'll crawl and pull up and climb. It's time for you to be aware of the sizes of things in your house. Your "on the move" baby is mastering the "pincer grip," that thumb to forefinger grasp that can pry incredible things out of tiny spots with the accuracy of tweezers. But your baby hasn't the least idea about what will choke him and what's chewable. It's that all-important exploring age, so keep an eye out for safety yet make sure there are interesting "pick-up-ables" lying about for discovery and mastery. Keep an assortment handy but only put out a few at a time.

PEOPLE

Although the researchers haven't figured out exactly why, babies notice and react to adults and other children in different ways. Size is thought to be a factor. The eight-month-old who is spooked by a strange adult will grin when an unknown six-year-old peeks into your kitchen. Babies love to look at other babies and at themselves in the mirror too. If yours is an only child, borrow your neighbor's children or brave up to a family reunion with cousins from time to time to give your baby "people" experiences with "big" and "little," "tall" and "short."

BODY

Your baby's body is the tool by which he measures the space about him. A crawler will manage to jam himself behind the toilet, a fourteen-month-old will manage to get his fist stuck in a cup and his finger in a bottle opening. A toddler will squeeze his head between the porch railings. A two-year-old will get his bottom stuck in the trash basket. Your child is learning what is "big" and "little" about parts of him and the spaces around him. The words "tall" and "short" don't mean anything to him, but he's beginning to extend his reach, crawling from chair to open drawer to dresser top, standing tall in spirit if reckless of physique.

FOOD

The size of food is very important from about eight months on because it's all involved in the child's growing ability to do for himself using important muscles as he practices. Practicing one skill leads to a more refined one. Those same two fingers that pick up a pea will practice for years before they can control a pencil or pen to form letters in school. Depending on your pediatrician's advice, you'll be moving to what is euphemistically described as "finger foods" (it is really more accurately "face and floor" food). At about a year, mastery of his new skills means practice, practice, and practice in picking up bits. The meals last longer and are more fun (for your baby, not for you). For finger foods see the food list in Chapter 2. For more fun make a line of dry cereals, beet cubes, hamburger crumbles. Let your baby pick and choose. Little foods are good for finger and hand practice. An occasional "big" item is a nice surprise and causes a toddler to use two hands to manage:

- A well-picked-over chicken or turkey drumstick. (Pull off the gristle that he could choke on.) The drumstick will graze nose and eye (a blink will save the eyeball) before a baby's arm can engineer the long bone into chewing position. He's learning long and short by experience.
- The tip end of a long loaf of French bread or pita bread
- A whole carrot, celery stalk, or peeled parsnip (if he has teeth watch for chewed bits too big to digest).

Don't worry that the spoon is out and fingers are "in." Nobody goes to college eating with his hands (at least not from our houses). When your baby's arm becomes adept at the movements necessary for spooning and forking, those skills will be exciting to practice. All in all nature is on the side of what civilized humans call growth and progress, though it may not seem so when your little baby has what Aunt Lucy would label "animal habits" at the table. Remind her that animals don't have thumbs and marvel at how your baby begins to use his thumbs.

BATH

Uncertainty about his size may affect a toddler at bath time. Toddlers may scream and wail when you begin to let the water out. They truly believe "big them" may go down the "little" drain. The solution is simple: take your child out of the tub, then drain the water. Before you pull the plug let your child play with containers in the water. Use any of the toddler texture "toys" that aren't paper, two or three at a time. Be selective—put in just bowls of different sizes or just spoons—not everything at once. Your order helps him order his world.

TOYS AND ACTIVITIES

Your baby's "toys" are anything he can encounter while he is creeping, crawling, and toddling. Feeling the rugs and furniture is fun, but he needs things small enough to pick up. He needs objects to look at and handle that have some details small enough to attract him. The size of things becomes increasingly fascinating as he gets older: "fitting" one thing into another, making his first crude judgments about which is bigger and which is smaller. In our experience many household items have gotten stuck or lost because the fit was tighter or looser than our child had supposed. In one house, for years we drank out of a double-decker plastic glass, unwilling to throw it away and praying that this tribute to an eighteen-month-old's misjudgment of size would crack some day, freeing the buried inner cup.

Your judgment about size allows you to maneuver a car between a delivery truck and another car parked at the curb. Your baby is beginning the experiences that lead to that skill when he pulls and bangs his wagon or toy stuck in the passage between the table leg and the sofa. It won't fit and he tries to force it. Let him practice. If you do it for him at the first sign of frustration he won't learn to solve his own problems. You can help him move the chair to make a wider space, but let him maneuver himself and things through space, judging the fit. "Practice makes perfect," and frustrations and resolutions at two, with your encouraging voice supporting him, will teach him. This practice will save dents in your car when he's sixteen and you're not there to move the delivery truck!

There are many different kinds of size toys; try one kind at a time. The list below has enough variety for weeks. A younger child will manipulate one or two at once, fitting one pot to one lid or nesting two cans. The near-two-year-old will begin to fit and build a bit or make little piles of pairs. Your child needs to have these simple experiences organized for him, not just a hodge-podge collection of size toys. Limit the number and kind of items you put out. One day just put out cans, another day little cans and little balls, another day big shoes and big boxes. The variety and the way you put them out will expand his concept of size. For size toys try these:

- Balls—Ping-Pong, squash, tennis, basketball, and beach balls. For an eight-month-old, one or two balls will do; for a twenty-four-month-old add more sizes.
- Cans—orange juice, tuna, baking powder, Crisco, coffee, institution-size cans, sequenced in height and width. For an eight-month-old two very contrasting sizes; for a twenty-four-month-old, a full series of four or five. Make sure there are no sharp edges.
- Cardboard cylinders—grits, oatmeal, salt, picnic salt
- Boxes—from baby shoe to worker's boot, from jewelry box to liquor store size. A real size surprise is an empty large appliance box for a playhouse.
- Sets—measuring spoons, bowls, plastic glasses
- Wooden spoons—large and small
- Wire whisks—several sizes if you're a gourmet cook
- Pots and lids—from small to giant, from egg coddler to lobster pot

Your child will be three years old before he judges size by sight, not by trial and error. The Montessori classroom has sets of beautiful wooden equipment which teach the size sequence skills your child can learn in the kitchen. The mania for fitting things into other things will mean your metal mixing bowl jammed into the dog's dish and many a small item deposited carefully into your empty trash basket. Big spaces cry out for little things to fill them; but remember, your child is learning "big" and "little," "large" and "small"—and check the trash!

LANGUAGE

Even though an eight-month-old is a long way from using a size word (he's at the "da-da" stage) he will listen to your voice tone as you give him a <u>BIG</u> ball or a <u>little</u> potato lump. Hearing you use the words as he has size experiences is the way he will eventually learn the words. By twenty-four months your child will repeat your words: a "big" boy, a "tall" tree, a "long" ride. Keep talking and those words you use will begin to bounce back at you.

Newly acquired language skills sometimes have their drawbacks too. A mother we know who had a verbally precocious toddler was embarrassed in a restaurant because her child had a vocabulary of size, but no social discretion. The table was approached by two waiters, one very tall and one very short. Out of the mouth of the babe came the language of a two-year-old, "look at the big daddy man and the little baby man" as everyone's face reddened. This child was on his way to a concept of size, but the practice of his new skills needed tactful guidance.

Two- and Three-Year-Olds: Your Child Finds Words for the World

The big achievement for a two-year-old is the definition of himself as separate from others. All those "NO's" and stubbornnesses and tantrums are saying, "I am ME," and "I make choices." Along with a sense of self comes an awareness of size; size for him is defined in a somewhat egocentric way. "Little is what I can see over, big is what I can't. Tall is what I have to turn my head up to, short is what I look down on." It's fun to see the wheels turning as a two- or three-year-old visually measures the size of a very tall person or a tree by looking up, up, up, then down, then back up slowly. Repetition is the keynote of this age, the practice for mastery as he climbs "big" hills again and again or gingerly walks back and forth over small objects. The toddling stagger of the eighteen-month-old is gone and being able to step over a toy truck on the floor is a proud feat for your two-year-old. By three, the same child may walk along a low wall, adding the challenge of height to his wanderings. Sometimes the motion of your two- or three-year-old is exhausting. It seems like motion for its own sake and it is. He can get about with reasonable facility and it's fun to move for the pure joy of it, like the teenager who has just learned to drive.

PEOPLE

Two- and three-year-olds are very interested in themselves: themselves as babies, themselves as big kids. They are establishing themselves as individuals in their own right and their need to "feel big" affects their

relationships with the people in their lives. Your child wants the tokens of "bigness"—grown-up underpants, not diapers; the move to a big bed from a baby crib. On the other hand, this very same child swings back and snuggles in your lap, happy to be a little baby. This "on again, off again" independence is a trial at times to preschooler and parents alike. You can encourage the steady growth of independence in many ways—talking about the things he can do, allowing him to make some choices, stretching his mental skills to pretending. Trying on Daddy's hat and sitting in Daddy's big chair give him a "taste" of being big. Pretending to be a baby is an acceptable way to be momentarily dependent. The pretending of a two- or three-year-old will pretty much be limited to the mommy, daddy, and baby roles that are familiar. He will say "no, no" to teddy and give a motherly kiss to his rubber duck. This is an exciting intellectual event. Your child takes on an active role, playing mommy and daddy, doing for others what was done for him.

BODY

A two- or three-year-old likes to try out his body to find out how big he is. In finding out just what his body can do your household furniture challenges him as much as the jungle gym in the park. You will find your child climbing on your sofa back, trying to fit in the dryer, or squeezing under the bed. Twos and threes put peas in their nostrils and seeds in their ears. It is all a matter of what fits!

Two- and three-year-olds love to measure each other with their bodies, standing belly to belly and nose to nose to see who's taller, or seeing if their forehead has reached your belt buckle yet. Children of this age love to hold up hands and feet and match with yours or a friend's to compare size. Your child's own body parts, not a yardstick or ruler, are the measuring tools of choice and comparison. Borrow a neighbor's baby or have one of your own so your two- or three-year-old can lie down and compare how long he is. If you're not ready to have a baby, a pet cat or dog will give your child the important experience of feeling bigger than something else, the superiority of size that everyone needs in the pecking order of life.

Mirrors are of endless fascination for a child getting acquainted with his own reflection—a full-view mirror for the whole body, a hand mirror for faces. Stand behind your child so he sees you towering over him, a different experience from looking at you face to face. Put teddy in too as the bottom of the line or on your head, taller than all of you!

CLOTHING

Your child will be fascinated by how little he was and how much bigger you are. Save some baby booties, a mitten or two, and his first shoe. The concrete experience of seeing that he can't get into clothes he once wore will give him a sense of growth he couldn't imagine any other way. At this age not only is it fun for your child to see that he can't fit into his baby clothes, but he will love to parade around in Daddy's hat, coat, and necktie or Mommy's stacked heels with necklace dripping to knees. Boys and girls will enjoy fitting into the clothes of either parent. If you're uninhibited try on his mitten or baby hat—it's all a way of demonstrating size.

FOOD

Sometimes two- and three-year-olds like to be able to manage their own food and drink, so a little table and chair, small cup, plate, and utensils will be a big deal. Just as you're basking in your success finding the perfect spot for your child's dining, he's eyeing the big table and wants a big fork. To make your child feel "big" at mealtime, make portions small, a teaspoon a serving for your picky eater or better still, a teaspoon to serve himself out of a cereal bowl "serving dish." Serving himself gives your child that sense of control he craves.

Two- or three-year-old children are used to many standard items of food and their expected sizes. For some reason the unexpected seems uproarious. It is the same with us as adults. One of our mothers has practiced an elaborate Thanksgiving joke on several sets of grandchildren by borrowing a hotel-size covered dish for the turkey and secretly cooking up a tiny quail. When the lid was lifted the shocked assemblage was told the turkey had shrunk. Your child will enjoy the same size surprises:

- A foot-long hot dog and tiny cocktail franks
- A big apple and little crab apple
- A little Cheerio and big bagel or donut served for breakfast
- A big hamburger for Daddy and a little hamburger for him, or the other way around
- A big pancake for him and a little pancake for Rover
- A beefsteak tomato and cherry tomatoes served in the same salad
- Big and little cookies baked by big and little hands
- Big and little pretzels (thick and thin too)
- His very own tiny Halloween pumpkin and the big family jack-o-lantern

BATH

Bath time is one time your child is confined to a relatively small space. Make it last as long as you can by providing interesting size bath toys:

- Sponges—big and little
- Kitchenware—metal or plastic spoons and cups which only last year satisfied his pouring mania will now be used for beginning rough measuring. He will transfer soap bubbles from the large to small spoon; will they fit? He will pour bath water from the small to large cup to fill it up. Your two- and three-year-old will not yet have a knowledge of size in relation to number, but the basis for a mastery of fifth grade fractions has begun.
- Plastic pill containers or little bottles that float and dare to be captured by small fingers.
- Brushes to paint tub, tile, and faucets using bubbles or bath water as paint. Vary brush sizes for excitement; offer a mascara brush or a paint brush.
- Bath towels can be size surprises. If your two- or three-year-old is used to a normal-sized bath towel, amuse him by wrapping him in a huge beach towel or give him four terry fingertip towels, one to dry each limb. He'll remember it for weeks.

TOYS AND ACTIVITIES

Your child enjoys toys that fit his size and capabilities, big crayons for his imprecise grip, large trucks and cars to push. There are lots of household objects that are fun to use as toys, too. Big and little things handle differently. Your two- or three-year-old will enjoy some of these:

- Cans of various sizes. Instead of just fitting little into big or building one on one, the plan now will be building tall towers with several cans, sometimes with the large one as the base and then with large perched on small for challenge.
- Boxes in different sizes. A big one is good to sit in; a little one makes a caboose for teddy to ride in; five boxes make a building for your child and teddy; three boxes make a tall tower to knock down.
- Balloons and bubbles that start out small and blow up bigger and bigger
- Paper—a little pad or great big pad to scribble on. Each size requires a different skill.
- Bags to carry treasures in, small and jumbo size
- Jars and lids of all sizes tossed into a box or spare drawer for you and your child

For you jars store leftovers, for your child they are a puzzle, a physical and mental challenge in finding the right size lid for the right size jar. At two-and-one-half, a child is able to make the turning motion to unscrew caps and will practice endlessly, finding the right top and screwing it on. Start your two-and-one-half-year-old with three jars and three lids to match and fit. When he masters these add more sizes. When your child tires of this matching and fitting game, trace the caps on a shirt cardboard and let him fit the caps to the outlines; then trace the bottle bases the same way. Matching two objects (bottle and lid) is much easier than this task of matching an object (lid or bottle) to a picture outline.

INDOORS AND OUTDOORS

Two-year-olds like to climb hills and look down; it's part of feeling big. Three-year-olds can climb a jungle gym higher than your shoulder, looking down on you and chanting "I'm bigger than you are." Take the time with your child to stand together under a tall tree, next to a tall building, or near the littlest plant beginning to grow. Some outdoor size activities for two- and three-year-olds:

- Collect big and little sticks and stones.
- Collect long and short pine needles.
- Find a big leaf and a little leaf on the same bush or plant.
- Find the biggest or littlest along the way if you can't stand the junk carted home. Compare what you've got and drop anything that isn't the most or least.
- Walk in tall grass, if it's taller than your child's head. It's much like an adult walking through a mature cornfield.
- Roll down a big hill, a little hill.
- Make big and little footprints in the snow, sand, or near a rain puddle.
- Make handprints in the mud—be bold and plunge in.
- Run in a big space, the nearby high school football field or auditorium. On the way home stand in a tiny space—a phone booth.
- Find the biggest flower in the flower bed and pick it.
- Take little steps to the mailbox, take big steps to bed. It's been a long day!

At this age, size is beginning to be an identifier and classifier, one way to tell one kind of thing from another, a dog from a horse, a flower from a tree. Two- and three-year-old children are beginning to sort animals, plants, and people into groups by size. Every now and then you will be surprised to discover that your two- or three-year-old is still limited in his views of classes and categories. He's calling the St. Bernard a horse or the Pekingese a kitty. You'll soon appreciate that size is not the only identifier he needs. The combinations of qualities is a sophistication to come in later years. The shapes of ears, the lengths of tails, and the sounds of cries and calls identify also. Two- and three-year-olds are at the level of gross comparisons, putting every new item into a familiar class (dog/cat) until they learn the refinements.

Expand your child's horizons when he's outgrown the neighborhood by visiting a farm or a zoo. Two- and three-year-olds, so recently babies themselves, love parent and baby animal pairs at a farm or a zoo: the big elephant and the little one he can touch, the pig and the piglets. Though little fingers can't be trusted not to crush bugs, your child will love watching ants and beetles in the grass if you show him where they live.

LANGUAGE

As your two- or three-year-old takes in the world, you are keeping an eye out, seeing to his safety, and tossing out a few new objects. But most of all you are "naming names," giving him the words he is eager for. As your child moves about, he will mumble the names and actions in his play: "truck, big truck, little dog, come little dog." His many naming experiences help to sort out his world and give him practice in talking. In addition to this constant monologue, twos and threes have begun to communicate to their families and in a simple way to outsiders and other children. The wish to communicate with this widening circle of people spurs his language. You can help by supplying refinements such as size words, which give precision to your child's speech.

Four- and Five-Year-Olds: Your Child Begins to Order His World

A four-year-old we know created complete chaos one evening as her parents were about to depart for a night on the town. When the baby sitter arrived, this heretofore unflappable four-year-old took one look at the sitter and proceeded to fall completely apart, wailing "You can't leave us!" Between sobbing and sniffling, the poor parents discovered what prompted this strong reaction. The baby sitter, although a high school student, was 4' 11" and in the words of a panicked four-year-old was "not big enough to be a sitter!" To a four- or five-year-old, size means importance, competence, and age. The bigger you are the more power you have, the more you can do, and the older you must be. The wailing four-year-old was not just being "ornery." She was faced with a real problem. Experience (all of four years) told her that adult baby sitters and children were of certain general sizes. This exception to her rule threw her into a tizzy.

A young child's concept of size will change as he grows physically and matures intellectually. The young child sorts objects in his world into distinct classes (large or small, tall or short, and so forth). At first everything is an either/or proposition. With experience and time the child's earlier classifications will begin to expand. He will begin to understand some of the complexities of size classification. Many experiences with perspective are needed to learn to judge the size of objects and people at a far distance. Amusing misconceptions may occur. The city child who has only seen pictures of farm animals may have no idea of their actual dimensions. In addition to practical matters, size is

spoken of in a relative way: one man's big may be another's tiny; basketball players have a different point of view from jockeys. You as parents can help your four- and five-year-old by providing and talking about size experiences.

PEOPLE

Piaget tells us that young children confuse size with age, assuming that taller is older. A very little girl who had a very tall college-age brother, taller than her daddy, knew that her daddy should be the oldest yet didn't think he was. How could he be? Her brother was taller. This is a puzzlement to a four-year-old. You can help your four- and five-year-old discover that people come in all sizes and gradually to grasp the subtleties of age and height. Ask your child to "think" who is taller, Daddy or Cousin Nancy. At first he needs to do some size comparisons with the people present so he can actually see the size difference, but later memory serves. Ask your child to order his family. Gross comparisons are easy to handle, the toddler cousin, the teenager, the tall uncle. Too many cousins or a set of twins will blow the fuse. A five-year-old can't handle subtle differences in size; in addition, his memory skills are just developing. Many experiences and maturity are needed before your child fully understands age and size.

Four- and five-year-olds are interested in the world outside. Little children like to practice being big. Your child will begin to imitate the jobs and actions of those community people he knows. Since play is the way your child learns about the world around him, he will try out other people's roles. This role playing is a very intellectual activity incorporating higher levels of abstraction as the play becomes more complex. Your four- or five-year-old will enjoy this kind of interaction with siblings, neighbors, and friends. The interaction of a group of role players stimulates language development and concept formation. Children need ideas for role playing—through visits to see people at their jobs, through conversation with you about what they saw, and through children's books about what firefighters, police officers, doctors, and veterinarians do. They need a few "props" to make their play exciting and realistic, plus some encouragement from you.

This is a good time to start a costume (and prop) box. Your props need not be fancy, just real enough to get the play going. Keep a collection:

- A white shirt to be worn backwards—for a doctor, nurse, dentist, veterinarian
- A length of old hose for a firefighter
- An old wig for a beautician
- A painter's cap and paintbrush
- An old suitcase for a trip

You will notice a change in your child's play alone and with friends as his "pretend" becomes more elaborate. If you help him with ideas and a few props (it doesn't take much) he can grow from the simple "mommy-daddy-baby" play of the three-year-old to more advanced ideas. The two-dimensional "super hero" characters get very boring to have zooming about the house, so a trip to the firehouse and a piece of hose may transform your yard into a fire station and leave Superman on television unwatched and unimitated for a week. If the weather is warm a real hose with water may keep the firefighter outdoors skipping two weeks of television!

BODY

Every child's interest in the world starts with himself and moves outward to other people. You may find yourself tripping off to Slenderella after being grouped with the "fatties" rather than the "thinnies" by your four-year-old. Your four- or five-year-old child, having survived the "identity crisis" of the two- and three-year-old, will be able to view his own body with a bit (and that's not much) more objectivity. He will be less concerned with his body as a whole than he was at two or three years and more interested in his body's specific parts. This is an awful show-off age when children revel in the unattractive. They laugh at big burps or sneezes and other unmentionable noises. They delight in making big and little bubbles with their own saliva. To channel the fun to more acceptable activities, have your child find these:

- Fat body parts (cheeks, tummy, bottom)
- Thin body parts (lips, ears)
- Large body parts (legs, back, chest)
- Small body parts (eyelashes, little toenails, belly button)
- Long body parts (arms, legs, tongue)
- Short body parts (neck, little fingers, toes)
- Thick body parts (tummy, thighs)
- Thin body parts (hair strands, little fingernails)
- Wide body parts (shoulders, waist, bottom)
- Narrow body parts (ankles, nose)
- Big and little (toes, voices)

With all this noticing your child may get "carried away" and call attention to the butcher's long nose or your minister's thin hair. Try to keep the noticing game closer to home and suggest that your child find large or small, thick or thin on a sibling or friend. The sociable nature of fours and fives makes this an exciting game. Keep an eye and ear out for body exploration which may go beyond what is socially acceptable in our culture.

For your four- or five-year-old playing alone or waiting for dinner, pull out a pocket mirror. The hand mirror or pocketbook size is great for looking at specific parts of the body. Your child will discover that depending on how far away he holds the mirror he can see his whole head or just an eyebrow. He will spend a long time fascinated by his teeth, his eyes, his fingernails, his tongue. The small size of the mirror opens up a whole new world. All this egocentrism leads to a necessary awareness of self. Formal intelligence tests score a child in how many body parts he includes in his drawing; knowledge of self is basic and is learned through direct and repeated experiences.

For the child who has some understanding of size concepts and knows the words but has a limited understanding of numbers, let him measure using his own hand or foot as the standard unit of measure. A clever teacher we knew had the class measure calling each unit by the child's name. The newspaper was five "Charlies" long and the aquarium three "Christophers." In primary school when your child is ready for standard units of measure (the ruler and yardstick), he will be familiar with the idea of measuring. Measurement is, after all, regarding one unit in terms of another. Have your child measure small objects with hand or foot. If he begins to measure your driveway he will soon get to numbers beyond the grasp of a four- or five-year-old.

For a size surprise take your child to the nearest shopping center which has a fun house mirror. He'll be amused at looking tall and thin, fat and short!

CLOTHING

Wasn't it pleasant selecting little outfits you liked in the children's department for your child's first three years of life? If your child is four or five you know the fun is over and the battle is on. Suddenly "short" pants are "out" for your five-year-old even though it's July and ninety degrees in the shade. The neighborhood dictates "long pants" and your son would rather sweat it out in corduroys than wear "babyish" short pants. Your four-year-old daughter will convince Grandmother to buy a "long" dress for the party even though she will hoist it above her bottom to dash out the door to greet a friend. For years long pants and dresses have been symbols of age and maturity; but every era has its counter trend. Watch for fashionable passing fads, such as safari shirts or jogging shorts.

Being social, your child will also be interested in and talk about what others are wearing. Without pushing the "best dressed list" it's fun to notice wide and narrow belts, big and little belt buckles, long and short hair, plaids with thick and thin lines, thick and thin jackets and sweaters, socks—knee, anklet, tall, and short—and shoes with thick and thin straps.

FOOD

Four- and five-year-olds love to try new things and taste new foods. Expand their knowledge of large and small, thick and thin, wide and narrow by letting them eat or cook the following:

- Large and small curd cottage cheese
- Big and little bread slices; a sandwich made on cocktail rye
- Big and little pickles and olives, one of each beside a sandwich
- Thick and thin bread and salami slices

- Thick and thin carrot or cucumber sticks or rounds
- Long and short celery or green pepper strips
- Wide and narrow, thick and thin, pastas in an unusual Italian dinner
- Thick and thin gelatin, pudding, soups, milk shakes
- Big and little biscuits cut with water tumbler and thimble

For a few size surprises make rice in a small pan and notice how it swells. Popovers and soufflés are size surprises worth watching. If you have a see-through oven door, turn on the oven light and pull up a chair and let your child enjoy the drama. It beats watching television!

TOYS AND ACTIVITIES

Your four- and five-year-old is probably a collector, acting much like a squirrel readying for winter. You will find a rock collection under his pillow and a toy car collection a hazard in the front hall. This collecting mania goes on for years so try to make the most of it. Classifying by size will enable him to clean up his toys; it's a way of organizing the grand mess. "Put all the little cars in a box and park the big cars under the bed." The challenge of classification may lead him to enjoy the "clean up" as part of the play. Seriation from large to small or thickest to thinnest, tallest to shortest, or vice versa, is a bigger challenge.

Four- and five-year-olds handle objects one by one, measuring one against the other to line up a series. They need concrete objects to handle and compare. Remembering sizes of objects results from the experiences of physically comparing them. Seriation of concrete objects by size, texture, or weight precedes the far more complex seriation of numbers, ideas, or events. Children of four or five enjoy precision and order and will line up a series of sticks (narrow and wide, thick and thin, long and short), paper tubes (toilet paper, paper towel, wrapping paper), clay (rolling long and short "snakes"), and buttons or rubber bands (little to big, thick to thin).

Become a hoarder yourself: forget your prechild housekeeping standards of the straightened dresser drawer. Save the giant pencil from the boardwalk at Atlantic City or the tiny pencil sent in a mailed advertisement. Your child of four or five will laugh at the size differences.

The mastery of the tools of creativity, such as brushes, crayons, and paper, open new possibilities for size exploration. Your child can at last hold the paper steady with one hand while he writes with the other. He will be looking at his old unbreakable crayons with disgust, wanting the status symbol of slim, breakable crayons. The slimmer shape is appropriate to his new finger precision. For special creative treats try these:

- Crayons for drawing wide and narrow lines (try the sides of crayons for wide lines)
- Paintbrushes in varying size and width
- Paper in tiny note pads or huge shelfpaper rolls
- A magnifying glass to create big from little
- Water experiments in bath or swimming pool (water magnifies too)

The basic tools of creativity—the crayons, paintbrushes, paper, tape, and string—are rarely given generously to children. They are considered adult property that is somehow an extravagance. In households where a $5.95 toy with batteries is considered a reasonable expenditure, tape is doled out by the inch. These materials involve your child in experiences of doing and thinking long after the $5.95 toy is broken or the batteries worn.

Size in many forms will delight your child: a big balloon as a present, a tea party with your after-dinner coffee cups. Soon your toy-oriented child will become interested in the sizes of letters and numbers, an intellectual event. Your four-year-old may show an interest in the letters of his own name. Your five-year-old may find the letters of his name on grocery store and gas station signs. If he goes to kindergarten he will know the difference between upper and lower case letters (capitals and small letters). Further down the educational road he will notice which letters are taller and shorter when he prints them. Remember the huge sheets of primary paper where you had to make some letters go all the way to the top line while others huddled below?

An interesting—and at some time necessary—activity is to let your child classify (sort) coins. As your four- or five-year-old begins to use his experience and knowledge in all concept areas you can ask him to classify the coins by size, color, or texture (smooth or ridged on the edge). It is at this age that children can begin to deal with two concepts at once. A two- or three-year-old may know that the penny is small and the half dollar is large, but the four- and five-year-old will begin to distinguish the difference between the penny and the dime, noticing subtle size differences, color differences, textural differences (the edge of the penny is smooth, that of the dime is rough). It's an exciting beginning as the thinker emerges!

INDOORS AND OUTDOORS

Going places with you is one way your four- or five-year-old will learn about the world and develop his concept of size. These are the years for experiencing, more than for reading about big buildings and tall ships. Sometimes your four- and five-year-old will accompany you on routine outings (the stuff of his dramatic role playing above) to the grocery store, the dry cleaners, and the hardware store; at other times your trips and visits will be planned just for his pleasure. He will learn from both kinds of trips. When you are not making a mad dash to the grocery to get the lettuce you forgot for tonight's dinner party, allow a few extra minutes for you and your child to find and laugh at the gallon jar of mustard . . . now who could eat all that mustard? Or send your five-year-old off to find the largest bunch of bananas or the tallest can of frozen orange juice. He will enjoy the independence and feel proud when he succeeds. You can still stick to your list while your child is enjoying learning.

The hardware store is wonderful for just plain browsing. It's a veritable paradise of size. Here you will find:

- An incredible array of nails, washers, screws, ropes, chains, and tubing, all in order by size
- Wide and narrow brooms
- Tall, taller, and tallest garbage cans, even with matching bags
- Screwdrivers with wide and narrow heads
- Big and little hammers

What is mundane to you is exciting and new to a child this age; it need not be an adult's idea of a special treat, such as the big yearly circus or a trip to the ice cream parlor for a banana split. Your child will enjoy and learn about size firsthand by visiting these:

- The tallest building in town, be it ten stories or one hundred ten. It doesn't matter to a child—it's just tall! You can stand outside and look up and then go inside and up to the top and look down.
- The airport and standing next to a plane. Where does your child come up to . . . the top of the tires?
- The fire department—which truck is longest, shortest
- A construction site—compare the cement mixer with a toy truck from home
- The sales area for road equipment—here even Daddy seems small
- The local post office—see trucks in all sizes, very small to very large
- The zoo. One day limit yourselves seeing only the biggest animals, the tallest, or the widest. Another day see the small mammal house. Who was the smallest, shortest, narrowest? Or who has the smallest head, the biggest teeth, the smallest feet? This approach will save dispositions too! Any zoo worthy of the name is too big to see in one visit.

Closer to home you can give your child many size experiences. Look for the following:

- A tree for your child to climb. Climbing a tree will make him feel big. It need not be a very big tree, just a sturdy one. He will grow in confidence and self-respect from the experience. It's worth a few gray hairs on your head.
- Wide and narrow canyons, rivers, and gulches to jump over. Do you think we've gone mad? A rope, a few sticks, an old beach towel; anything can become the obstacle to conquer, to jump over. As skills increase the "rivers" and "canyons" can become wider.
- A patch of garden. Your child can plant his own seeds. Sunflowers and small zinnias are hardy and offer great size contrasts.
- A patch of dirt. Give your child a shovel (a trenching shovel from the surplus store is far sturdier than a toy shovel and just the right size) and let him dig the biggest hole he can. Better pick the spot before he does. This is also a good challenge for the beach. Maybe you'll have a chance to read a book while he tries to dig to China.
- A snowstorm. Roll the biggest snowball and build a snowman. The body should be in different sizes. A conventional first grade teacher will hand out three white circles graded in size and your child will be expected to know that the big one goes on the bottom. Defy convention in your backyard and give your snowlady a wasp waist. Maybe it'll take four circles if you must have a head!
- The tallest tree on the block or the longest car, the smallest pebble, the shortest name on a mailbox, the largest television aerial, or whatever comes to mind
- Stars, searchlights, or floodlights from your backyard. Take out a penlight and a flashlight and let your child compare the beams; dance one light into the other.
- A small house, a mansion, a wide street (boulevard), or a narrow alley
- A large zucchini and a small tomato

Keep your eyes open and your sense of humor handy and you and your child will thrive. After all, there is something very humorous about a zucchini as big as your arm, isn't there? All this makes for companionship, sharing, learning, and fun. What more can you ask?

LANGUAGE

Four- and five-year-olds are big talkers. Their ideas are more complex and their language richer than two- or three-year-olds. An older child has more experience with reality and begins to enjoy fantasy. Tall tales are typical of this age and parents turn to "lying" in the index of the child development books to figure out whether or not their child knows right from wrong. Size words are great for exaggeration, as anyone interested in fishing knows, so let your four-year-old have his ten-foot-tall talking fantasies, but give him a wink to let him know you're aware that he's kidding. This way he won't lose his own grip on the truth.

Back to reality, he is constantly seeking out the right word, trying new words and qualifying his nouns by the adjectives of size, color, shape, weight, and so on. Remember that the more experiences your child has had, the richer his language will be. Sometimes a child knows the words in one context, but is limited in variety of experiences. One of our children's kindergarten teachers made the mistake of overestimating her class' grasp of size. The well-intentioned teacher told her class the traditional Thanksgiving story about the Indians and the hardships the Pilgrims endured. In her poetic telling of the tale she said, "The Pilgrims had very little food." This same tale was retold by a five-year-old using the same poetic phrasing, however, the five-year-old inserted a descriptive gesture: "The turkeys were this big"—all of five inches! It seems something of our American heritage was lost in the translation.

It takes many years to grasp fully size concepts. "Little" must be understood as a relative term. "Tall" or "short" must be applied appropriately to people or buildings in the vertical plane, "long" and "short" to lines, pants, and hair. People are fat or thin, objects are wide or narrow. Absorbing the conventions of word use and applying them appropriately take time and experience. Misconceptions and misapplications of words are part of every preschooler's growth. You'll smile when your four-year-old asks for fat noodles or talks of tall instead of long legs. Bit by bit the confusions and contradictions disappear as your child tries new experiences, new words, and new ideas. Besides size experiences, you can encourage language development by selecting and reading nursery rhymes about size, for example, "Little ships must keep to shore" and "I had a little husband." You can also select and read children's classic tales that involve size, such as "Jack and the Beanstalk," "Goldilocks and the Three Bears," "Little Red Riding Hood," "The Three Billy Goats Gruff," "Tom Thumb," and "Thumbelina." Your child will also enjoy children's books that tell about big people, firefighters, doctors, dentists, and space explorers.

You can also encourage language development and creativity by playing "thinking games." Please do not assume teacher/pupil roles or turn the games into wrong and right answer sessions. Make them enjoyable activities for you both. This is a great time passer while your four- or five-year-old is waiting for his brother's trumpet lesson to be over and a great way for you as parents to see how your child's mind works. Try these:

- Making lists together of things that are wide, narrow, tall, short, big, little. Remember size is personal! That dog next door may be big to your child and small to you.
- Making lists of big things you like (extra large deluxe pizza) and small things you like (a kiss)
- Making lists of big things you don't like (the dog next door) and small things you don't like (ants in the bread box)
- Playing a game. "What's bigger than our bread box?" "Is it smaller than a school bus?" This is good for analytical thinking about size.
- Playing what if . . . you were as tall as your toothbrush, we lived in this shoe box, or your feet were as long as your legs?
- Combining two or more concepts. "What animal is big and gray?" (an elephant)
- Being silly (your four- and five-year-old's level of humor). Since your child has a basic grip on some concept areas, his sense leads to an appreciation of the absurd, enjoying what is beyond the usual or the expected. The clown car in the circus, a tiny car that opens to spill out body after body, is wildly amusing.
- Teaching your child a classic game: "Mother may I . . . take a giant step, baby step," etc. Four- and five-year-olds love the power the "Mother" exerts and the control required by the players.
- Talking about careers related to size: the thin man, the fat lady with the circus, basketball players, jockeys, miniature-makers, stilt walkers
- Remembering animals by size, the littlest and the biggest your child has ever seen
- Singing a size sequence song, "I know an old lady who swallowed a fly" or "There's a hole in the bottom of the sea"
- Encouraging your child to make up his own jokes and riddles about size. The results may not be funny to you but will probably be hilarious to another child.

Remember, creativity is what you are after. As a parent you are encouraging the mental manipulation of concepts. You are also whiling away long waits at the doctor's office or long car rides with activities that are fun for your child and delightful to you. You will enjoy the revelation of how your child thinks by his answers to playful language games. By five some children have not reached the level of abstraction necessary to handle games which involve thinking about two concepts at a time or putting sizes in order from memory. Adults' use of size words such as "tall tales," "narrow misses," "big deals," and "small change," may conjure funny images in a child's mind. At five a child is still tied to the concrete experience. A "tall" tale may seem like the other end of a giraffe, a "narrow" miss may emerge from the Slenderella Salon, a "big" deal may fill the room and "small" change may seem the size of rice! All children proceed from the concrete manipulation of objects to the abstract manipulation of ideas. The experiences, the words, the back-and-forth of talking with you about everyday or imaginary happenings will move your child along the continuum until he is ready to "think like a grown-up." You can't force it. You can enjoy seeing it happen. If your child is especially adept at conceptualizing size you may be watching the seeds of tomorrow's city planner, architect, or engineer sprouting.

Chapter 4

"As Round as an Apple"
How a Child Learns
About Shape

STARE AT A NEWBORN BABY'S HAND or watch a time-lapse film of a flower blooming and the excitement of shape will hold you once again. Watching your child discover shapes in the world will bring you to observe forms that you'd stopped noticing. Your hurried glance will spot a rabbit hopping by, but your child's ponderings about what he has seen, noting its shape, size, color, and texture, will make you look back again and see more. You'll find symmetry together in flowers and ponder how the keystone stays up in a Roman arch. Your eyes will be reopened to the wonders of the world.

Knowledge of shape is both practical and aesthetic: shape is an identifier and an eye pleaser. Shape comes in pure form in picture books and in combinations in objects. Shape differentiates one animal, flower, letter, or number from another. Shape comes in the reality of objects or in the symbolism of letters. In five short years your child learns to handle them all, the pure shape of the two-dimensional square in a picture book, the three dimensions of a cube of ice, and the symbolism of an H. Your child will experience shape in many ways. Babies first discover shape by mouth, biting and chewing around curves and corners. The young scientist at one year tosses object after object off high chair and out of playpen. Some roll, some don't. Hundreds of dropping "experiments" later, he begins to understand that the balls and beads wander away and the books and blocks land close at hand. Toddlers feel shape toys with their hands as well as their mouths. At each age shape is explored in many ways. For a child it is a difficult task to abstract the "shapeness" around him, such as the roundness of the tabletop or the squareness of his sandwich. A child may know a triangle in a picture book but be thrown when the triangle is presented tilted, set on one point, or with the sides unequal. Even the four basic shapes are not learned in one rainy afternoon. The preschooler may spend a year or two testing and retesting his theories. "This is a circle, right? This is a triangle, right?" Though your child may chant shapes to "Sesame Street" cues, it is a long reach to recognize shapes wherever he finds them. The child who knows his basic shapes upside down or right side up is ready to know the shapes of the world: the oval of a grape, the diamond of the road sign, the cube of gelatin, the cylinder of his drinking glass. He can use his knowledge of shape to describe differences in the tail of a bird or the petal of a flower. Like the listener who knows something about the composition of a symphony, your child's appreciation of his surroundings is increased by his knowledge of shape.

SHAPE CONCEPT WORDS

Least Difficult	*More Difficult*	*Most Difficult*
straight—crooked	edge—corner	flat—slanted
round	curved	
circle—triangle	oval	
rectangle—square		diamond—cube—cone

The Infant: Birth to Eight Months or Crawling Age
You Bring the World to Your Infant

In the past it was thought that newborns lived in a visual blur, but careful study has shown that babies can see clearly from birth. They are nearsighted, though, and focus best at an object less than a foot away. A number of research projects have been conducted to see what sort of patterns and shapes interest babies. Variations of contrast, contour, size, shape, and color have been studied with measurements made of baby's heart rate and length of attention to different stimuli. The results of all the research projects point to one ideal shape to catch a baby's interest: the human face. The three-dimensional face of a real human sparks the most interest in a baby, but pictured ovals with eyes and hair and chin lines win a baby's attention over abstract designs. Nature has planned the baby to show the most interest in the face of the human beings who care for him. This visual communication between you and your baby will draw you together just as the body language of touch does.

TOYS AND ACTIVITIES

You won't be holding him or hanging over his crib all day, so benefit from the results of the research and give your baby some other favored "look" toys. Babies like change; put a new toy up from time to time. Hang these toys about eight to ten inches from his eyes. They should be

about the size of a tennis ball and have some detail or contrast. Babies have been found to like complexity of design. Try:

- A striped pattern or bull's-eye. Your older child could paint one as a gift for your baby. These tested patterns are surefire baby pleasers.
- A face picture from a magazine
- Gift paper or wallpaper samples cut into simple geometric shapes hung above the crib or stuck to the wall to be looked at as he's fed and burped
- Designs in your shower curtain. Clean out your medicine cabinet while your baby sits in his infant seat and stares at the designs.

Nature has not only created the marvel of baby's interest in the shape of the human face, but also the marvel of how breast and thumb fit baby's mouth. Bottles and pacifiers are designed to imitate natural shapes suiting the baby's mouth and sucking action. Babies not only find and mouth their fists and thumbs, but they discover their hands as toys for visual amusement. When your baby first visually discovers his own hands at about ten or twelve weeks he will spend substantial amounts of time watching them and waving them about. Flailing hands will strike some of the shape toys you suspend above crib or carriage and the motion of these toys will attract him. The visual toys you suspended before four months were for infant looking, not grasping. Once your baby can grasp, safe toys suspended on a strong cord are necessary.

It takes several months before your baby will be able to coordinate hand and eye in order to reach for a toy and grasp it. At three or four months, his efforts look like the giant crane which moves shakily and crudely toward its destination. He must look at his hand, then at the object, then back and forth from one to the other as he closes the distance between hand and object. He touches the object without grasping it, then with a swing of the arm the whole project begins again. Between four and six months he will no longer need to look at his hand when reaching for an object. He will also learn to open his hand and adjust his hand grasp to fit the size of the object he encounters. Once he has learned to grasp, it is a good idea to choose suspended objects that fit his hand and are within his reach. Secure such toys on a cord across crib, carriage, or playpen. Don't let the toys dangle from separate strings, as baby's hands will send the toys swinging through space before he can grasp them.

When he sits supported in your lap or in his infant seat you can hold out toys for him to grasp and mouth. Resist the temptation to put the toy into his reaching hand. Let his hand make the journey and he will reap the rewards of his own efforts. Some shape toys which his hand can grasp and mouth can feel are standard rattles and teethers that you already own or toys listed in Chapter 3, such as measuring spoons, cups, spools, bracelets, large beads, or rubber sink stoppers.

Between six and eight months, as your baby learns to sit alone, these same toys will interest him. Give them to him on stroller tray or feeding table but present them one by one. He will pick them up and look at them, mouth them, and pass them from hand to hand. It is thought that babies can't construct a mental image of an object until they see it from every angle. You will be providing these experiences by bringing objects into range before your child can crawl to new experiences himself.

The Baby on the Move: Crawling Age to Twenty-Four Months
Your Crawler/Toddler Goes to the World

During his second year your baby becomes a great experimenter, trying to see how everything in sight works. Sticky finger marks all over your house attest to the attraction of shapes and spaces. Years ahead, your child will laboriously copy shapes in a handwriting workbook, but now he vigorously rummages the feel of shapes with fingers, fists, and even toes and tummy. His first sense of the shape of things will come from manipulation and exploration with his whole body or parts of it.

This feel of shapes precedes the refinements of the copy book, so

when you despair as your eighteen-month-old fingers the hole in your antique chair, think that he may be "practicing" the even strokes of Elizabethan script!

You'll be amused as your child discovers the functions of various shapes, watching dropped objects stay put or roll away from high chair or playpen. He'll try to stand a square block on its pointed edge or be surprised when his plate lands on its edge and rolls like a ball. Learning the functions of shapes is far more complex than memorizing the names of circle, square, or triangle when the outline is presented. There is a wealth of information your child must accumulate before he can make the shape of things work for him in the world.

PEOPLE

Babies explore people the same way they explore objects. If you've ever watched an adult hold a wiggly ten-month-old where the child can't be put down, you know about a child's interest in shapes. After an initial struggle to get down the child settles into happy play, tracing the adult's ear, and poking his finger into the just fitting nostril of the shocked adult.

At about a year, babies delight in imitating adult facial expressions. Play a game: make your mouth into an "O" and watch your baby pucker back. See if your child enjoys imitating your grimaces and hand gestures. The novelty of seeing your mouth form unexpected shapes may delight one child and alarm another. Your baby may be a born clown or a more predictable and conventional creature.

FOOD

The kitchen is a great learning place for crawlers or toddlers. Food shapes can encourage the independence of self-feeding. Tiny bits encourage finger coordination. If you let your child handle food before you prepare it he will learn some of the shapes of the world. Even an eight-month-old can be given a washed orange, grapefruit, or green pepper to roll about his feeding table as you cook dinner. A one-year-old will be surprised when the curve makes a banana totter and topple. An eggplant, lemon, cucumber, or apple to pat and stroke will familiarize him with the different shapes of fruits or vegetables. Knowledge of shape added to knowledge of texture, size, and color will ready him for recognition and identification in the years to come. You are not trying to raise a two-year-old greengrocer who can rattle off the characteristics of exotic eatables; you are raising a child who knows by touch, taste, and sight that the world is full of an infinite and exciting diversity. Give your child shapes to grasp:

- Cubes of cheese
- Ovals of rusks
- Triangles of apple
- Circles of banana or cooked carrot
- Rectangles of chicken, meat, or toast

• Cooked noodles. Draw up a chair and prepare for a show when your child first encounters the "shape surprise" of limp cooked noodles. His struggles will remind you of the statue of Laocoön and the Serpents.

TOYS AND ACTIVITIES

You'll be terribly excited when your baby learns to pick things up but see if you can manage the same level of pride when he learns to release and throw down. At about ten months this developmental milestone leaves the floor unexpectedly strewn with everything you have just placed near your child to amuse him. A crawler can retrieve his toys but a child in a feeding table or a playpen is soon faced with a bare territory and fusses for you to retrieve. Some parents react as if this new skill calls for disciplinary action. They fear a lifetime of thrown toys. Like most new achievements there is a flurry of practice and then the feat dies out and another takes its place. Take this new achievement in your stride (literally) and think what a few weeks of running and bending will do for your waistline. This throwing and fetching is a variation of the "Rover" game you will find in Chapter 5. At about one year the ability to pick up and let go will lead him to the next stage—putting small objects into a container, dumping them out, and filling once again —a happy amusement. In addition to throwing, dumping, and picking up, your child will experiment with fit. In the same way that he was unaware of size fits he'll be confused by shapes. Many a square peg will be pushed at many a round hole before he gets his shape perception in order. Trial and error is the rule.

You'll be cheered to know that some substantial amount of a child's time in the eight- to twenty-four-month period is spent in staring at things, visually examining their shapes. It really won't seem that there are pauses between actions but they've been statistically proven.

Your baby will probably be given a shape box for his first birthday and soon he will begin to fit in the simple shapes. The circle (cylinder) is the easiest to insert because it can fit in any direction. The triangle comes next and the progression follows, the block with the most angles being the most difficult to manage. Put the shape box out with only one shape (the cylinder) and add challenges as your child's eye–hand coordination progresses. Simplifying the initial variety promotes learning. If he is dealing with a single shape, your baby will notice the match of one block to another (circle to circle) or match the shape of the block to the shape of the empty space. A basketload of shapes promotes random guessing or howling frustration depending on your child's skill and temperament.

Whether or not you have a formal shape box, your household abounds in shape toys. Bought toys alone would not be enough because your child needs variety. He doesn't need a collection of objects all at once but interesting shapes one at a time or in small groups, a changing challenge. There is a reason for simplifying and varying your child's experiences. Young children can attend to one stimulation at a time. Too many objects are confusing and overwhelming. When a child catches sight of a new delight he drops the barely explored toy and moves on. The mental task of concentrating on two objects at once is like the adult motor task of patting your head and rubbing your stomach. In a few years your child will be able to scan casually one toy while managing another, to run and chat at the same time, but for now keep it simple as that is how he learns best. His attention span is fleeting in the second year, barely clockable, but some household shape toys may be your child's favorites. You may see his short attention span lengthen as he plays with the ideal toys for this age—household equipment, accessible, sturdy, easily manipulated, multipurpose, and available for him to use independently. Because of your child's short attention span you need this ready collection to dole out to him so you can get something done yourself. In the second year you can see traits of persistence emerging, the child with physical skills barely developed who challenges himself with tasks worthy of his new skills. One of our children used to put one shaky toy car atop the other and insist on pushing them double-decker, a tottering feat but possible. Matching challenge to ability is something most children do for themselves if you have a variety of toys and opportunities. You have to keep an eye out for your child's frustration level, walking that tightrope between providing him with boring, easy tasks or overwhelming ones. There are no rules about the right amount of challenge, as children differ in powers of concentration, motor coordination, and disposition. The same child may be patient in the morning but cranky and short-fused at noon. As you observe your child you will absorb the cues to his style and even learn a bit about yourself. You may find it's better to give your child simpler toys when *you* are cranky and not up to supporting his efforts at mastery. Your home can provide the range from simple to more complex. Many of the items in other chapters are suitable for shape exploration too. Make these "toys" available :

- Pots and lids in the kitchen (start with one little pot at eight months and progress to three or four pots at twenty-four months, varying from saucepan to percolator)
- Empty soft drink cartons in which to fit plastic cups or blocks. A toddler will love to carry them about.
- Soup cans, food boxes, and freezer cartons to build with; increase the selection as your child becomes more skillful
- Empty cans and boxes to nest (the same ones listed in Chapter 3, from tuna to big juice cans, from jewelry to grocery carton)
- Bracelets, spools, and balls to combine with any of the above. They fit into, on, or around the other shapes.

INDOORS AND OUTDOORS

One of A. A. Milne's poems has the refrain "Roundabout and roundabout and roundabout I go." This dizzying verse describes crawler and toddler alike, each circling whatever lies in his path. If your coffee table is round your toddler will learn the property of round from the endless circling of its periphery. Its height and size make it his first form of jungle gym. If your table is square or rectangular he'll have to make a whole series of different body adjustments to get back where he began. Unlike the continuum of a supporting circle he'll learn the abruptness of a right angle when he can't quite make it around. The invention of the round playpen a decade or two ago took cognizance of this difficulty.

You'll watch your eighteen-month-old make further exploration of space, this time using his backside. An eighteen- to twenty-month-old toddler can take a few steps backward and will be interested in seeing what he can sit upon. A little child-size chair or rocker is fun because he just fits, but boxes, trash baskets, laundry baskets, balls, and books will all be tested as proper perches. It will take your child a while to learn when his body can adjust to the shape of things and when it can't. To him, hollow spaces seem to demand to be filled with solid shapes. Empty spaces or openings invite exploration. Tiny fingers will poke through fan grills, but where safety is not involved you can dignify this household sabotage with the name of problem solving. Many an item will be maneuvered in and through such openings as the mail slot in the door, a heating grill, the opening in a chair back, and a drain hole. It would be interesting to know if plumbers keep statistics of what toddlers manage to put down toilets and into pipes. Once a neighbor's child was at the height of her powers of fitting shape to space and discovered the opening of the storm drain at the curb. It's rectangular opening is like a giant shape box. This particular child had also just learned to remove her shoes, another triumph of shape control. Before the nearby mothers noticed, she had a single shoe off her own foot and one from each of her three companions. Each shoe was dropped gleefully into the slot. There wasn't a pair of shoes left on a toddler! This same child loved to insert her foot, shoe and all, into a coffee can and clomp about the neighborhood Long John Silver style. These childish inventions are not as conventional as form-boards or shape boxes but the learnings from them are of equal merit.

LANGUAGE

It's hard to realize how many learnings must take place before the abstraction of shape words has any meaning. Show a young crawler a realistic color photograph in a picture book and see him try to pinch the cookie off the page surprised that it has only two dimensions. It takes years to know plane and solid forms, their variations and functions. Your crawler or toddler will experience roundness in a real cookie, container, ball, or pot lid, and in the oval of a grape. First he feels, sees, and tastes; then he recognizes two-dimensional pictures and solid geometric forms; lastly he abstracts shape by words like round or square. You'll label the shapes in his world for him long before he labels them for you. Long before he says shape words his recognition of shape in the world will help him mentally label objects and people. His first recognition of form will be those things and people who are important to him: his bottle, his parents, his dog, his shoes. For a year or so these forms and their names may be the labels of a whole similar class. All men may be Daddy, all dogs, even all four-legged creatures, bear his Fido's name.

Two- and Three-Year-Olds: Your Child Finds Words for the World

Two- and three-year-olds begin to emerge as distinctive people with particular focuses, talents, and interests. Some especially delight in texture, others in color or shape. If your child has particular interest and talent in spatial qualities, he will be a puzzle doer and block builder, and in later years be recognized as the neighborhood wizard of design and construction. The child with spatial talents will lock and unlock your door with the masterful precision of a safecracker, build tall towers with an eye to how one box or block fits on another, and do puzzles your other child didn't touch until age five. Any child needs to get the feel of how one shape relates to another, but some children are particularly fascinated by it. If you're not that kind of person yourself, it will be especially interesting to notice and appreciate this genetic surprise in your child.

CLOTHING

One of the encounters two- and three-year-olds have with shape is getting the right body parts into the right-shaped opening as they learn to dress themselves. Getting a round head into a round neck hole or arms into rectangular sleeves is an ardent and serious task. Dressing

oneself is one of the major accomplishments of a three-year-old. Four-year-olds who can dress themselves like to put the wrong clothes on the wrong body parts, two legs in one pants leg or underpants on head, perhaps in celebration of their new skills in dressing. When your child is eager to "do for himself," put his pajamas or shirt and pants out on the floor where he can feel and see the shapes that must match to his own body shapes. Many a shape experiment will occur before success. Matching body shapes to clothing shapes takes practice and endurance for parent and child. Some mornings neither of you will be up for the challenge, a perfect time for "Mommy's turn." Once pants, shirts, and sweaters are managed, your child can escalate to socks, shoes, and mittens. Many a proud two- and three-year-old has gotten shoes on feet successfully, but the wrong shoe on the wrong foot, unable to handle the subtle differences between curve of right and left. This shape distinction takes a year or so to conquer; sneakers and corrective shoes with less of a curve make the task impossible. Strangely enough, these achievements are important accomplishments, and children need encouragement and time to "do it myself." For quite a while it will be easier to do it for them, but the emerging self needs ever-expanding control over clothes, toys, and actions. Supporting a child's perseverance in getting his sock on with heel in back not festooning the ankle front may lead to his being a persistent teenager who doesn't give up and hand in an unfinished geometry paper.

FOOD

Food shapes are fun for two- and three-year-olds who can feed themselves. They have moved beyond grasping shapes of "finger food" and are becoming adept at using eating tools of civilized man. The combination of food shapes and tool mastery challenges the "stick-to-it-iveness" of a two- or three-year-old. Scooping up round peas with a spoon requires refined eye–hand coordination and an intimate knowledge of shape. Before this task is mastered completely, many a clever child will insert an intermediate step of taking a pea in hand and solemnly placing it on the spoon. He wants the grown-up status of silverware, yet is wary of shape demands. For snacking or restful periods without spoons and forks your two- or three-year-old may enjoy these:

- Cookie and cracker shapes—round Ritz, square graham, round oatmeal, and square Fig Newton
- Apples and oranges cut into wedges—it is fun to fit them back together to see the whole again.
- Tiny pieces of any food placed in shapes on plate or food tray. What fun to start breakfast with cereals in a big "O" shape or lunch with carrot sticks making a triangle. Use raisins and other decorative foods to enliven shapeless ones.

TOYS AND ACTIVITIES

Two- and three-year-olds remind you of what it must have been like for Stone Age people when the wheel was invented. They discover the wheel anew and they dote on it. The trike is turned over and the wheels spun. The record and top are studied as they spin (and stopped with little fingers). The classic set of children's blocks is experimented with to see what happens to rectangle, square, and triangle when they are combined. Puzzles are a big interest at this age. Some children do puzzles by matching colors, but most see the shape, matching the solid shape to the empty space. Puzzle doing is a great lesson in parenting. At first you are tempted to do it for your child. Now is the time to set up your relationship as helper or resource, giving your child a growing confidence in his own increasing capabilities. You can put the "right" piece facing the right way invitingly near the space, or place it on the table nearest the side it will fit into. You can help little fingers make the exact fit once the place is discovered. You can beam at the achievement, but if you do it for him he won't grow in confidence and competence, and you'll spend a lifetime doing his homework.

Two-year-olds can experiment with shape by rolling and kicking balls. At two a child can balance briefly on one foot long enough to kick. Catching a ball in the air requires the coordination of an older child, but your seated child will enjoy "catching" a rolled ball as you aim it into his spread-out legs. Make sure the ball size is larger than a tennis ball, but smaller than a beach ball. Three-year-olds can begin to experiment with shape by catching balls with both hands. Make sure the ball is large enough for small arms to encircle easily. It will be many years before you will play a real game of "catch," but with these primitive back-and-forths you've begun. Gradually you'll move farther and farther apart for tossing, and just about the time your back threatens to give out from years of constant bending, stooping, and retrieving your child's throws, his accuracy will improve. The age cycle between parent and child is a wondrous thing. In addition to balls of any size he'll enjoy these:

- Cardboard boxes of unusual shapes in grocery, ice cream, appliance, or department stores
- Clay or play dough to pat and punch into shapes. Two-year-olds will be able to pound flat pancakes and poke round holes with curious fingers, while three-year-olds will be able to make the more complex shapes of

"snakes" and "balls." With maturity of eye–hand coordination children become more capable.

- Balloons—round and long ones to see blown up with the surprise of shape as well as size. Have you ever seen the master of balloon shapes create dogs and rabbits by combining the basic shapes?
- Bubbles—just as the size change intrigued your child so will the shape change from oval to perfect roundness of the bubble
- Laundry baskets and dishpan in round and square shapes to sit in, play with. Add some water and toy boats so your child can see what happens when they float past curves and corners.
- Crayons and pencils to lead your two- and three-year-old to create his own shapes
- Popped balloons and burst bubbles are shape surprises

There is a definite progression in the ability to draw shapes. The young child cannot draw a circle, triangle, or square until he is neurologically ready. This task which seems so simple to adults is a reminder of the complexity of learning and its dependence upon physical maturity. The toddler who is interested and ready to grip pencil or crayon will soon try scribbling. Scribbling is the first stage of writing and drawing, just as cooing and babbling precede speech. This random scribbling will evolve into drawings of shapes as your child learns from experimentation. Drawing shapes is a self-taught art that gradually evolves from experimentation, not instruction.

There is a progression in shape, drawing capability from the first scribbled circle of the two-year-old through the hand-drawn diamond of the five- or six-year-old. Three-year-olds can draw crosses and V shapes. Four-year-olds can draw triangles and squares. Only at five can a child begin to manage a diamond shape. The physical eye–hand coordination required for stars and hexagons is beyond the preschool years. After a period of accidental discovery your child will want to draw shapes, copying them from shapes you draw for him. It is easier for your child to imitate a shape after watching you draw the shape for him than it is to copy a completed shape.

INDOORS AND OUTDOORS

Your two- and three-year-old will discover shapes where you had forgotten they existed, as his toy cars and trucks are driven around the rectangular border in your rug pattern. Plaid wallpaper will become a busy intersection for converging cars, and kitchen floors with repetitive patterns will become streets and houses to visit. If you don't have built-in shapes, make a track in a kitchen or recreation room corner with masking tape. Your two- and three-year-old will find shapes in your sofa pillows and lamp shade tops, light fixtures, vent grills, chair backs, and furniture designs. Though he cannot name shapes at this age, he is learning to recognize their likenesses and differences, a necessary first step.

Outdoor shapes lead two- and three-year-old children to activity. Two-year-olds want to do pleasurable things again and again; three-year-olds want to share new skills with friends and family. Both ages will enjoy the following:

- An old tire which invites little feet to go round and round—twos may need a steadying hand
- An old inner tube to circle bouncing-bottom style or to lie astride feeling the curve of a circle in fingers, toes, and chin
- Flagpoles and trees which beg to be circled
- A circular driveway which beckons like a racetrack
- Ring-Around-the-Rosie game. It's fun if there is a group.
- Trikes and kiddie cars. Two- and three-year-olds will enjoy driving on big lines on a school playground. Three-year-olds also delight in the tiny, tight circles they are able to make on their tricycles, turning handlebars to an angle and peddling madly.
- The sandbox, a favorite outdoor place. Your sandbox could be a standard square one or an old tire filled with sand. A few battered cups and muffin tins will help your child make endless creations of "birthday cakes," packed in and turned out to be admired. A stick or dull knife will slice the shapes into other designs. A stick in the sand is a good tracer for round roads.

Animals in the backyard, farm, or zoo will interest two- or three-year-olds. Two- and three-year-olds are still in the active process of identifying objects in their world, and animals become known by their shape as well as by their other qualities of size, texture, color, and sound. To the two-year-old, the basic body shape as well as size, color, and texture of a cat and rabbit may seem the same, but ear and tail shapes signal a difference. Shape is becoming an identifier for your thinking child. Help your child in his discriminating efforts—look at lots of animals together, noticing the shapes of bodies as well as feet, beaks, paws, ears, and noses. Beak and foot difference is the one sure way to clear up the classic mix-up of duck and chicken in the mind of a two- or three-year-old. Absorbing the essential qualities of each animal takes time and experience, and the unknown or unusual can unnerve even an old hand at animal observation. A class of four-year-olds once had a visit from a furry Abyssinian guinea pig complete with long plumes of hair on his back. He was an enigma to these sophisticated barnyard experts. It was thought to be a sort of cat, rabbit, or dog, none seeming quite right, when suddenly a little boy spied the plume of hair and boldly announced, "I know what it is—a rooster." The group solemnly agreed. Moral of the story: learning about the world requires experience and conceptualization, not memorization. Perhaps this is why most zoos and pet farms are wall-to-wall mommies, daddies, and preschoolers on Sundays. Join the crunch!

LANGUAGE

By three years of age many children know the names of the basic shapes—circle, triangle, square, rectangle. They may not apply them to the right shape, but they know these labels are shape words. There's the verbal skill of naming names, the motor skill of drawing and block building, and the visual skill of picking the figure from the confusing background of other circles or triangles. Your child will be six years old before he's accomplished all this, but two- and three-year-olds have begun. Help your child get to each stage by naming the names of shapes before he's ready to name them himself, and listening and being proud when he points out the circle on your new shirt. Your child will use his awareness of shape to recognize an increasing number of objects, people, and pets. Together you can discover the many shapes in the world and your sharing will enrich both your lives.

Four- and Five-Year-Olds: Your Child Begins to Order His World

Four- and five-year-olds are collectors of words, people, and ideas. They begin to turn from home and hearth to society. Depending on experience and interest, your four-year-old will name and identify basic shapes, in books as well as in the world. As your child's world view widens he will use mental tools to organize and classify new experiences. Shape recognition will be a help in sorting people and animals, buildings and cars, food and furniture, letters and numbers. As your child grows older he will be expected to notice subtle differences in shapes, the "S" from the "5," the "M" from the "N." Your four- and five-year-old is beginning to refine his perceptions to notice and to name. Getting to know shapes is a complex affair. Your child will be wrestling with the confusions of shape—the static and fluid conditions of shape and the relationship of one shape to another involving parts and whole configurations. He will discover the function of shapes—the round of gears, the slant of the roof. He will learn that some shape is purely decorative.

Two-dimensional shapes must be recognized no matter what axis they lie on. Children first recognize a triangle planted on its base but cannot recognize the triangle if it stands on a point with sides elongated

or tilts right or left. This necessary recognition step is called "form constancy." No matter where the child finds a shape or which way it is tilted, he must recognize it as the same shape. The mover who stands and thinks, looking at sofa and door frame, and then comes up with an upside down angled approach that leaves your paint intact has native spatial abilities. If your child has these talents your house will be less marred and scarred from wagons and toys.

In addition to learning two-dimensional shapes and the shapes of letters and numbers, your child will be learning the properties of three-dimensional shapes. A four- or five-year-old will not name solid forms, beyond the familiar cube, ball, or ice-cream cone shape. His handling of three-dimensional concrete objects will familiarize him with their properties. Annoying as crayon and can peeling may be, these activities lead to perceptions about cylinders. The wrap is rectangular around a circular form. Dignifying mischief with educational benefits may not be helpful, but having tolerance for children's need to explore may make the list of what you call mischief shorter.

Once children know the shapes of things they can recognize the whole from seeing only a part. After seeing only the tail and ears your four-year-old may exclaim "rabbit." Years ago one of us went to a children's movie preceded by a delightful short film of Picasso executing drawings as the camera followed his pen. In the darkened theater families watched two or three lines become people and animals. At one point Picasso drew two distinctive "UU" shapes, and in the pause before he drew the woman's shoulders and head a tiny voice piped up, "Look Daddy, just like Mommy's!" As the lights went on most of the audience whirled to see the well-endowed young mother, her face as red as her hair. This child excelled at visual closure, the name for recognizing the whole shape from seeing an incomplete form.

There are no simple lessons that will further a child's knowledge of shape. The variation, functions, and properties of shape cannot be memorized or taught. To understand and use shape your child must experience it with his body, in his clothes, food, toys, and around him at home and in nature.

BODY

The body of a four- or five-year-old is a wonder capable of bending, stretching, twisting, and turning into new and exciting shapes. Give your ever-moving creative child the challenge of finding body shapes. If your child is particularly interested in body shapes let him look at pictures of dancers or gymnasts. A finger play or shadow play book from the library may intrigue your child. To start him off let him view himself with these:

- A little hand mirror to find shapes in his face. A. A. Milne's "Jonathan Jo has a mouth like an 'O' " may be all the priming he needs to get going.
- A big full-length mirror to look for circle shapes. Did he notice eye pupil, belly button, freckle?
- A full-length view of himself making big circles, two arms and fingers touching; a tiny circle, index finger and thumb touching; a big triangle, legs spread apart; smaller triangle, hand on hip; a moving shape, somersault; or many shapes at once

Your four- and five-year-old may go on to find curves, corners, and geometric shapes in nails, skin, veins, and bones. Don't be offended when he points at the triangular crow's feet, the semicircular bags under your eyes, and the many V formations of your varicose veins! Your observant four- or five-year-old will also notice the variety of body shapes in the world. A pregnant woman's pear shape and other ladies' hourglass shapes; short, stocky, square, lean, and lanky rectangular body shapes will capture his attention as much as the classic endo-morph, ectomorph, and mesomorph fascinate the clinical psychologist. Fortunately, most four- and five-year-olds are growing in discretion and their observations can be contained within the family circle.

FOOD

Four- and five-year-olds have the disposition of honored guests at a Japanese picnic. They properly "ooh" and "aah" at each aesthetic surprise of color, size, and shape as it is presented on platter and plate. Attractive and unusual food shapes become a still life to be studied and admired. Eye appeal can equal taste appeal. You need not master the oriental art of cutting a turnip ten ways nor succumb to the sales pitch of purchasing a "slicing-dicing vegamatic" to satisfy your preschooler's aesthetic sense. Simple pleasures will suffice:

- Carrots or squash cut in a variety of shapes—circles, semicircles, cubes, sticks, or on the bias for ovals
- Cucumbers cut in serrated circles. Run a fork lengthwise before slicing.
- Melon balls
- Pineapple circles or wedges
- Radish roses or fluted mushroom caps if you are a shape-artist gourmet
- Pasta in fancy shapes: bows, tubes, shells, and letters
- Square graham crackers which break into two rectangles
- Square sandwich cut in interesting shapes—two big triangles or four little triangles, three rectangles or four squares. Your child will enjoy separating the whole and then reassembling it again, an elementary lesson in shape composition. (Note that the basic handling of sandwich, getting it from plate to mouth without losing the innards, is a four-year-old's shape accomplishment in itself.)

We have never been able to master the feat of making the rabbit cake with two round cake tins or the gingerbread house from a sheet cake but if you can, more power to you! Your child will be impressed with your skill in using shapes. Your four- and five-year-old will enjoy his own shape experiments in cooking. Let him try these experiments:

- Make sandwiches on unusual bread shapes—a bagel, muffin, or pita bread, or bread baked in coffee cans. These circle shapes are a pleasant change from square sandwiches. Try peanut butter on a round apple slice for a shape treat.
- Fit round pieces of sandwich meat, tomatoes, or cucumber on square bread, or square cheese on round bread

- Make free-form pancakes, letting him pour and name the shapes he creates
- Make tortillas—mix corn flour and water, form balls, flatten into pancakes between wax paper using pot bottom or plate. This is an easy shape experience with a new taste to boot.
- Make cookies and pie crust using free-form hand designs or cookie cutters. A handcrafted "cloud" can be as beautiful as a cut-out star.
- Mix a cocktail snack with cereals, nuts, and pretzels—shape variety for a pleasanter nibble

With their developing sense of the absurd, your four- or five-year-old will enjoy the peculiarity of shape surprises. Chuckle together at these unusual sights:

- Square pies
- A layer cake slightly off balance. Does the imperfect shape dull your appetite?
- Hamburgers made in the shape of hot dogs and served in hot dog buns
- Ladyfinger cakes
- Fortune cookies
- Molded aspics, Jellos, mousses, and patés
- The half circle a bite makes in a sandwich
- Shape catastrophes. It may not amuse you, but your child will laugh at your fallen soufflé and melting aspic.

TOYS AND ACTIVITIES

In your child's efforts to understand the world he remembers what he has seen and imitates its shape and design in his play. Creations are often a group product, as four- or five-year-olds are sociable creatures. At school hollow blocks, unit blocks, table blocks, Lego blocks, Lincoln Logs, Tinker Toys, and art materials are used in the mastery of shape and space. At home you can provide these same sorts of experiences if you recognize your child's need to experiment. His creations are invented, destroyed, and invented again. Two- or three-year-olds delight in destroying a just-completed building or flattening a clay creation. The process not the product is what matters at two. Four- and five-year-olds have coordination enough to execute a recognizable product and they want their creations saved to be admired by neighbors and friends. This sort of play is at a high intellectual level. Watch a four-year-old struggle with the proportions of a remembered elephant's trunk as he attempts to have his clay model look right. Watch a five-year-old study how to make a window without weakening his block walls. The solving of these problems leads to further observation, further curiosity, and knowledge of the world beyond his home.

At this age your child also imitates the shapes of the world with blocks, dough, crayon, pencil, and scissors. The fine motor skills of handling drawing and cutting tools develop rapidly at this age. All these skills are necessary to successful performance in kindergarten and first grade. New skills bring motivation to exercise them. The capabilities to draw, cut, or mold are a matter of physical maturation. Children differ radically in acquiring this maturity. Boys are generally later than girls in fine motor development. You need to be sure that the skills and motivation move in tandem and that the motivation is the child's, not yours. Trying to color in the lines or cut on the line is impossible for some four- or five-year-olds. They are not neurologically ready. This has nothing to do with intelligence, just physical development. Just as some children walk earlier, some children cut or draw letters earlier. Since these skills are closely related to early school expectations, they often get mixed up with notions of how smart a child is. Some super-competent little girls may neatly write their names at four while their bright five-year-old brother reverses his letters and makes shaky-looking numbers. Praise both for their motivation, and don't judge intelligence by eye–hand coordination.

Shape discovery is important, be it through body and blocks or pencil and paper. By the time your child is four or five, you will know his approach to learning. Your mover and doer may be experiencing shapes by stuffing himself in empty trash cans and making mud drawings on the sidewalk. Your thinker and looker may have observed carefully and be ready to shape the letters of his name. Watch and wonder at the many ways to learn.

At four or five years old your child's mud, clay, or sand creation will take on a realistic shape. His experiences and physical skill will enable him to make a form recognizable to you. A group of four- or five-year-olds may rename their creation as it changes form. The sand birthday cake may turn first into a castle and then into a mountain. In the forming and reforming of dough, mud, sand, and clay your child may notice the shape of a familiar object, then stop there and name his creation. Whereas just a year or two ago he was content with the process of muddling and not interested in a product, now he usually wants to "make something."

Paper, pencil, and scissors are popular with four- and five-year-olds because these tools lead to tasks that have the flavor of school, that important occupation your child is preparing for. Don't try to make your home a "Little Red Schoolhouse," but do provide the important materials children like to practice with at this age—paper, pencils, crayons, and scissors. For four- and five-year-olds, cutting with scissors is as hard to learn as handling chopsticks is for adults. Some very adept three-and-one-half-year-olds may learn to cut, but cutting usually is a four- or five-year-old's accomplishment. For the first few weeks your child will tear more than cut, just as you give up in hunger and trade your chopsticks for a fork. Experience helps and so do good scissors. Children's scissors are usually neither sharp nor efficient, and though they are safe they are barely useful. Supervise for safety and start your child with small sharp scissors, left-handed ones if your child is showing a preference for his left hand for writing or eating. In mastering cutting there is a definite sequence. There are also two skills involved in the fine motor skill of manipulating the scissors and the eye–hand coordination feat of cutting along a designated line. Cutting also involves holding and maneuvering the paper with the other hand. Start your child with stiff paper such as brown grocery bag squares and hold the paper for him for his first few experiences. Cutting soft fabrics or intricate designs takes years of practice. Your child's first cuttings will be single snips, cutting for the fun of the process. Nursery school teachers who understand this send the proud scissor wielder home with a bag of scraps, his first cutting successes. Learn the general sequence of skills so you don't expect more than your child is ready to produce. He will progress from:

- First featherings. These are single snips which fringe the paper but don't go anywhere unless the paper is narrow, then one snip-cuts across.
- Cutting a number of snips across a paper. Opening and shutting scissors repeatedly is hard.
- Cutting along a wide line. You can put a wide pencil line on his paper for him to follow.
- Cutting "W"-shaped diagonals. He must turn the paper and change direction.
- Cutting along curved lines
- Cutting simple shapes out of paper
- Cutting out complex pictures

Your child will discover more forms and shapes as he plays with a "feel bag" of string, wire, and paper. He can do the following:

- Feel odd shapes you've placed in a bag or pillowcase. You are giving him the experience of recognizing a tube of toothpaste or spool of thread by feel alone. Four- and five-year-olds who can name or describe many objects in their world are ready for this new challenge. They can feel without peeking most of the time.

- Draw a shape on another's back and try to guess what it is.
- Loop a twelve-inch knotted string over his fingers and discover shapes or beginning "cat's cradles."
- Make designs with a single length of string on rug or table. Your child will discover that a single "line" can twist and turn to become circle, square, or triangle.
- Bend pipe cleaners or the wires from inside telephone cords to create shapes. Bendable bright wires are phone company throwaways.
- Fold paper squares, circles, or rectangles, then discover shapes within shapes—the two triangles in a rectangle, the squares within a square. This is a precursor to a lifetime interest in paper hats, paper airplanes, water bombs, and trick creations any origami master would admire.
- Set the table. Give your child the job of folding the paper napkins at dinner in "new ways."

Four- and five-year-olds enjoy arranging patterns of shapes drawn, printed, or cut out. Let your child make his own pattern design or start a pattern and ask your child to continue it. Patterning with parquetry, tangrams, and block designs of all sorts involve the same sorts of skills necessary to make sense of letters, numbers, and words. Letters and numbers themselves are combinations of shapes; words are patterns of letter shapes. The shapes of letters begin to interest four- and five-year-olds. Before your child knows the name of any letter he can recognize the shape and match identical letters. Visually matching similar forms precedes copying, just as a child's first grade reading skill proceeds faster than his writing skills. Noticing the triangular shapes of A or V, the curves in C and U, the circle of an O, will help in letter recognition. Remember not to rush this learning. There are only twenty-six letters in the alphabet and any able child will learn them during his school hours. Share his interest but don't push. If he is interested at five there are many ways to practice letters outside school—writing in the sand, making his body form letters, tracing letters in advertisements with his fingers. If you ever skated the figure eight you have a feel of the number beyond what your pencil brought you. For your child, wiggling in an "S" shape like a snake is better preparation than paper and pencil tasks for which he is not ready. Readiness is a state of body and mind. You can't affect the pace of maturity but you can keep motivation, awareness, and curiosity alive. Most of all you can enjoy your child's mental growth. No matter what the pace of maturity, your child will read during the second grade unless he has learning problems.

INDOORS AND OUTDOORS

As your four- or five-year-old is discovering the many shapes in the world and is talking about circles, squares, and triangles, give him meaningful household jobs. He will expand his knowledge of shape and at the same time be proud of his helping. Some good "shape discovery" chores might be the following:

- Setting the table—"Can you set the table using round shapes?" (place mats, plates, bowls). "Find the oval mats." "Use the square tray."
- Sorting silverware from dishwasher to drawer
- Sorting drawers and shelves of buttons, dishes, and jewelry by shape. Let your child set up his own classification system. He will enjoy organizing your clutter.
- Sweeping, vacuuming, and dusting. These jobs can draw the eye to shapes in floor, furniture, and fabric design.
- Folding pillowcases and towels. Do you remember your own discoveries about shape the first time you learned the ritual of flag folding, going from large rectangle to small triangle?
- Sorting your kitchen sponges, oval and rectangular
- Sorting round and square freezer containers
- Sorting a deck of cards by suit so you can see if they are all there

Finding shapes in the world can be a mind boggling experience, as the list below will attest, but four- and five-year-olds are undaunted and plunge in, delighted by the complexity and variety. They've become experts of plane and solid shapes and take great pleasure in practicing their new skills of identification. A four- or five-year-old who is "into shapes" will sharpen any adult's powers of observation. His eyes will lead your eyes to see patterns in manhole covers and elevator doors. He will notice the triangular design of animal footprints on the snow and the "V" form of migrating geese. Go exploring together looking for shapes in roads, houses, museums, pet shops, zoos, and in nature. Don't go in a task-oriented frame of mind but rather let these ideas jog your perception of space and see what you can see. On walks and rides look for some of these:

- Sidewalk squares
- A cul-de-sac (half of an oval or circle)
- An oval high school track. Jog it together and your child will know the feel of a big oval
- A baseball diamond—walk the bases so your child can feel the angles.
- A triangular slide—the greater the slant the scarier the ride

- A place to have a tricycle slalom. Feel the pull up a slanted hill and the whoosh down.
- Ramps in sidewalks for the handicapped. Let your child think of the reason for the slant.
- Ponds and pools, oval and kidney shaped
- Drains, grates, and storm sewers, from giant ovals to squares
- Fences, rectangular board and round posts, and garden gates with peepholes
- Road signs; your child will soon know the hexagonal stop sign by its color and shape, the "S" curve sign which warns of road shape ahead. He will also enjoy the feel of the "S" shape in the motion of the car. With eyes closed the curve seems more exaggerated.
- Mazes in formal gardens
- Rocks and stones; enjoy the natural shapes or the shapes as they break at their natural cleavage. A special find would be an arrowhead.
- The moon in its various phases
- Clouds—lie on your back and study cloud shapes
- Graphics of arrows, numbers, and shapes in public buildings to interest your five-year-old. Find out what these shape statements say to him.
- Logos—another shape creation. Together figure out what the picture–symbol means. If you're stumped, call the company and ask.

Transportation   If your child has been around and seen lots of vehicles, he'll enjoy thinking about transportation shapes. You can name a shape and have him think of vehicles or their wheels, wings, and sails.

Buildings   Look for houses and buildings in odd shapes:

- Triangular tents
- A cylindrical silo or lighthouse
- Recreation homes in unusual shapes—"A" frames and hexagonal designs
- A theater-in-the-round, circus tent, or merry-go-round
- A racetrack
- Art museums-in-the-round—if you're near the Guggenheim in New York, or the Hirshhorn in Washington, D.C., take a tour. Your child will enjoy the curved ramps and feel the slant in his muscles.

Think about the way you feel in rooms and buildings of different sizes and shapes: the cozy corner and the lofting dome, the soaring cathedral or the snugness of the salt box. Let your child discover these shape feelings. In books, share with your child pictures of unusual home shapes: hogans, tepees, yurts, and igloos. Besides looking at whole building shapes, take apart buildings indoors and out with your eyes and mind, and see the shape parts that make up the whole. Look at some of these:

- Window and window-pane shapes, portholes, and triangular clerestory
- Circular stairs
- Roof lines—peaks and gables
- Shapes in woodgrains and marble
- Shape surprises like round beds and bathtubs, area rugs in hexagons, chandelier baubles, and faceted doorknobs instead of the usual round ones
- Conversation pits and convention halls. Think about how shape affects communication. A meeting with chairs in a circle is more democratic than one with a podium facing chairs in rows.

Birds   Birds have beaks of different shapes (some woodpeckers peck round holes and some oblong ones), build nests of different shapes (the "U"-shaped nest of the Baltimore oriole in contrast to the usual round shape), and have feet of different shapes for different functions. Think about curved branch-holding toes versus triangular webs designed for walking in a marsh or swimming. Keep an eye out for bird footprints too. The beach is a good place to see patterns of bird tracks.

Bugs   Insects are identified by shape as well as color and size. The oval of the beetle and round of the ladybug are easy to spot for young children. Notice what's at hand in park and garden; if your child gets excited, then look at the pictures in a library book. Some insects and butterflies have shapes that look like big eyes on their wings to frighten their enemies. Look up the "Eyed Elater."

Beasts   Last year the oval bunny ears intrigued your child, now he will notice more unusual shapes: the design on the diamondback rattler and the spiral of the snail. Take a trip to the zoo or pet store, concentrating only on shape of ear, tail, or paw.

Flowers   Look at leaf shapes with your child. You don't have to know the names, but notice differences, and if you ever want to learn names this noticing will help. Have you ever seen the heart-shaped leaf of wild ginger? An interest in flower shapes may spur you on to find dutchman's breeches, lady's slipper, or elephant's foot.

The Arts   If you are a museum- or symphony-goer, share your interest with your four- and five-year-old. He won't be up to the monthly visiting artist show or a season ticket to the symphony, but he will enjoy an occasional visit to a museum or gallery. A touch museum is best, one that encourages fingers to feel spaces. If your town is still of the "look but don't touch" museum philosophy, a brief visit to look at shapes is still fun. Together you and your child can find shapes in pictures and sculpture. Talk about the negative space shapes in modern sculpture.

What does it do? There is no answer, just speculation and thought shared by you both. What a giant step from discussing the hole in the donut to the spaces within Henry Moore's figures! For symphony-goers, start your child out at the local music store. He will be interested in looking at instruments close at hand, noticing the basic shapes of drums, banjos, flutes, and violins. As he takes in the overall shape of each instrument he will also begin to see shapes in the parts of each instrument, the circular horn openings, the "S"-shaped sound openings of the stringed family, the rectangle of the keyboard.

LANGUAGE

The language of shape is much more theoretical than practical. Most four- and five-year-olds are able to recognize a cutout of a circle, triangle, or square. This seemingly simple school task of knowing and naming shapes is minor compared to the conceptual use of shape in sorting out the world. Like texture, color, and size, shape tells us what things are and are not. The shape of a pear and apple are different although the texture, size, and color may be similar. The shape difference groups apples from pears. This intellectual task of classifying has become part of a four- and five-year-old's thinking process. Two- and three-year-olds are at the matching stage (something is the same or it is not; a pear is a pear or not a pear), but four- and five-year-olds are beginning to group things considering two or more qualities. Your child will be using his knowledge of shape not so much in a verbal way, asking for a circular cookie or a square sandwich, but in a conceptual approach in looking at the world, noticing shapes wherever he finds them, in animals and people, cars and trucks, flowers and trees. His ability to recognize shapes will spur him on to observation of more and more of the world, and his interest in the people, events, and objects he encounters will increase his language ability. A four- or five-year-old child has four or five times as many words in his speaking vocabulary than he did at age two. Knowledge of shape is one way that he identifies and classifies the increasing diversity of words and ideas.

For passing time in a doctor's waiting room or on a lengthy car ride play some language classification games. Your child will be able to recall shapes he has seen or touched and any of the activities in the preceding shape chapter could get you started. Think about food shapes: what shape is a pizza or a loaf of bread? Classify fruits or vegetables into basic shapes. Talk about shapes in clothing: round buttons and square belt buckles. What article of clothing could be a triangle, square, or rectangle shape—a scarf. On the road, play a family game looking for round, square, or triangle shapes. The driver calls the shape to be sighted and the passengers hurry to spot the shape first. Healthy competition sure beats back-seat squabbles. For imaginative games, ponder together: what if balls were square, what if tricycle wheels were triangular, what if your house were shaped like a honeycomb?

Books can be a great source of visual stimulation. Adult specialty books on photography, art, architecture, shells, flowers, and birds are fun to share with your child. Finding shapes and talking about things together is a great way to enjoy your child's growing language abilities.

Chapter 5

"Roses Are Red"
How a Child Learns
About Color

Focus on color and you bring the rainbow out of the sky to share with your child. As adults we hustle by the blur of green leaves, birds flying, and flowers blooming, thinking "Spring is here." We don't stop to notice that the willow is more lemon yellow and the spruce more blue than green. Children notice. They see the rainbow iridescence on the grackle's back, not the bird as a pest; they see red dots and yellow fuzz down in the flower bloom, not just one splash of color. Look longer and see more. Take a little time to share your child's fresh observations. Grow by seeing through your child's eyes and sharing his sense of wonder at the colors in the world.

Color has different meanings to different ages of children. The infant's world is a kaleidoscope of changing colors. Color says "Notice Me!" to the infant in the crib or the crawler exploring the house. To an older child color is a way of sorting out the world: apples from oranges, bluebirds from cardinals. Besides being an identifier, color can give poetry to a child's life, sunlight can be seen as gold, raindrops as silver.

Color can make your baby's room and crib an exciting place to be. It can attract a crawler or toddler to stop and play: a bright red ball to crawl for, a cheerful yellow cup to finger. Children will be attracted to colors long before any color has a name. Over a period of several years a child will learn the names of the colors and how to use the names. Your two- and three-year-old will use color names to get his favorite Jello or shoes. Four-year-olds are serious about "knowing their colors." Knowledge of the shadings and intensities of color come at a later age.

Color, like size or shape, is a way your child recognizes and describes objects. The zebra is known by its black and white stripes. The richer the child's color experiences and the more you have talked with him, the richer his color vocabulary will be. One of our children described her friend's dark red hair as "maple colored" remembering the leaves on the maple tree in her yard. For your child the sky need not always be the same blue.

For children and for adults color has many emotional associations we rarely think about. It affects the clothes you select on a given day, the paint you pick for your bedroom. To one person white may mean the excitement of white caps on a stormy sea or to another the stark white of a nurse's uniform and fear. It is interesting to see color as your child sees it and find the roots of some of your own associations.

COLOR CONCEPT WORDS

Least Difficult	More Difficult	Most Difficult
primary colors	other colors	shading of color
red	black	light—dark
yellow	white	(combinations of
blue	orange	colors, light to
	green	dark, dark to
	purple	light)
	brown	
	gray	
	pink	

Some color words from experiences are lime, lemon, cream, coffee, and sand.

The Infant: Birth to Eight Months or Crawling Age
You Bring the World to Your Infant

Is it possible to bore your baby? We think so. Color is a way to make the world a more interesting place for you and your infant. Think of it— an infant lying helpless in a crib is much like an adult confined to a hospital bed: white walls, white sheets, and white ceiling. The surroundings are bland. Some focus of attention, some interesting color or shape entertains the eye. Even a fussy baby can sometimes be quieted by the diversion of color or light. Your baby will thrive on the visual liveliness you create for him. You need not hire an interior decorator, dip into your savings account, or become an arts and crafts director to change your baby's environment and stimulate his mind. Our suggestions are quick and easy. Your efforts will be rewarded by the interest your baby shows in his colorful surroundings.

Where to begin? Let's start with the baby's first home—the crib. White sales have become bright sales with rainbow, polka dots, tartan plaids, and zebra stripes on sheets and blankets. Take advantage of this variety. The infant pastel tones are sweet, but dull. Try using bright, single bed sheets on your baby's crib (just tuck the extra sheeting under

the mattress). He won't outgrow these sheets either. For additional color excitement get the gaudiest crib bumper you can find. Purple elephants and chartreuse kangaroos are beautiful when you're four months old! Your baby will look at these during his waking hours and give you a few moments peace.

TOYS AND ACTIVITIES

Find other spots and swatches of color to hang about your baby's room to attract and delight the eye. Bright cellophane or tissue paper squares taped to a window are fun. Move your baby's crib near the window so he can enjoy the sun shining through the bright colors. The colors can be changed occasionally if you have an extra minute or two. Can you tell if your baby responds to sunny yellow or bright blue? These colorful papers or bright fabric samples can also be snapped into an embroidery hoop and hung by yarn in a window. This makes an unusual and useful gift for a new baby. One mother we know hung plastic sandwich bags filled with colored water in her baby's window— bizarre but beautiful, and her baby loved it! Another unusual color experience for your infant is to place a cut-glass vase or bowl in a sunny window to catch the light and transform it into a sparkling rainbow. A new use for Aunt Martha's wedding gift!

If your baby has finally gotten into a regular eating and sleeping schedule and you are interested in providing something for your baby's waking moments, try making a quick and easy color mobile for looking, not touching. Most store-bought mobiles are not apt to interest your baby day after day. He wants new shapes, colors, and sizes to look at almost daily. The directions for making this mobile are simple: tie one end of a piece of yarn or string to the top of a hanger, and attach the other end to the ceiling or overhead light fixture. A few pincer clothes-pins (these come in colors too) are used to attach swatches of bright colors to the hanger to complete the job. Any spot of color will do. The bright red cookie box liner or lemon yellow thank-you note will delight your baby. Remember, your baby will enjoy the variety of colors and be unconcerned about the mobile's artistic qualities.

The Baby on the Move: Crawling Age to Twenty-Four Months
Your Crawler/Toddler Goes to the World

This "into everything" age baby turns your household inside out in his explorations. In this most trying of ages you have to keep an eye out to see what new trouble your baby can get into. Color may be one of the keys to your survival in the eight-to-twenty-four-months period. Be sure there is color in your house to attract your crawler/toddler. Those bright objects he can reach urge him to lift and roll, to test and fit.

Even as early as eight months children differ radically in their per-sonalities and approach. There are "lookers" and "doers." Some chil-dren from the moment they begin to play have a thoughtful, staring, tentative approach to any object; others fairly charge along, physically fearless and quick to "run through" whatever objects they encounter. These two different types will need different numbers of objects to ex-plore. The "looker" will be slower and more thorough. Color will at-tract him to touch and handle. The "doer" will demand more variety of stimulation. In going through a basketful of objects, colorful ones may hold his attention longer.

Just as children differ in the vigor and depth of their approach, they differ in the degree to which color, sound, and motor activities interest them. One can almost sense the beginnings of the artist, musician, or gymnast. The child who is attracted early to color may be the four-year-old who insists on matching pants and shirt. He knows whether they "go together" or not, and his eyes enjoy the blend. Another child less conscious of color might put on plaid pants and a flowered shirt without a shudder. These differences are fun for both of you; enjoy your child's budding individuality.

FOOD

Had you thought of how color might affect your child's eating? Picture a one-year-old faced with creamed turkey, potatoes, and banana. It's hard to tell where one food leaves off and the other begins. Even you are cheered by the cherry and orange wedge in your drink. For color interest give your child the colorful foods listed in Chapters 2, 3, and 4, plus orange wedges, green noodles, and pink grapefruit.

TOYS AND ACTIVITIES

One of any child's favorite toys is the light switch, which bestows the wonderful power of turning dark to light and back again. If the energy crisis isn't severe, rearrange your child's room, moving his bed or crib near the switch. He'll be amused for hours by his own magical powers. The 10¢ on your electricity bill gives far more pleasure than a $5.95 toy.

Although most bought toys come in bright colors, your child will not confine his play to bought toys; everything in his path will become a toy to manipulate. Bright color is a beacon. Your crawler or toddler may scale great heights to reach the red plastic top of the can of hair spray. Put the spray on a high shelf and give him the bright top (carefully washed) to play with on the floor.

INDOORS AND OUTDOORS

If you're putting pictures in your child's room the bright modern painters will probably appeal to him. Your favorite Mondrian, Klee, Pollock, or Miró print will be far more interesting to him than the blurry pastel lamb or bunny pictures that usually adorn children's rooms.

Color attracts outdoors too. If you aren't wary, your red tulips will be neatly beheaded by curious hands, a poor imitation of "picking flowers" but logical to a toddler. Keep him moving by rolling a bright ball or giving him a red sock stuffed with old rags to throw and fetch. You may feel that it's a little like playing with Rover, but this game gives your child healthy motor exercise, and you some moments of peace.

LANGUAGE

A toddler is just learning the names of the important things in his life: "Mommy," "Daddy," "bottle," or "cup." Refinements like color names are very unimportant. Before two years you need not "teach" your child the names of any colors. However, he will be aware of differences in colors even though he won't name them. He will recognize the color of an apple as different from that of an orange. He will also benefit from hearing color words as you talk with him. "Here's one you will like, a blue one." "Mommy will get your yellow sweater and we'll take a walk." A year later these words will peg specific colors and one by one a child will begin to name the colors that make up the world.

Two- and Three-Year-Olds: Your Child Finds Words for the World

Some parents begin to think of "teaching" their children at age two or three. One of the first concepts parents try to teach is color. They feel a great surge of triumph when their child "learns his colors." They can check that learning off the list and move on to memorizing shapes. A parent *could* get some bright squares of the primary colors and make the child repeat the color names on presentation of the proper swatch, but that's not the way children really learn color.

Color is very complicated. The red of a wool skirt is not the same red as of an apple or a balloon. The balloon deflated is not the same color as the balloon inflated. Children begin by noticing things that are alike in color. They don't know the name of the color, they just notice that things match. The charts in the child development books tell you children "know their colors" at four and one-half. Really knowing is what you're after, not the "push-button" memorization of the color of a few objects.

Two-year-olds love to sort things, putting a pile here and a pile there. Color is one of the ways they sort. They don't have to know one pile is green and one is blue. Sorting by distinguishing likenesses and differences in color is an important mental activity.

Color is everywhere to interest your two- or three-year-old, play dough, finger paint, lemon gelatin, cherries, fire engines, ambulances, flowers, birds, clothes, and picture books. He'll be excited by his ever-expanding experiences of the world and color will be an enticement to learn more and more.

FOOD

Two- and three-year-olds love to help in the kitchen. Take the time to give your child some cooking experiences with color:

- Making gelatin—you handle the hot water and let your child stir
- Making vanilla, caramel, and chocolate pudding
- Icing cup cakes. If you can bear the somewhat bedraggled appearance of the end product, give a two- or three-year-old white icing, a few drops of food color to stir in, and a dull table knife or Popsicle stick for a spreader. The result will be gorgeous to him. Even icing a vanilla wafer for a tea party is great fun for your child.

TOYS AND ACTIVITIES

The Crayola people are telling you something by offering a small box of crayons with only eight colors. Save those sixty-four shades for the five-year-old's birthday party. Simple beginnings with limited numbers of colors are right for a two- or three-year-old. Here are some other color toys to offer your child:

- Play dough—add a few drops of food coloring when he's bored with white
- Finger paint—in one color at first, then add one or two more
- Water play—a drop of blue or green food coloring will add excitement to the bath water. If you can stand it, try yellow or red.

By the time your child has a sense of the usual colors of things he'll enjoy the magic of color surprises. Changes of color are fun even for adults. Show him some of these:

- Sunglasses and colored cellophane, which change the world
- Tops and pinwheels, which blur and blend colors
- Rainbow colors in oil drops in a puddle, on bubbles, and in dancing mirror reflections

When two- and three-year-olds match colors they need concrete objects that can be placed near each other. Give them experience by suggesting they help in household "chores" such as sorting by color:

- Mittens and gloves to straighten out the hall closet
- Socks to help with the laundry

- Place mats and napkins into piles
- Buttons or thread into an egg carton to tidy up your sewing basket
- Apples, oranges, lemons, and limes in the fruit bin. Maybe they don't really need sorting, but a two- or three-year-old will enjoy the organization he creates if you let him. Practice at an early age will mean an independent and trustworthy shelf straightener later on.

If the idea of all this housework makes you weary we've got a sure-fire way for you to catch forty winks and still supervise your child. The only necessities are a package of colored rubber bands and your bare foot. To start the project, put a different-colored rubber band on each of your toes (every other toe if your child is not yet finger dexterous). Now stretch out and your child will be content matching colors, reds on the big toe, blues on the little toe. In the meantime you know just where your child is. You may need less sleep than we did, but this idea was born of desperation. It works for twins too if you take off your other sock.

OUTDOORS

Your child will delight in the spots of color he comes upon traveling low to the ground. The dandelion which you view as a failure of your lawn program is a golden gem to him. The dots on the bugs eating your flowers will intrigue him. The blue cornflower isn't a roadside weed, but a match for the early summer sky or his new sunsuit. Many things we take for granted or check off as pest or weed are discoveries of color to a child. Watch a storm gather, light changing to dark. Take a walk at dusk or see the stars and moon at night. Familiar objects have different colors in these changing lights.

LANGUAGE

Just because your child can't name the color of everything in sight at two or three doesn't mean you shouldn't use color words. He will learn all his words from you until he gets out into the world of school and playmates. You use the color words but don't demand them back. Let your child experience, absorb, and compare. He'll begin to express his wants and needs, "red Jello, not green," "my big blue ball, not my yellow one." His words will be applied to a much wider range of objects than the colored blocks of a "teaching toy." These words will come when his eyes and mind are ready and when they are of use in getting about in the world.

Four- and Five-Year-Olds: Your Child Begins to Order His World

Color adds a dash of excitement to the world of the four- and five-year-old. Color attracts as it did in the earlier years, but by now your child has mastered some of the color likenesses and differences and is interested in learning all the color names. Besides being a way of identifying and selecting objects, color for the four- and five-year-old is a way of establishing his own identity. Allowing your child to make

choices is one way to promote his growing sense of self. Let your child choose the color of his new sneakers or birthday cake icing—easier for you than letting him choose his bedtime or menu—and it makes him feel "grown-up."

Color for four- and five-year-olds has become an emotional issue. It is loved, hated, discussed, and argued about. Every four- and five-year-old has a favorite color. You will find your child selecting or rejecting clothing, food, toys, and even candy on the basis of color.

Any nursery school teacher will tell you that pink and purple are the favorites of four- and five-year-olds. Black and brown crayons and paint are often left untouched. For the four- and five-year-old, the gaudier the better. Only the bravest of mothers would allow a child of this age to select the colors for his room. Do you have the courage?

BODY

You will find four- and five-year-olds talking about who has blue eyes and who has brown eyes, who has light hair and who has dark hair. They may speak of having "blond hair," not "yellow" hair as they might have a year earlier. If they have experience with children of other races, at this age they will begin to notice and inquire about differences in skin color. Encourage your child to discover other body colors and shadings, such as pale, sunburned, and tan skin; bruises; freckles; blue veins; pink nails; red noses; and tattoos (do you know a sailor?). If your child has a clear understanding of color and is able to deal with abstractions, try expressions like "You're white as a sheet," "You're red as a beet," and "You can ask 'til you're blue in the face."

CLOTHING

Four- and five-year-olds are choosy about their clothes. They want to dress like their friends. Not until the teenage years will peer group pressure about clothes and appearance be so great. "Everyone" will have red sneakers, wide belts, or matching barrettes. Fours are socially clubby, using color as a way to be "in" or to leave someone "out." Listening in on a group of four-year-olds, you'll hear one say, "We all have red sneakers. You don't have red sneakers. You can't play with us." Fives are a bit less socially pressured but care that they go off to kindergarten looking like the rest of the class. If you can bear to let go of some of the control of your child's wardrobe, allow your four- or five-year-old to pick his own outfit to wear to school. It may be red socks, red shirt, and red sweater—all different and clashing shades—but your child will feel like a "million dollars" and will be the fashion model for his peers. As teachers, we could tell the four- and five-year-olds who picked their own outfits for the day. They may not have looked like fashion ads, but they were the children with blossoming self-confidence.

Four- and five-year-olds are interested in other people's clothing too. They notice the color of uniforms: the doctor's white, the police officer's blue, and the football team's purple and gold.

If you watch yourself and your child, you can tune in on your moods and the clothes you pick: the sunny yellow shirt that cheers up a dull day or the old beige when you're feeling down, that peachy shade that picks up the lights in your hair when you want to please someone or the brisk business gray to wear to a job interview. Watch this grow in your child. It's part of the fun of daily living, the depths and dimensions in simple things that we forget to think about.

FOOD

Many of our words for color come from foods. We speak of chocolate-brown carpeting in an apple-green room. For these words to have meaning, the young child must have tasted chocolate and seen a green apple.

Your four- and five-year-old will be interested in new foods and their colors. Family menus will be perked up, too, by a new fruit or vegetable, a welcome change from the familiar yellow banana and green peas. Enjoy together the more exotic colors and flavors of black-eyed peas, sweet red peppers, and fried green tomatoes. Have three colors of apples or grapes in your fruit bowl for the evening dessert. Serve a ruby-red pomegranate to your four- or five-year-old. Its jewel-like brilliance will appeal to his special sense of color.

When your child knows the difference between a plum and an apricot it's time to introduce him to the colors of spices: the yellow mustard powder, the green mint leaf, brown cinnamon. Even black and white pepper are fun. Your own color sense is heightened by experience. Would reading about a monk's saffron robes mean anything to you unless you had once made saffron rice?

Have you ever thought of the many colors used in food names? You and your child will enjoy making brown bread, "brown Betty," or brownies; green tea; white sauce; snow pudding; or black bottom pie.

Your child will also be interested in the color changes in food as it is grown or cooked. Ripening changes the color of bananas, tomatoes, pumpkins, and apples. In the kitchen let your young chef try his hand at browning butter for vegetables (yellow to brown), popping corn (yellow to white), frying hamburgers (red to brown), making toast (light to dark), and toasting marshmallows (white to brown or black).

Four- and five-year-olds love to sort out objects. Their sorting ability is greater than that of two- or three-year-olds. A two-year-old is content with two piles, the red and the not red. A four-year-old is ready to handle more categories. When he has a bag of jelly beans you will find your child eating all the "red ones" first, then the "yellow ones." This is usually done with an air of solemnity and seriousness of purpose. Some children love ritual more than others and perhaps become the adults who approach a dinner plate systematically eating one food at a time.

To those of us who happily mix it all together, this is inconceivable, yet we too sorted out jelly beans by color as a child. Some very special color treats for sorting are: fruit cocktail; granola mix; light and dark raisins; yellow, orange, white, and blue cheese; colored candies; and your homemade health snack—a combination of coconut, dried fruits, nuts, and seeds.

Does your four- or five-year-old know the primary colors (red, blue, and yellow)? If he does, it is great fun to create other colors using these three basic colors. Don't tell him that blue and red make purple, let him experience the joy of discovery. All he needs is food coloring (red, yellow, and blue) and several containers of water. Avoid concern about spills by doing this outdoors. Back in your kitchen you and your child can make new and unusual gelatin desserts. What happens when you mix lemon and cherry flavors? Call it "orange fruit supreme!" For the real color enthusiast try a few drops of food coloring in milk!

Four- and five-year-olds like to think and talk about foods and their colors too. Some suggestions:

- Selecting the evening's green or yellow vegetable from the freezer, cupboard, or store
- Playing a memory game—"Which is darker green, broccoli or lima beans?" "Which is lighter, beets or radishes?"
- Making a collage of foods by color. Seed catalogues and magazines are good sources for pictures.

TOYS AND ACTIVITIES

The best "color toys" for four- and five-year-olds are materials that invite creativity. This is the time for you to visit the stationery store, office supply store, or art store, to select a special toy. Fours and fives will love these:

- Crayons—the greater array of colors the better. For a five-year-old happiness is a box of crayons that has a flesh tone and a lemon-lime.
- Felt-tip pens—look for the washable variety
- "Craypas"—a soft crayonlike chalk
- Chalk—soft artist's chalk to use on paper and hard blackboard chalk (in assorted colors) to use on blackboard or sidewalks
- Paper—colored construction, tissue, and cellophane can be used for painting, drawing, tearing, cutting, folding, pasting, or origami

Remember our advice in Chapter 2 and become a scavenger and pack rat. Save from holiday wrappings, sewing projects, and decorating binges:

- Yarn, ribbon, fabric scraps, fancy foils, and papers to tie, weave, and create
- Rug, paint, and wallpaper samples, often free from paint or hardware stores. These samples can be used to classify (sort by colors): "All the blue ones in this pile, and all the green ones in this pile." Don't be rigid about categories, turquoise may be blue to your child and green to you. Or he can seriate (order from light to dark or dark to light). This is a challenging task.

Cleanup time with all of these materials is more likely to happen if you provide containers that invite sorting by color and kind.

Because your four and five is a social being, he will enjoy sharing an activity with you or a friend. For some color fun try board games that involve color such as checkers, Winnie the Pooh, and Candy Land; dyeing the corners and edges of folded paper towels with food-colored water; and tie-dyeing fabric swatches and old T-shirts with cold-water dyes. If you want to give your child a very special color "toy" (that will be enjoyed by any adult as well), buy a kaleidoscope or prism. The kaleidoscope moves colored shapes into ever-changing designs; the prism reflects a rainbow onto light surfaces.

OUTDOORS

You don't have to be a naturalist to enjoy color in nature with children. Their curiosity may spark questions you can't answer, their powers of observation will challenge your own. The answers don't matter, the sharing is what is important.

Your child is interested in sorting out his world, classifying trees, animals, flowers, or birds. Identifying and comparing the colors in nature is a wonderful beginning. You and your child may be a long way from identifying one hundred or even ten species, but this doesn't matter. What is important is noticing, being interested in what is around you.

Birds A collection of bird feathers found on a walk and a children's nature book listing the birds in your area (from your local library or the Audubon Society) is a beginning to knowing a blue jay, cardinal, goldfinch, or crow. Five-year-olds will be fascinated that the male of the bird world is more colorful than the female.

Bugs Insects, caterpillars, and spiders are of interest to a four- or five-year-old. Your child will notice the striped and the dotted patterns of color. A dragonfly's iridescence or the firefly's light will delight him. It won't take him long to know that red ants sting and bumblebees have stripes.

Beasts The patterns of color on animals help children tell them apart. Fours like to figure out classes of animals. A younger child smiles benignly at any floppy-eared bunny, but to a four-year-old a rabbit is black or brown and white. Fours and fives who now find tropical fish with dots and flashes of color entertaining, found a single goldfish exciting enough a year ago. It's time for a tortoise-shell cat or a chameleon from the pet shop!

At the zoo the polar bear will be more novel than the brown bear, the peacock with all his color, the crowning glory of the trip. Ten trips later your child might be distinguishing the mountain lion, the jaguar, and the leopard on the basis of the color differences. A five-year-old who has seen a number of animals will find animal color camouflage very interesting. The coloration of an animal as it relates to its natural surroundings leads to levels of thought far beyond simple recognition of color.

Flowers Flowers picked or planted interest most children. Some flower activities are:

- A walk looking for flowers of only one color
- Collecting fall leaves and sorting by color
- Letting your child choose one color of flower when you plant your garden
- Picking a bouquet of wild flowers. You may never learn the names but the memory of the little yellow flower by the mailbox will cheer your winter conversation.

If your child shows a special interest, find a person or a book to teach him the names of your local blooms. The flower show or a florist shop will be a special treat.

LANGUAGE

Words are part of the richness of the world for fours and fives. They love words: color words; silly words; and bird, animal, and flower names. Once children know the names of the basic colors, they carry the labels out into a wider world. Color is no longer tied to an object at hand, it is something children can use to describe things they remember. They are eager for new experiences and the words to describe those experiences. They want to talk, not just to an understanding parent but with a friend their own age or a neighbor.

Color word games which use imagination and creativity are fun for your child and his friends. When you play word games with your child, don't feel you have to know the answers. Your child will surprise you, thinking of the yellow pages while you're still proud you thought of canaries. Some games are naming your favorite color; a bird, a mode of transportation that's green, yellow, and so forth; an animal, fruit, or vegetable for every color; happy colors, sad colors; holiday colors; flag colors; jewel colors (your child's birthstone); or a meal in one color. (For St. Patrick's one of us had green noodles, green dip, green beans, green Jello, and green milk.)

Reading about color in books is fun too. "Little Red Riding Hood," "Goldilocks," "The Little Red Hen," "Snow White," "The Red Balloon," and "The Color Kittens" are just a few of the children's books that focus on color.

Noticing colors, and talking and thinking about them will make the world more exciting. A person who can describe her new blouse as lilac, violet, lavender, or heather colored is more fun to listen to. Share your child's color experiences and his growing vocabulary will become a tool for creativity.

Chapter 6

"Rings on Her Fingers and Bells on Her Toes"
How a Child Learns About Sound

"Muzak" PROVIDES a constant sound background as you work or shop. Climate-controlled buildings separate indoor and outdoor sounds from each other. Adults who grew up in another era remember silences broken by a peep of a bird, a train in the distance, the tolling of a church bell. Listen to your child's sound environment, the beautiful sounds and the noise pollution. Imagine what memories these sounds will evoke for your child when he is older.

Out of the general whir about them children must learn to listen to and isolate the sounds of speech, music, and noise. Listening helps children sort out the objects and people in their world. Without looking babies can tell Mother's footsteps or Daddy's voice. As they are learning where sounds come from, they are also making sounds of their own. Some of these sounds become speech, some music, and some noise. The baby's babble becomes speech as adults repeat baby's sounds and encourage communication. Early music comes from thumping spoons and pounding feet. Parents can tolerate the babbling and the banging if they know these sounds are the beginnings of language and music.

One-, two-, and three-year-olds recognize sounds and their sources, the moo of the cow and the bark of the dog. Sound becomes another identifier of the objects in the world in the same way color, size, or shape has helped him know his surroundings. He learns that the refrigerator door click means the beginning of dinner preparation or the "woof" of his dog means company coming. In older preschoolers fascination with noise is not diminished. The organized gang of cowboys and Indians roaring through the house replaces the randomly banging toddler.

As speech becomes more developed, children play with the sound of words: new words, rhyming words, poetic words. Creativity is a hallmark of four- and five-year-olds. A child with a rich background of language and musical experiences may surprise his parents with poetry and music of his own creation.

SOUND CONCEPT WORDS

Least Difficult	*More Difficult*	*Most Difficult*
loud—soft	high—low	noisy—quiet
sounds from child's own environment: household noises, animals, pets, familiar transportation (for the city child a bus noise, for the farm child a tractor noise).	sounds from wider environment: city or country noises, animals (zoo or farm), other transportation	general onomatopoetic words as in: pop, hiss, buzz, screech, squeak, etc.
		consonant and vowel sounds
		musical scale sounds

The Infant: Birth to Eight Months or Crawling Age
You Bring the World to Your Infant

Infants, like plants, need to be talked to. Although the research on plants and sound isn't convincing to every "green thumb," the research on children's language development is clear: babies learn to talk by being talked to. They learn to talk by listening. At the classic christening party, aunts and uncles hang over the bassinet talking baby talk in voices as high as they can raise them. Maybe you are revolted by these antics and would just as soon be caught dead talking to your baby that way as be caught reading Plato to your philodendron. Fortunately babies are more responsive than plants and even if they can't talk back you will begin to see clues that tell you talking to a baby makes sense. Uncle Harry at the christening talked "funny" because he instinctively intuited what science has discovered. Infants respond to the high tones best. Unless his mother has a Greta Garbo voice, a baby usually alerts to his mother's high voice first.

Within the first few months your infant will notice the sound of your voice and it will often stop his crying. He's begun to connect the sound of your voice with you and what you do for him. Infants don't understand any words, but they alert, turn their head toward your voice, and enjoy the tone and communication. It may be on the vibe level, not the vocabulary level, but it's an important beginning relationship with other people. That connection by voice may mean you can stay where you are finishing the last touches on your hairdo because your infant is assured of your presence by your voice. A voice on the radio won't give him the same sense of security; he needs your voice and your presence. Parents

of babies even a few months old seem to know this intuitively and chat with their infants about news and nonsense. Research studies confirm parental instincts that the human voice is the most interesting sound to infants, just as the human face is the most interesting shape. The sound and rhythmic beat of the human heart is also thought to be comforting to an infant. You can buy a recording of the sound or just be aware that holding your infant for feedings is important, providing him with pleasant sights and sounds as well as nourishment. Your speaking voice may be most significant in your child's listening world, but your singing voice has a function also. Singing lullabies is a parental prerogative. You don't have to be operatic quality to please your infant, so close the windows if you must and take your one chance to solo with a captive audience. Infants have the wonderful ability to block out unpleasant sounds, usually by dropping off to sleep, so you may never know if your talents are appreciated!

TOYS AND ACTIVITIES

For the first few months most babies will be startled at a sudden loud noise and alert to your voice, but they will show little interest in toys until about four months. At that time babies begin to find one hand with another and to grip those rattles they got as presents. For the few months before they crawl and get to things on their own, sound is very important. Swiping at chime balls and kicking cradle gyms causes sounds, and this startling effect will make your baby try again. Sound is a feedback from the object and invites repetition. For "sound discoveries" string some sound toys on a strong cord across your baby's crib or carriage to be knocked by hand or foot. Some suggestions are Indian bells from import shops, jingle bells, or a plastic syrup bottle (the kind with a handle to put the rope through) with pebbles, marbles, ball bearings, or tiny bells inside. Glue the cap on.

Often parents-to-be are concerned about the effect of a baby on their lives. At each extreme are parents who believe their lives will be either unaltered or drastically different. One of the first tests of philosophies after homecoming happens at baby's nap time. There tend to be two camps here, the Mozart-on-high-volume group and the tiptoeing group. Generally the issue is resolved if there is a happy match of parents and child. Sometimes hi-fi buffs have jumpy babies who need a library's hush for napping, or tiptoers waste whispers on their placid babies who can sleep in the middle of a parade. Familial bliss often requires a compromise between parental philosophy and infant personality.

Think of your baby's sound environment. Is it the teenager's rock and roll records or the quiet of a country house? From time to time stand and listen to what your child hears. Remember all babies, regardless of their personalities, need pleasant and interesting sounds to listen to part of each day. Loud and sudden sounds may alarm or overstimulate your baby. Repetitive sounds like tires on the road, the vacuum, and television seem to lull an infant to sleep rather than stir him up. If you have a fidgety baby repetitive sound may calm him down. For awake moments plan some pleasant sound experiences for your infant:

- A wind chime made from old keys, nails, or chains strung on coat hangers or a length of doweling, not pretty but surprisingly musical. Be sure to place the sound chime in a safe spot where your baby can't reach it and a strong breeze won't knock it into his crib.
- A music box to be wound as you leave the room. The simple, repetitive melody will soon became familiar.

- The classical music program you enjoy before dinner or a favorite record during his bath

Someday when you are feeling loose and uninhibited, have a little dance with your baby to your favorite waltz or polka. He will love the feeling of moving to music and being close to you. You will relish his responsiveness and there's no problem about who's in the lead either; Arthur Murray would be pleased! When you weary of waltzing, wander through the kitchen together and clink a few glasses or "play" a pottery flowerpot with an old table knife and watch your infant's reaction. He will also be surprised at the single sound you make blowing into an empty bottle or whistling on a blade of grass. Your older infant (four to eight months) will surprise you by recognizing the footsteps of his sister, the dog, Daddy, and Mommy. He is beginning to discriminate one sound from another and you'll see him begin to jiggle and wiggle the way he always does when he knows "Daddy's coming" just by hearing a familiar step. Notice your baby's look when he hears the click of the refrigerator door or the key in the front door. Your infant is associating sounds with meaningful events.

LANGUAGE

The listening to sounds and voices, music and familiar noises is readying your child for language, music, and noise of his own. Your baby may be destined to be a trial attorney or basso profundo at the opera, but at this point in his life your infant is much like Rover in his reception of language. Your tone is what matters. You can say "bad dog" to Rover in a pleasant voice and he will continue chewing on your slipper with tail wagging. One of us often rocked a particularly cranky baby to sleep sweetly singing the gruesome nursery rhyme:

> Baby, baby, naughty baby,
> Hush, you squalling thing,
> I say.

The dulcet tones quieted the baby and the ghastly lyrics made the mother feel less angry about the baby's demands. Keep talking, and remember your infant prefers the sound of the human voice and is learning from it; soon meaning will connect with sound.

You too must operate on the primitive level of language, becoming skilled at identifying the meaning of your infant's cries. All new parents worry that they won't know what each cry means, but within weeks of living together the messages begin to emerge—"I'm hungry," "I hurt,"

"I'm overwhelmed," or "I'm bored." Parents quickly become experts on their own child's crying and respond accordingly. As needs are met the child feels secure. This is the beginning of what Erik Erikson calls an important "sense of trust"; with this developing trust, the basis for communication has begun.

At about two months old, infants add cooing sounds to their repertoire. These are happy little social sounds composed of vowels— "ooo's" and "aaa's." This cooing ability along with an infant's irresistible smile makes social interchange blossom. At about three months old infants develop a marvelous laugh full of chuckles and chortles. Its contagious, deep-throated quality makes parenting a joy. Six-month-old babies respond to their names, another pleasure. The research of T. Berry Brazelton and others on early mother–child interactions shows that the experience of dialogue begins long before true language is developed. By the use of slowed-down movies it was possible to detect a definite give and take between parent and child. It was noted that the child made the first move (smile or coo) to which the mother responded, then she waited for the child to make the next move. This exchange was compared with the exchange in adult conversations. You and your baby will be communicating long before he says a word.

Have you ever found yourself in the midst of a foreign-language-speaking group? Fascination soon leads to frustration. Everything sounds alike with no beginnings, no ends, and no meaning. Apparently infants are more gifted than adults in their language ability. In the first six months of life an infant is able to make all of the sounds required for any language. After the first six months the sounds in languages not his own drop from his babbling. The infant spends the second half-year of life concentrating on producing the sounds of the language he hears around him: French sounds if he hears French, English sounds if he hears English.

Your infant will be cheered by the sound of his own gurgles and coos. He'll repeat and repeat the same happy sound for the simple pleasure of it. His solo vocalizings will take on the same rhythm of conversation, pausing and listening, then cooing again. The sounds of the older infant (five to eight months) become "babblings" as consonants are added to vowels. He may now say two-syllable words: "ma ma," "da da," "na na." The more you talk to your infant, the more he will babble and his vocalizing lead to verbalizing. Remind yourself that he needs to be talked to and bear in mind that verbal competence often determines success. Your "talking to" can take the form of imitation. Have you ever cooed a baby's coos trying to hit just the same note?

Baby noises are fun and your child will delight in your imitations. Your babbling sounds, "baby talk," tonal inflections, response to his cries and coos, even your high-pitched voice like Uncle Harry's give your infant what he needs for the development of language. In eight months he has mastered all the sounds necessary for speech, learned speech intonations, and is practicing the real give and take of communication.

The Baby on the Move: Crawling Age to Twenty-Four Months
Your Crawler/Toddler Goes to the World

As your child begins to get about in the world interacting with objects, he will associate objects with the sounds they make. He will crawl to the sound of the refrigerator fan, chuckle at a clattering toy, and toddle toward a purring cat. His hearing will take in a full range of environmental sounds. As you listen with him you'll hear sounds you have ignored for years: the light rattle of your dishwasher timer signaling a change of cycle, a branch scraping against the house. As adults we have the ability to ignore the general whir, attending only to those sounds which have meaning for us. We concentrate on speech over the clatter of dishes. We listen for the letter carrier and barely hear the neighbor's mower. This ability is known as "auditory figure ground." Children with auditory learning disabilities sometimes have a figure ground problem; they can't sort out what's important and meaningful and repress what is not. They are bombarded with sounds of equal and confusing merit. Before this ability is fully developed in children, they are alert to all the sounds around them, giving attention to whatever catches their ears. Gradually individual sounds take on meaning. Televisions and radios which play all day create a sound background confusing to a child. In the frustration of hearing too much, a child may tune out everything including your voice.

Children not only listen, but during the eight-to-twenty-four-months period they begin to talk, they say words you can understand. This exciting moment is the beginning of speech, yet looking back you realize how much communication went on from birth. Most of all, you realize you've been interacting and enjoying each other. The words of the second year are the icing on the cake, signaling the beginning of the fully communicative vocabulary your child will have at four or five.

BODY

Your child's listening and talking will alternate with moving about for several months. Early crawling and walking take such concentration of energy that you'll have one or the other but less frequently both at once. Savor this brief period, for as soon as your toddler can jog about easily he will add noise to his movements just to see what jiggling and jogging does to the sound. He'll sound a bit like a Plains Indian circling a campfire as he holds a tune that varies with each bounce. Crib rocking and repetitive jumping and jiggling are the rhythms of your waking child. His vocalizations are hardly musical, yet the child development texts say at eighteen months he may begin to hum. Watch for that moment, hardly of operatic quality, but a happy independent self-amusing sound.

An eight-month-old may bang spoon to table and repeat it, delighted in his noise creation. A fifteen-month-old will enjoy banging on pots and pans, feeling the vibrations in his hands as well as hearing the "bang, bang." A twenty-four-month-old will enjoy the noise a collapsing tower of blocks makes and may even cry out "boom" as it topples. Although the cacophony of sound discoveries may exhaust most parents, the noise dies down in the years to come. Noise for the sake of noise lasts through age two. Sound has much more of a purpose in later years, though when your teenager takes up the drums you may remember his pot banging years and it may feel the same!

The body sounds of hand clapping lead to one of baby's first games, an imitative Pat-A-Cake at about one year. Not only do babies imitate sounds you try to teach them, but they also imitate the odd sounds other people make: coughs, sneezes, and nose-blowing sounds they hear around them. We know one visiting grandmother who taught her nine-month-old granddaughter to cough. They coughed away at each other, amused at the communication. For weeks after the grandmother left, the parents didn't know whether to laugh or to call the doctor. A kissing sound might have been a better choice for Grandmother's lesson.

TOYS AND ACTIVITIES

In the investigation of the world about them, children are intent on sound and its sources. Babies differ in their sound preference and reactions. One eight-month-old might drop off to sleep lulled by a favorite music box while another would stay awake until it stopped playing. Watch your child for his musical preferences and reactions, and hope they match your own. One of our friends liked nothing more modern than Bach but her lusty baby swayed in glee to the sound of rock and roll.

Toy manufacturers create push-and-pull toys with tinkling, whirring, and clanging sounds. Toddlers love to go about pushing or pulling something which makes noise. Your toddler will delight in the sounds he makes pulling a plastic syrup bottle filled with gravel or small bells across the floor. He can easily pull the bottle if you tie a spool on the cord end he holds. It will follow your child as he totters about the house, changing sound as he crosses the rug or bare floor. He'll like the "doing," the ability to create the sound himself. Some crawlers and toddlers bask in big sounds, the crash of pot lids used as cymbals, the bang of wooden spoon on pot bottom. Others seem alarmed at their powers, stopping in apparent horror at the sound they have created. For the soft or loud sound devotees try the following:

- Cardboard boxes to beat upon with wooden spoon (soft)
- Plastic containers to beat upon with rubber spatula (soft)
- Tin cans tied together to pull about (loud). Tie a string on the indentation on the side of a coffee can and put noisemakers inside. Nuts and bolts would make a large noise!
- English tea tins, the square metal kind with tight-fitting lids with a variety of sound substances put inside. Rice, bottle tops, paper clips, pennies, or beans make sounds. Which does your child prefer? Stay nearby his play to make sure noisemakers stay inside.
- Smaller tins from tea sampler sets, film canisters, or metal and plastic cigar tubes with sound makers inside. These smaller sizes are easier to grasp in baby's hands, but also easier to fit into a shape-testing mouth. These sound toys can only be used if you are present. One of us saved these special toys for the family dinner hour so baby could be happily amused in the high chair while the rest of the family could dine in peace.

Just as your child may have a preference for toys that make sounds, your child may also be afraid of certain sound toys. Both of us had a child who was reduced to wails and shakes at the sound of a particular toy. The jolly music box Santa with a windup nose and the "friendly" lion that talked with the pull of a cord sent by doting grandmothers brought tears, not smiles. Respect your child's fear and put the toy away for another time, another child.

INDOORS AND OUTDOORS

As your baby crawls or walks about he will seek out sounds in your house. At this age your baby will have many new experiences each day. He has no built-in ideas of safety. You must constantly keep an eye out for what he is into and how he might be injured. He may be as willing to investigate a growling dog or the refrigerator motor as he is to fondle a musical toy. You will soon learn to hear what he hears and know that sound entices him and his next step will be exploration. Experience and your admonitions will make him more cautious as the months go by. Some children seem to have more built-in caution than others. The sound-sensitive child may wail when you turn on your vacuum cleaner. The sound lover may run to join the fun. One of our children used to hop aboard happily, riding atop the roaring, pulsing bronco, feeling the roar in every pore. For the fearful child, sound imitation may modify the fear. Before you turn on the vacuum, the power mower, or the circular saw, look at it with your child and imitate the sound. You may find your fearful child laughing in recognition of the dreaded noise. If sound imitation doesn't rid him of the fear, save the horrible noises for his nap time. Fears of particular noises are temporary in most children and disappear with time.

As your child gets more tuned into the sounds of the world you will get by with less. He will know when you open the refrigerator to eat or when you open the hall closet to put on your coat. In a crude way he monitors your whereabouts by sound in the same way you monitor his.

A child's listening skills are vital to his development. For the first several years of school all directions will be given orally. He will be in second or third grade before he can read well enough to follow written instructions. To help listening skills develop, encourage your child to notice sounds such as these:

- Bell—clock chimes, the doorbell, the dinner bell, the telephone, the kitchen timer, and an alarm clock
- Pet sounds—barks, peeps, meows, or the baas and moos of the farm
- Machine hums of the refrigerator, drier, sewing machine, vacuum cleaner, electric mixer, or blender

Though the radio, television, and record player won't stop his motor drive for long, they will be of passing interest. By two years of age your child will sit and listen to a simple record, but he is more likely to stop and start the record with his hands than sustain an interest in the story or tune. One of us, desperate for a few moments sleep, used to pick up the bedside phone so our toddler could listen to the repeated recorded message. It's worth about eighty winks. Though these amusements may not hold him long, a creaky door or squeaky drawer will delight him. Don't oil the squeak for a few months but be grateful that you have a free new toy.

Because noise is a way of life as crawlers and toddlers push, pull, bang, and investigate your apartment or house, take them outdoors where the open sky absorbs the sound. You'll have a chance to hear your own thoughts and your child will exercise his volume control with the knob mostly on the loud side. Sit near the park fountain and let its "white" sound drown out the yells that are getting on your nerves.

Outdoor sound will lead your child to investigate a much larger world—the helicopter overhead, the motorcycle passing by. He'll soon recognize the sound of the school bus bringing big sister home or the car as his grandfather drives up. The sanitation truck's crash and crunch may be the highlight of his week. He'll point out the peeping bird and imitate its sound.

LANGUAGE

Language is acquired slowly during the crawler/toddler period. Your child's first word usually appears before he is a year old, and by twenty-four months he may have a vocabulary of more than two hundred words. However, your child will understand two or three times as many words as he can utter. You can ask a ten-month-old who has not uttered a word, "Where's Mommy?" and see him look in her direction. The understanding of language is called a child's "receptive vocabulary," and for years it is far greater than his "expressive (speaking) vocabulary."

Long before your child can utter words or sentences comprehensible to a stranger, he will be muttering gibberish that has the flavor of the language around him. The intonations and inflections follow the same sound patterns as the adult speech he hears. During his second year a toddler talks only to his parents or familiar sitters and to himself, rarely to another child. His speech is still so rudimentary that other children cannot understand him. Some of a child's first words are often words of his own invention, "ba" for blanket," for example. It is vital for parents to understand their child's meaning rather than correct his pronunciation. The focus of early language should be communication, not articulation. Communication with you is the beginning of communication with the world.

Your child's utterances may be single sounds or words, but they convey whole thoughts. As your child's speech becomes clearer, other people may understand some of his words, but not his meaning. His one word "horsie" doesn't just mean horse, but may mean "Here comes a horse" or "Let's go see the horse" or "Is it a horse?" In this phase of language acquisition you are very important to your child. The words and sounds he makes are important, but more essential is the feeling of understanding and being understood. Just as you take a foreigner into your world, you translate what strangers say to your child into the words you know he can understand and you translate his words for others. His first words will be labels for the here and now, those items that are most useful to him—his own body, family, toys, food, clothes. As his words emerge it is important that you give your child a chance to communicate, to express his needs in words; he should feel his growing vocabulary has impact on the world. If at a wrinkle of his brow you say "Do you want milk? cookie? teddy?" you remove his need to speak, you take over for him.

In a sense this age requires a great change of style in parents. For the first eight or ten months you did all the talking in words and your infant responded with smiles and babbles. Your child was content to hear the sound of your voice; the topic didn't matter to him. He was equally pleased to hear about your grocery list or the state of the union. During the first year your child was absorbing the sounds and rhythms of speech, not learning words. Now he uses words, and you need to respond so that his words are effective signals. To communicate effectively with your young child who is just learning to speak, change your own conversational pace, speak directly to your toddler and talk about the here and now which interests your child, emphasizing the key words you want him to understand. Understand your child's words and extend his communication. If your child says "doggie" you might reply, "Yes, I see the big dog, Liz's dog."

Studies have shown that a child doesn't learn language from television, records, or radio but from the adults who care for him and talk to him. A child's speech reflects the tonality, patterns, and style of his parents' speech. Young children need human contact from a caring adult to learn. One research study discovered that educational television had little effect on the growth of language or ideas in young children without an adult nearby to make comments, ask questions, and draw the child into active participation.

All of this low-level childlike talk wears on most adults. The claustrophobic parent may prolong conversation with the grocery checker to hear the sound of an adult voice and participate in a real conversation beyond "doggie," "milk," and "bye-bye." Be aware of your need to communicate fast and freely, and join any adult group you enjoy. Go back to your one-year-old ready to talk some more, for by four or five years he will have much of his language learned and can communicate freely with other children and adults. You are vitally important in the first stages, for only a close companion knows what a one-year-old is talking about. You are your child's link to the world.

Two- and Three-Year-Olds: Your Child Finds Words for the World

Your two-year-old is the "King of Din," a rival to any New Year's noisemaker. He's learning how things work and what they do, and noisemaking is one of his major occupations. Three-year-olds seem

quieter by comparison. Fortunately, your two- or three-year-old is also growing in language skills and is able to use words instead of actions at least some of the time. These first tentative steps toward civilization are a boon to both parent and child. The one-year-old who sat screaming in the high chair and pointing to a particular food on the dining table knew exactly what he wanted. Unfortunately, the rest of the family didn't and the frustration escalated. The two-year-old can now label milk, bread, and apple, and at least "get by" like a traveler with a Berlitz phrase book in hand. The three-year-old uses many words effectively and can be a family conversationalist. Within these broad age characteristics there are individual styles. Some two-year-olds are "talkers" and some are "doers." The "talkers" will gallop ahead in speech, wanting to communicate; the "doers" may be sparing of speech.

BODY

Two- and three-year-olds are very proud of their own bodies and all the sounds their bodies make. They'll be as pleased and proud of the noises we consider socially unacceptable as the ones we consider refined. Leave the burping and other unspeakables to be enjoyed with their friends and remember there were eras in history and cultures when these body noises were considered polite adult behavior. Some sounds they will find fun and you can find acceptable are coughs and sneezes, tongue clicking, straw sucking, bubble blowing, and last-drop slurping, hissing, clapping hands and thumping feet to rhythm, and humming the tune of their first song.

Note that most two- and three-year-olds do not have the language or tonal ability to "sing a song" as in a rendition of a popular song. If your child can sing nursery ditties recognizable by someone outside the family, then start a piggy bank for music lessons in grade school because your child probably has what music teachers refer to as "an ear."

Musical sounds may not be every two- and three-year-old's bit, but noisy tantrums are. At least once during these two or three years you will be subjected to your child's screams of rage and frustration, often accompanied by pounding feet or fists. The intensity, length, and volume of tantrums can be frightening to both parent and child. Keep in mind that the rage is bothering him more than you and most children outgrow tantrums.

FOOD

Two- and three-year-olds love the bold noises of food. They will relish and exaggerate the pops, snaps, and slurps. It's all part of the "I can do it" feeling. Your child will enjoy listening to or making: the pop of popcorn, the snap of carrots, celery, and beans; the slurp of soup; the gushy swoosh of pudding; the ghastly sound of exhaling through applesauce; and the sucking smack of lollipops and candy canes.

TOYS AND ACTIVITIES

Most two- and three-year-olds like musical and noisy toys. Your child will practice with sound toys, fascinated by his own ability to control the volume. You will know your child's special sound interest and tolerance. One child may love the nerve-racking noise of a toy lawn mower and another the soft plink of a music box. See if your child enjoys these:

- Records from the library, such as Mother Goose and simple stories. Let your child experiment with the volume knob, a heady power.
- Megaphone of paper towel and toilet paper rolls. If you "jump out of your skin" with the yells, he will collapse with giggles.
- Sock puppet for cow "moos" and kitten "meows." Puppetry skill for two- and three-year-olds is limited to simple sounds. Conversation and role playing are too advanced.
- A noise box for guessing what's inside. Put some obvious sound items in a shoe box and jiggle it. Is it a Kleenex or a shoe? Don't be too subtle. Two- and three-year-olds will have to practice for a year or so before they can tell a pencil from a paper clip.

INDOORS AND OUTDOORS

Most of your appliances have noises you take for granted. Children love to imitate sounds they hear. Can you brave up and join your two-year-old in trying to sound like the vacuum or try to match tones of the hair dryer with your three-year-old? Shedding inhibitions will keep you young anyway! Together you can notice the sounds of:

- The spin cycle of your washer
- The ice maker working
- The start of the air conditioner or furnace
- The slow hiss or loud bang of a screen door shutting
- The squeak of a window being cleaned
- The splash of water filling sink or tub and the gurgle of water going down the drain
- An echo in an empty room
- Hard and soft things falling—a shoe, a block, a book, a feather, a flower, a scarf

Your two- and three-year-old will also enjoy the magic of quiet. Use the Montessori technique of asking your child how quietly he can shut the door, park his tricycle, climb into his chair. The challenge will please you both. Two- and three-year-olds will hear remote sounds from outside and shudder at the unfamiliar. The cry of the wind whistling through a crack or a neighbor's cat howling may be terrifying to your child. Young children need lots of time and experiences in order to feel comfortable with sounds; they are a bit like adults in a new home who feel unsettled and slightly insomniac until the creaks and groans of the house become familiar.

Two- and three-year-olds love to be outside. Go on a sound walk and listen for these sounds:

- The tap of feet on the pavement, the crackle in dry leaves
- The sound of a stick dragged along fences or garbage cans
- The buzz of a bee, the croak of a frog
- Bird chirps, peeps, and squeaks
- The quiet swish of a bike passing
- Airplanes, close or distant
- Trucks, big and little
- The ice-cream truck bell
- Sirens

Buildings will interest your child. The noisy or quiet sounds will be remembered long after the visit. At your office your three-year-old will be impressed with the buzz of the typewriters or the clickety-clack of the ticker tape. Knowing that you are office manager or a stockbroker means nothing to him, but your office sounds will speak his language and impress him. Together listen to other building sounds:

- The quiet of a church or library
- The hubbub of a school cafeteria
- The echoes in an underground garage
- The bustle of a railroad station or airport

LANGUAGE

Your two- or three-year-old will be most comfortable in talking to his mommy, daddy, brother, or sister. Your worlds are one and communication is easy. A visiting uncle or new teacher demands new listening skills; verbally able young children often clam up in unfamiliar social settings. With other children your child will be more interested in doing than talking. Two-year-olds playing side by side can often be heard talking to themselves. Both the play and the talking of two-year-olds are self-directed. Even three-year-olds who talk less to themselves speak sparingly to friends in play. Their play may now be more involved with another child driving trucks side by side, but the talk will usually be single words or short phrases. Your three-year-old may save his lengthy conversations for you at home after the play session is over.

Your child needs someone to listen to him and someone nearby to provide words or extend his thoughts. He may speak of his "big truck." Try adding, "Your truck drives fast. Your truck is full," to encourage him to enlarge his vocabulary and extend his thinking. Delayed speech in two- and three-year-olds may be caused by a number of factors, from physical hearing loss to individual maturation, but environment plays a part. A two- and three-year-old who is slow to speak may be cared for by a foreign-speaking housekeeper or be number four in the family pecking order and have all of his grunts translated by older siblings. Twins are notorious for language delay and often develop their own language in the early years. Your child will grow in his language skills by leaps and bounds during these years; his particular pace is determined by his personality and learning style, and by the environment you create for him.

All children of this age need language competence not only to make needs and wants known, but also to label concepts. The two-year-old is beginning to "think" about things for the first time, not just play with them. He can talk about "the duck" even if the duck is not in the room. Two-year-olds need more and more words for their ideas and feelings. Words and ideas are a linguistic "chicken and egg" situation, but educators agree that words and ideas go round in a circle, language expressing ideas and ideas demanding language.

It may seem that your two- or three-year-old is on a talking jag, and he is. His practice with you is readying him for talking to the world. His constant "whys" are not a search for causes and "life's real meaning," but a surefire way to prolong a conversation. Whining is also a technique used by children hoping to engage others in dialogue. It is a more advanced attention-getting device than screaming, but equally annoying. Try to ignore your child's whine and tell him you'll listen when he can say it in a "nice voice."

Two- and three-year-olds need an enthusiastic listener capable of understanding all. They need simple explanations, not dissertations on the ways of the world. Some parents overwhelm their children with reasons and explanations beyond a child's comprehension. Two-year-olds are a pleasure, zooming full speed ahead and verbally identifying everything in their path—toothbrush to transistor. They greet each new word with gusto, savoring the sound. Three-year-olds are usually beyond sheer labeling. Between ages two and three an exciting moment comes in language development. Your child is not simply parroting the words he has heard; he is quietly devising linguistic rules and applying them. He may begin using pronouns saying "I" and "you" correctly most of the time. You may hear him speak of his "foots" or "feets" or tell you he "ated" his breakfast. He has abstracted the general rule for plurals and past tense adding an "s" or "ed" when needed. He will apply his new rule in odd ways before he learns the exceptions, but the moment is one to treasure not to laugh at. He's on the way to mastering the language. Often the ideas of three-year-olds come faster than their words. This can cause stuttering, which occurs typically at age three-and-one-half. Maturation and time usually get thoughts and words synchronized, and stuttering disappears within a year. If this speech pattern doesn't disappear, have a speech and language center screen your child's speech.

Your child will want to try his new language skills on the telephone. Two-year-olds are like tourists in a foreign country: they can get by speaking face to face with the natives, but the phone is another matter entirely. The message gets lost when they don't have gestures and facial expressions to go with the words. Your two-year-old will want to talk to Grandfather long distance but may only nod and shake his head in response to his questions. Three-year-olds with practice will be able to carry on limited phone conversations, particularly if you are nearby to prompt. It will be a bit like Edgar Bergen and Charlie McCarthy, but it's a beginning. In years to come when your child is a teenager with "telephonitis" you will forget that it once was an acquired skill.

Books will help bridge the gap between the familiar and the unfamiliar, the concrete and the abstract. Your two- or three-year-old will learn about the world first by active exploration, but seeing pictures and words will help in symbolizing. The best books for two-year-olds are simple ones with clear representational pictures and little text. The subject matter should be familiar: family and home, toys and animals. For your two-year-old, "reading a story" means "talking a story." What he will like best is skipping the story line and identifying the objects or actions, asking you "What's that?" or better still, having you ask him "What's that?" This labeling mania abates a bit in three-year-olds, and one-event stories begin to have an appeal. Your child won't want dozens of different stories, but will demand repeats of favorites. Bedtime ritual for some two- and three-year-olds consists of the same dog-eared book read in the same way night after night until it is memorized cover to cover. During these years you will find yourself able to quote pages and pages of "children's literature" with the ease of a Shakespearean scholar. Unfortunately no one wants to hear about the adventures of Benjamin Bunny at a dinner party, so your talents go unnoticed. No matter; your child is growing in language ability and his lifelong love of books has begun.

Four- and Five-Year-Olds: Your Child Begins to Order His World

Four- and five-year-olds like organized, purposeful noise. They talk with other children and adults, imitate voices, shout or whisper, sing songs, and make music. Their creativity is evident in their language, music, and noise. Many children at this age are at school, away from someone who can interpret what they say, and they wish to be understood.

By age four or five you have some sense of your child's style—the "looker" or "mover", the "talker" or doer." Some children are very sound oriented; they learn best by what they hear. Adults who recognize their own learning style will say, "Just a minute, spell your name for me and I'll remember it," or "Let me write it down. Once I've looked at it I can remember." For the child who learns best by listening, you'll want to look ahead and choose a school that emphasizes verbal instruction and encourages the give and take of discussion, rather than one which emphasizes silent, self-motivated study. You may find that your sound-oriented child has a flair for music or is adept at foreign language. If you are a quiet, inward person and your child is a talker, give him chances to chat with your more talkative neighbor. If you are both talkers, you'll have to learn to take turns.

PEOPLE

Four- and five-year-olds notice other people's sounds and speech. Uncle Herbert's throat-clearing tic is subject to imitation. They will also notice high and low voices, big and little voices; varieties of laughing styles, belly laughter, the muffled titter; foreign languages and accents; speech defects; and the sweet sounds a happy baby makes. They will become experts on occupational sounds, such as the construction jackhammer, the dentist's drill, the fire siren. Their play becomes a mirror of their experience.

BODY

Four- and five-year-olds' general interest in their own bodies extends to the noises they can make. The whistler and finger snapper are the envy of the neighborhood gang. Other body sounds four-and five-year-olds can make and listen to are hiccups; whispers; laryngitis or sore throat voice changes; teeth chatters; heartbeats; stomach rumbles (called borborygmus in the dictionary, a triumph of onomatopoeia!); squeak of shampooed hair; knuckle cracks; clicking heels; and tap dancing. A sound game to think about is what body part plays what instrument. Your four- or five-year-old would have to have seen each instrument played to succeed at this game. For a body and sound surprise locate a one-man band!

CLOTHING

Clothes-conscious four- and five-year-olds will listen to the subtle sounds clothes can make. The squeak of sneakers skidding on a linoleum floor means your preschooler is announcing his self-confident arrival. He'll listen for and be delighted in onomatopoetic words such as zippers zipping; snaps snapping; the whoosh of cordoroy pants leg to leg; the rustle of nylon ski jackets; the swish of the satin or taffeta of your best dress; the crackle of a plastic raincoat; and the slap, slap of flip-flop sandals.

FOOD

Two- and three-year-olds can rarely eat and talk at the same time, but four- and five-year-olds are more conversational. Four-year-olds interrupt each other and share silly words at a twosome lunch hour. Five-year-olds are more grown-up. For them snack time with friends may sound like the give and take of a board meeting. Now it is possible to enjoy a full meal exchanging talk with your four- or five-year-old. His increased memory span means he can recall some events of the day and share them with interested parents.

Cooking can become a new adventure as your child helps with snapping beans, grating carrots and cheese, sizzling hamburger, and blending soups or milkshakes. He knows the familiar kitchen sounds and is not afraid of the roars and rattles of beaters and mixers. He will like feeling part of the family and sharing in meal preparation.

TOYS AND ACTIVITIES

The best sound toys for four- and five-year-olds are the very same toys your grandparents played with happily. Your child will like:

- Balls to bounce in a rhythmic beat
- Balloons to fill with air; then pinch the neck between thumbs and forefingers so the slowly released air produces an ear-piercing shriek
- Combs with tissue paper to blow like a kazoo
- Rubber bands of various sizes to stretch across a shoe box for a gently plucked banjo. Does the wide band make a higher or lower noise?
- Jelly glasses to fill with water at different levels, clinked with a spoon to create a song

By age four or five most children can listen to a story without having to look at pictures. If you enjoy reading aloud you can begin your own story hour. For children who like to listen, search your public library to take out records of poetry, fairy tales, folktales, and folk songs. Some telephone companies have Dial-a-Story and some radio stations a Story Hour. Stories read by famous performers give children an ear for the rhythm and cadence of spoken language. There are several children's recordings which feature orchestra instruments and their sound: "Tubby the Tuba," "Peter and the Wolf," "The Sorcerer's Apprentice." Picking out an instrument sound from all the others is a difficult auditory figure ground task. All children think the sound effect records most libraries have for radio or theater performers are a howl. If you can stand the noise try the sound of cannons to let your children know dinner is on. Your reputation will be made with your child's friends. If your library doesn't have sound records, try the end of the "1812 Overture" for a morning wake-up on a school day!

OUTDOORS

There are many outdoor experiences which are explorations in sound. The wind sounds differently blowing through various kinds of leaves. The muffled stillness of snow is broken by the sharp crack of ice. Rain, hail, and thunder are part of nature's orchestra. Speed changes the sound of cars, trucks, and trains. The sound of nuts falling from a tree is a surprise; the sound of rain falling can be peaceful. You and your child may want to take an Indian walk, putting your ear to the earth. What's coming? Take your dog along and watch his ears perk up to noises you can't hear. Dogs can hear higher frequencies than humans. Even humans vary in their hearing ranges. Does your child put his hands over his ears when he passes the ultra-high frequency burglar monitor in stores? The alarm system is shut off in the daytime but the monitor is left on. This sound actually is felt as pain in some people's ears. For hearing pleasure listen to some sounds in the list below.

Birds Woodpeckers have a rhythmic peck. The crow and dove have identifiable calls. If there's a mockingbird nearby it will treat you to a full range of birdcalls. A bird feeder will entice an assortment of birds for watching and listening pleasure.

Bugs Mosquitos are easy to identify by sound, but hunt for the beetles that click when they turn over or the tiny cricket that makes a huge noise in the brush.

Beasts If they've heard them before, the farm sounds are too tame for adventurous four-year-olds or inquisitive five-year-olds. Visit the zoo to hear the wild and weird: snake hisses, monkey chatters, elephant trumpets, and hyena laughs. Your child will marvel that animals communicate by sound and that the giraffe doesn't make any sound. See if your child can make up the sound a giraffe would make if it made one.

The Arts Visit your junior high school orchestra or your music store and listen to the sounds that are made by different shapes and sizes of instruments. Don't go to the symphony, as your child is still too young to sit still and be silent, but the junior high school will accept your coming late and going early. They will be flattered at your interest in the instruments after the concert or rehearsal. If you get a chance, compare the bass with the violin. Notice that the bigger the drum, the bigger the boom. Your child will have a chance to combine shape, size, and sound concepts. Listening to the same instrument sounds on a record and identifying instruments is a more sophisticated task.

LANGUAGE

The nursery school teacher's admonition to four- and five-year-olds is "Use your voice. Don't hit. Use words." A four-year-old usually has a large vocabulary and clear enough articulation to use words to make things happen, to ask questions, to express his feelings. But when emotions are strong, words don't always come before actions. Five-year-olds, however, live more by the rules and can usually "talk things out" even if in a loud and angry voice.

Four- and five-year-olds relish talk with peers more than talk with adults. At four, much talk with other children is in the boasting line: "My cookie is bigger than your cookie," "My Daddy is stronger than your Daddy." At five, realistic conversations are more the mode. Four-year-olds play with language, trying words the same way they try their bodies on jungle gyms. They make ridiculous word combinations, rhyme words, or make up nonsense words. Their humor is absurd but fun to share. They know enough right words, functions, and actions to delight in the absurd. "The chair ate a hamburger" may be the joke of the week. Four-year-olds like to rhyme, attending to the sounds in words that will make reading easier in two years. Five-year-olds may listen for initial letter sounds in kindergarten, bringing this curiosity to cracker and cereal boxes, asking you to spell the letters for them. Fours make up bathroom words like "do-do" and use them like swear words. Parents who have a big reaction may see a dramatic increase in these words. If you swear, children will pick up the words quickly and use them with swagger and bravado. They may not know the meaning of what they say, but they pick up the drama. Fives are more conventional and will be less embarrassing. The letters of the alphabet and "numbers to ten" will be important conversation to them. Both fours and fives like classic childhood chants, and their shouting and singing will bring back your childhood memories.

Four- and five-year-olds can understand much of what you say to them or to other adults. Their language skills have increased in the same way their motor skills increased at earlier ages. They can remember events that happened in the past and talk about events in the future. They can make up and tell a story. They can follow directions. When your child was eighteen months old you could give him a single direction, "Give me your shoe." Gradually a child's memory grows until the child can follow a three-level command at four years, such as "Go get your shoe, put it on the shelf, and then bring me your sweater." Listen to yourself as you give directions and see how well your child can follow. Some children (and adults) are less talented at this memory sequencing act; if your child has difficulty, back up and give him one or two directions at a time or wait until one phase of the job is over before announcing the next. Family jobs are good practice, for in kindergarten the teacher will say: "Hang your belongings in your cubbies, get your crayons and workbooks out, and sit down at the tables." Years of shoe fetching will pay off in ability to attend in kindergarten classroom and college lecture hall. The standard reading readiness tests assess this same skill. For an auditory memory skill combined with an expressive language skill, have your child call the telephone number for the correct time when you need to double-check your clocks. This skill of listening and then repeating verbatim what's heard is another necessary school skill. For four- and five-year-olds, stick to telephone time calls; the weather announcer with wind velocity, forecast, and air index will be overwhelming. Play some language and sound games with your child:

- Creating tunes on homemade or bought instruments (drum, tambourine, maraca). If you purchase instruments, be sure to buy quality instruments from a music store, not the toy store. Your child will grow accustomed to quality sound, distinguishing music from noise, and will learn to treat instruments with special care if encouraged.
- Making "poems" with rhyming words. You say a line, let him do the next.
- Making up simple songs. Musical ability doesn't matter.
- Imitating animal noises and letting everyone guess what animal you're pretending to be
- Classifying sounds as high or low (brake squeals or lion's roar, violin or drum); indoor or outdoor (trash truck or vacuum); big and little (elephant or mouse, jackhammer or sailboat sailing); transportation (siren and horse's trot); noisy or quiet (dump truck or snowfall); city or country (traffic or cows); animal or people (people can make animal noises, can animals make people noise? Find a parrot or a myna bird.)
- Remembering noisy and quiet, loud and soft, food sounds—Which is quieter, biting into a cream puff or potato chip? Which is louder, biting into a cracker or a piece of bread? What is the softest sounding food—mashed potatoes?
- Trying simple tongue twisters together

- Thinking about scary sounds (thunder, fireworks, big barks, growls) and nice sounds (lullabies, cuckoo clocks, baby's coos)

If your child is imaginative and can shift from reality to fantasy, try some way-out games. If a color or a shape had a noise what would it be? Does red yell and pink whisper? If a chair, a bowl, or a sweater had a voice what would it sound like?

Take your child to a mime performance and think of the unspoken communication. Your child may be perceptive enough in the mime of everyday life to know now if you mean what you say: "Isn't it nice Auntie is coming" may be said through clenched teeth. Be careful you don't give him mixed messages. He'll be confused by the dichotomy between your tone and your words. You'll want *him* to mean what he says. The language skills your child is building both by listening and talking are the bases for his social and intellectual growth in the coming years. Watch your child pretend, imagine, and play with the words and sounds he has learned through his experiences.

Chapter 7

"Up the Hill and ... Down Again"
How a Child Learns
About Position in Space

"POSITION IN SPACE" sounds a bit like a concept for astronauts. It's not. It's the everyday art of getting around, indoors and out, without bumping into chairs or falling into holes. It's a slow process. Babies learn by trial and error where their bodies end and objects begin. Toddlers practice, repeating their successful maneuvers, by activities such as walking from chair to table and back again, or putting pegs in holes.

Position in space is not only important as your child moves his body and objects through space, it also applies to his management of the printed page. A child who has position in space problems may have learning problems. In school the teacher may tell him to "read from the top to the bottom of the page," "subtract from the bottom to the top of the problem," "sit in the middle seat of the back row." No amount of memorization of these dizzying directions can really prepare children for tracking letters and numbers up, down, and across pages. A child must have the background of many physical experiences, a background acquired before he ever starts school.

POSITION IN SPACE CONCEPT WORDS

Least Difficult	More Difficult	Most Difficult
in—out	into—out of	inside—outside
	indoors—outdoors	
	by	toward—away from
side	beside	close to—far from
	next to	together—apart
	to—from	

		near—far
up—down	high—low	right side up—upside down
		above—below
	open—shut	float—sink
on—off	over—under	
top—bottom	on top of—	
	at the bottom of	
through	around	middle
		across
		between
front—back	in front of—	behind
	in back of	before—after
	forward—backward	
here—there		left—right

The Infant: Birth to Eight Months or Crawling Age
You Bring the World to Your Infant

Just as you bring other experiences to your infant, you are responsible for his position in space. In the first few months an infant is unable to change his position at all. If you put him face down or face up in his crib there he stays, unable to turn over. You make the decision, but early on he communicates to you what his favored position is. You know by his settling down or restlessness whether he is a tummy-down or tummy-up type for nodding off. You know by his coos and gurgles whether he enjoys back-lying kick sessions or tummy wiggle sessions for his wakeful play. Some babies are most content when toted in a carrier or backpack, changing position as you change yours. Others who seem tense or overstimulated by too much contact may prefer the regularity of a rocked cradle or the placidity of a quiet, stable crib. Some older infants thrive on being carried facing away from your body, looking at the world. Some infants are easy to hold; in spite of floppy heavy heads they lean in and curve to your body. Other infants have limp bodies like overcooked spaghetti: they need to be supported limb by limb. Some parents have ample shelflike chests or bosoms that easily support a tiny form. Others are worn out at the task of carrying about an infant whose body keeps dropping or sliding from their grip. No matter what shape your torso, you will need to adjust to cradle and hold your infant.

All babies enjoy change in position from time to time—picking up, turning over, propping up. Change in position means change in light, with new things to look at and later new things to reach for. Be aware of what your baby can look at or reach in his new positions. By experiment you'll find your baby's favorite change of positions and you'll learn your own tolerance for these kinds of interactions. Sometimes you'll happily let him use your body as a jungle gym. Other times you'll depend on that collection of furniture which seems to come along with babies:

- Carriers and backpacks to give your infant a chance to be upright. He'll be six months old before he can sit up on his own and a year before he can walk. He will experience all the directions your body goes in as he feels your motions in his own body.
- Pillows on your sofa to prop up your baby before he can sit himself. Grandma used this technique before infant seats were invented.
- An infant seat on a table, in a chair, on the floor, anywhere near you. You and your infant can chat back and forth and you can occasionally change what he looks at (or handles, if he's four months old).
- Baby carriage, rocking chair, or cradle for a change of pace. The steady back and forth, side to side motion will be a pleasant change.

BODY

As your infant's body develops, his growing capabilities in handling his own head, hands, and feet mean a new relationship to the space around him. Wobbly head and flailing arms gradually become directed and controlled. Babies differ in their eagerness to change their positions. Some snuggle in cribs in swaddled contentment and others struggle and kick from birth on. At the tender age of three days one of our babies had a brush-burned nose from lifting his head. He had neither the strength nor control for this feat and soon his head thumped down. Whatever his pace and vigor, your baby will follow a general developmental pattern, gaining strength and coordination from head to toes. Watch his changing relationship with the space around him:

- Holding his head up to look around when you hold him on your shoulder
- Lifting his head in the crib to look forward
- Turning his head from side to side as he lies on his back
- Rolling over from front to back (about four months)
- Rolling over from back to front (about six months). You can no longer settle him down and know he'll stay put!
- Getting to a sitting position (at six to eight months)
- Getting up on all fours preparing to crawl (six to eight months)

Postural changes mean new vistas for your infant. During the same period, your infant is gaining control over his hands, arms, and feet. (See section on use of hands in Chapter 4.) In his encounters with toys he will gradually explore more and more objects as you bring them into his range. The accidental encounters of flailing arms and hands grow more refined. As his eye–hand coordination develops, your child will relate more and more to the objects you give him. He will bring toys to his mouth and explore them his way. At six months he has a rough whole-hand grip, but by seven or eight months, fingers and thumbs work in opposition. You will want to be sure that the objects you give him to hold demand different grasps so your infant can practice his growing skills. A bracelet requires a different grasp from a ball. Some of the objects will be hung over his crib to be hit by hands or feet, but others should be loose so he can handle and mouth them.

TOYS AND ACTIVITIES

The toys listed in the texture, size, shape, color, and sound chapters will provide your infant with looking, touching, and manipulating experiences. This growing physical ability is the beginning of the mastery of the world about him. His physical exploration and management of his body in relation to the objects in the world and the objects in relation to each other leads to an understanding of the complexities of space in and out, behind and beside. When you understand an infant's relationship to the objects in the space around him you have a peek at how his mind works. If he can't see, mouth, touch, or handle an object it simply doesn't exist for him. Watch a five-month-old enjoy a toy. If it rolls out of sight or drops from his hand he doesn't search for it. Out of sight, out of mind! It's hard for us to imagine such a world. It must be completely unpredictable: objects and people appear and disappear, having little stability. The world may seem filled with a hundred balls when one day your infant's ball is in its crib, the next on the floor, the next in a chair. As your infant's eyes and hands coordinate, the world becomes a bit more stable. Your infant can follow the path of a slow-moving toy, tracking it a short distance. You can attach some objects to a cord over his crib so he can hit them with hands or feet again and again. He can learn to coordinate his looking and reaching if the toy is within grasping distance. If the toy goes out of his view, even if it's in his reach, he won't search for it until he's more than eight months old.

There are some handy aspects to this characteristic of infants. You can take a toy away and substitute another and your infant won't miss the one you took away. You can put a box in front of your infant's bottle if you want him to forget he saw it. If he's not fussing from hunger pains he will be distracted and play with a toy.

LANGUAGE

Children less than one year old can't use or understand position in space words with the possible exception of "up." If you say "up" when you are about to pick up your infant he may begin to recognize it as a word and jiggle and posture to be lifted.

Infants associate voices with familiar faces at an early age. Even though people appear and reappear from different directions, infants gradually begin to expect familiar voices to come from familiar faces. People in the infant's world seem as unpredictable as the appearing and disappearing objects. Some research was done on infants less than five months old with the child's mother appearing in three images over his crib. One was the real mother, the other two were created by mirrors. When the three mothers spoke with the same voice coming from one then another, the infants cooed happily to all three. They were used to their mothers' faces appearing and disappearing from many locations. Two months later a baby would cry out in confusion at this same test. He would have established a more permanent view of the world and would recognize the triple mother as a contradiction of his new view. Keep in touch by voice as you come in and out of your child's view. In the first eight months your tone is more important than your words. In the next few years as you watch his wanderings through space, you will label his actions. Your labeling over a period of years will enable him to grasp the intricacies of spatial words, an understanding he will need to manage ideas.

The Baby on the Move: Crawling Age to Twenty-Four Months Your Crawler/Toddler Goes to the World

The practice of movement through space and manipulation of objects is the hallmark of the eight- to twenty-four-month-old baby. At this age the constant practice of new skills, rocking on knees and hands, pulling up, creeping, crawling, and finally walking is a change of posture and therefore a change in the baby's relationship to the space around him. All this moving about brings him into contact with an expanding world. He can see more, reach higher, and go places. Hands that were just the end points of wiggling arms become sophisticated tools able to pick up and drop objects. Thumping feet become a way to move about. At the same time your baby's body is developing competence, his mind is intensely curious and leads his body into an era of exploration of places and things which is (thank heavens!) never repeated with the same

intensity in the growing years. The "ins and outs" and "ups and downs" of this age try even a physically active parent. Remember that all this physical experience is readying your child for thoughts and some of the quieter activities of later life.

BODY

The "on the move" baby learns about the concepts of "forward" and "backward," "inside" and "outside," "on top of" and "next to" by doing. His own body is the best teacher. The baby's approach to the world is like our approach to a complicated new board game: listening to instructions can't compare with getting the "feel" of it by playing the game. Your crawler/toddler will "play the game," exploring his world and perfecting his body skills nearly every waking moment. The "on the move" baby should have an "on the move" person caring for him. Toys are less important than the freedom he needs. Playpens should be avoided except as a safety zone for a quick time-out while you stir the stew or answer the phone. The restraints of the playpen will frustrate your child's natural curiosity.

All babies go through the same physical skill progression, although the rate of development will be individual. Just as you can't "teach" your baby position in space concepts to accelerate his intellectual pace, you cannot teach motor skills in hopes of reaching physical goals at an earlier age. Your baby will develop at his own rate, with you nearby to support mobility and to encourage curiosity.

Just as there are individual development rates there are individual styles of "moving." Crawlers have various methods of getting about. Some babies creep before they crawl, using a drag-the-body approach, and others practice rocking on all fours until they are experienced enough to move in that position. Some babies crawl backward before they are able to crawl forward, causing untold frustration. As they make the motions to go forward they move in the opposite direction. Toddlers' walking styles show the same variety. Some toddlers hesitantly move from base to base and back again until they feel confident enough to venture out. Other more adventuresome souls seem to go at full tilt regardless of ability and rely on sheer momentum to keep the toddling going. Moving about gives your baby a new view of the world. The creeping and crawling baby sees sofa bottoms and people's shoes at close range. This ability to move independently allows him to crawl behind chairs and between crib and dresser. Often a new crawler needs help in getting unstuck, but the panic is momentary and the exploration is on again. New vistas open up for walking toddlers. Tabletops are investigated; shelves and drawers are rummaged. You may need the Alice in Wonderland experience of making yourself as small as your toddler to see what he sees. A year or more of looking at people's feet or even knees seems incredible to us and yet that is what the toddler sees from his vantage point. From time to time crouch to see eye-to-eye with your youngster. It will give him a new view of you.

Body games with a change in position in space amuse some children and terrify others. Some babies like being held high in the air or being swung upside down, others shriek in fear at the sudden change of position. Roller coasters and Ferris wheels exhilarate some adults and intimidate others, and babies seem to have the same range of reactions to motion.

CLOTHING

It's great when your year-old baby can control some of his body positions and begins to "help" with dressing. He is aware enough and coordinated enough to push or thrust to get hand through shirt sleeve.

Be grateful for his assistance. Your toddler will be able to completely undress himself by the time he is two years old. The "undoing" is easier than the "doing." When you find him stripped at your front door remember that practice in taking off clothing helps in the later skills of putting on. Babies as young as a year are able to take off hat, shoes, and socks. Shoelaces will be unlaced triumphantly. Older toddlers (sixteen to eighteen months) will be able to unzip a large zipper from top to bottom, but it will take a few more months before they will be able to zip up even after someone else "starts" the zipper. Unbuttoning and buttoning skills are beyond the toddler unless the buttons spontaneously pop open when tugged. Toward the end of his second year your toddler will be able to pull stretchy underpants up or down and put on his shoes. He has no idea of front or back or right and left, but his first dressing successes will cheer you both.

FOOD

Feeding himself is a position in space feat for your child. One of the ways to build a child's ego is to give him the time and space to practice body skills. If a child feels good about what he is capable of doing, he feels good about himself. During the second year of a child's life his muscles are ready to handle some of the table tools society insists upon. If the cereal is thick enough it will hang on the spoon until a fifteen-month-old gets spoon to mouth. If the vegetable is firm enough it can be picked up in thumb and forefinger. To have an independent toddler you may have to limit his menus to easy "pickupables." Some children at about one year refuse to be fed by someone else and are limited to a diet of foods that they can manage. Other children are more amenable to taking turns; you feed one spoon and they another. The graduation from bottle to cup occurs during the crawler/toddler age. At first your child uses two hands on a mug or cup, but eventually he can lift it with one hand. Prepare for "many a slip from cup to lip" as he practices. It's an art, moving a cup from table to mouth, and transferring liquid from one place to another. See Chapter 11 on volume for sequence of drinking skills.

Toward the end of the toddler period your child will take great pleasure in "undoing things"—packages, candy bars, or bananas are all the same to him. This position in space skill which combines mental know-how with finger dexterity will make the birthday unwrapping as much fun as the present, the banana peeling as much fun as the banana. We don't advocate monthly birthdays or a steady supply of candies, but some unwrapping activities are a cookie or cracker in a paper napkin bundle to be opened at snack time, or little boxes of dry cereals or plastic baggies with apple slices inside for dessert. Make the undoing easy and use no ties or twists. Supervise any plastic near a baby because nonporous plastic can cause suffocation.

TOYS AND ACTIVITIES

There are certain favorite toys at this age, all having a great deal to do with your child's growing awareness of the space around him and his ability to change the position of himself and objects in space. He will love riding a rocking horse, tilting back and forth; knocking over tippy clowns or other toys that bounce back; knocking over block towers he just built up; and rolling a ball to you.

Toddlers are busy refining eye–hand coordination skills, and their fill and dump preoccupation satisfies this urge. Pincer grip of thumb and index finger makes dropping smaller beads and blocks in containers a triumph. The ability to transfer objects from hand to hand lets things be viewed from every angle. This new skill is often shared with adults. Your fifteen-month-old baby will love to give you a toy and then take it back again, a new game you'll tire of before he does.

Your eight-month-old is beginning to enjoy toys on strings. He can sit and pull a wheeled toy toward him as many times as you are willing to pull it away again. Pulling something on this plane allows for instant success. Retrieving a toy dangling from a string requires the additional dexterity of hand-over-hand hauling motion. Often when the toy is within reach the baby lets go of the string to grasp the toy and all is lost. With repeated tries the baby eventually develops a two-handed technique that works. Tying favorite toys on strings not only provides problem-solving opportunities for your child, it saves you from bending and picking up tossed toys. At first, use string a little shorter than his arm to make pulling back easy. If you are hanging toys from crib or playpen where your child may be playing unsupervised, for safety use easily breakable yarn in case your child becomes entangled. Sometime between age one and one-and-one-half years, your child will be able to pile carefully one block on top of another, building a tower of two to three blocks. By age two your child may be able to build a block tower of six or more cubes, each additional block requiring precise position in space skills.

At about eight to twelve months your child will reach one of his great intellectual milestones. He will begin to grasp the permanence of objects and people, and this will affect his relationship with the world. He will know that objects exist independent of his own actions on them. He no longer has to see, touch, or mouth something to know it's there. Suddenly you will find your baby trying to look in your hand for the cookie you were holding or under the newspaper for the dirty ashtray you just tried to hide. Your old techniques are becoming less effective and your baby may cry or try to locate the disappearing object himself. At first his attempts will be fleeting, a glance at you as if to say, "What's happening?" or a peek where it was last seen. With experience and maturity your child will gradually develop a longer memory and will search more effectively.

The notion of the permanence of objects and people leads to pleasure in several baby games such as Peek-A-Boo and Hide-And-Seek. Peek-A-Boo confirms your child's understanding that the same people come and go. He can giggle at you behind your hands or the door because he is an "old pro" and knows you are there ready to pop out. Once your toddler has some understanding of "object permanence" he will begin hiding things throughout the house. His memory is still fleeting so the "finding" will often be accidental. It is standard procedure to find a block behind a sofa pillow or a cookie under the dining room table when visiting a house where a toddler lives, no matter what the housekeeping standard. Because of his short memory he is a better hider than finder. Your toddler's discovery of a hidden treasure will be reminiscent of Rover finding a buried bone, but unlike Rover your child will probably want to share his find with you. At twelve months a child's use of a pointing index finger makes poking into cup or container possible. Tiny objects can be retrieved from cups with this new finger dexterity. The toddler's focus on filling and emptying containers seems to give him the needed experience in "now you see it, now you don't." For hiding and finding and filling and spilling activities your toddler will enjoy some of these:

- A plastic laundry basket and an assortment of toddler-safe unbreakables; the more there are the worse the mess, but the longer the fun
- Shoe boxes to hold collectibles. At about age twenty-one months your child will be able to position the lid on and off, another challenge.
- Scarfs, tea towels, or a diaper to play hide teddy, find teddy—a toy variation of the Peek-A-Boo theme
- Plastic pitchers or bottles to put small things in and to shake out of

When your child tires of putting in and dumping out, play the old carnival shell game by inverting the containers. "Where is it?" "Which is it under?" This is howlingly funny to toddlers even when they've seen you put an object under the container; they are so close to forgetting what they can't see. Try putting a favorite animal or car under the bed or bed covers to be found; on a shelf just high enough to reach; in a cabinet—the fun is opening the door; behind another animal; or upside down at the bottom of a box. All these changes from the usual will stimulate your child; he'll imitate and make some changes himself. If you have a color cone with rings that stack on the center post, your toddler will practice the on-and-off positioning again and again. If you don't have one, your child will enjoy putting your bracelets on and off your arm or the bedpost and your necklace over your head. Sit on the floor and practice your meditation while serving as a spindle. Your toddler will also enjoy positioning your body in space. He'll love tugging and pushing you to stand up, sit down, or lie down, a heady power (sometimes) to have you where he wants you. He will occasionally use your hand as a tool, pushing your arm to reach things he can't reach himself.

Both crawlers and toddlers like wheel toys to roll back and forth, push ahead of them, or pull behind them. Cars, trucks, wagons, and kiddy cars are all tried for quick back-and-forth rollings. Toddlers have no destinations in mind, the to-and-fro movement is enough. Beginning toddlers enjoy push toys on a stick. The movement keeps them walking and the stick often steadies their rolling gait. Confident walkers enjoy noisy pull toys that follow behind, each duck's quack, quack echoing "Look what I can do."

INDOORS AND OUTDOORS

The ability to self-propel enlarges a baby's play space. Your whole house becomes an area to explore for the crawler/toddler. Off-limit areas are difficult to enforce. Doorknob rotating is a two-and-one-half-year-old's skill, so with a toddler a closed door will still mean privacy. The crawler/toddler has two interests: exploring and keeping you in sight, and these tendencies are often at odds with each other. A baby "on the move" keeps checking over his shoulder to make sure his mainstay is still there or returns from explorations periodically to check on your whereabouts. Your baby seems to belong to the school of thought that he can wander from you, but you can't do the same. Crawler/toddler babies, despite their urges toward independence, seem to shadow your every move. They like to play near your feet while you are doing the dishes and read next to you on the sofa while you scan the morning paper. This constant "togetherness" can drive parents wild. The last straw is often a wailing baby on the outside of your bathroom door. As maddening as his constant connection with you is, it's a very important phase. If he feels sure of having you when he needs you he will have the courage to become more and more independent in later months. To help your baby who is torn between dependence and independence, create some mini-play stations throughout your house, a basket of his

books near your favorite reading chair, a plastic dishpan of toys in your laundry area, a low drawer in the kitchen for his kitchen toys. Encourage his independent play no matter how brief it is and stay within his eye range when he is off exploring. This takes care of his ambivalent feelings about your permanence and your feelings about his safety. The mobile baby poses certain risks, but you can minimize these by surveying your house with an eye to your baby's skills and interests. Your crawler will probably be at the peak of his explorations. This, coupled with his new mobility and low-to-the-ground position in space, will bring him face to face with dangers such as wall outlets. Don't assume that you will always be at his heels to avoid his pokings into electrical sockets. Cover them with child-proof caps.

Your baby will not be content to move on the horizontal plane only; he will also explore the things above and below him. Climbing into chairs and onto sofas, and out of strollers and cribs will keep you on the alert at all times. You cannot curb this motor drive, which is an important step toward self-sufficiency and self-confidence. Be aware of your baby's physical skills and of the physical feats he will be attempting. You can also stay near your practicing baby until he can climb into the armchair with ease. Positioning oneself in space requires practice, whether the child is a fifteen-month-old climbing into a stroller or a fifteen-year-old negotiating a difficult skateboard maneuver. Accidents will happen, but your presence and support while he is practicing will reduce the probabilities. Restricting your crawler/toddler will just postpone the inevitable, and your two- or three-year-old will have to go through the same positioning practice. Let him try to crawl up the stairs. Don't do it for him, for he needs the confidence of knowing he's competent to get about. If all this physical fitness business leaves you cold, consider the fact that changing one's position in space requires considerable problem-solving ability.

Your baby's fancy for climbing probably reaches its zenith in his fondness for stairs. Stairs entice a crawler/toddler; the power of looking back and down at what's below, the struggle to get up even crawling one step at a time. The effort is worth it in the change of scene. Your baby will be able to go up stairs before he is able to come down with the same ease. His creeping on stairs will gradually become walking although he will need your assistance or a stair railing to hold onto until he is three. Your baby will be two-and-one-half before he will be able to climb up stairs with alternating feet and four before he can go downstairs alternating his feet. So the stairs are a great plaything for years. If you don't have stairs in your house find some for practice.

Your wandering toddler will be interested in the objects he encounters along his way. He will experiment with what opens, what sinks, what falls over when pushed. It will take your baby a few repetitions to realize the reasonable array of positions each object can assume. Your crawler/toddler will be interested in the following:

- Pillows—to crawl over, hide under, perch upon, fall into
- The radio and television—channel changer and the on/off button
- Emptying ashtrays, mail baskets, your purse. They are all fair game unless positioned beyond his reach.
- The toilet bowl—dropping objects in, dabbling in the water. His interest in this wonder will force the whole family to put the lid down.

Your crawler/toddler needs bigger spaces to explore too. The backyard or park offers a whole new set of challenges for climbing, stooping, squatting, jumping, and rolling. Ramps and slopes are fascinating; those hills that invite a toddler to get just so far before he begins to stagger backward, unable to manage enough control to get the next foot forward. If you can find a slanting walkway in a park or auditorium you can read a whole chapter of a book while your child runs up and down feeling the change of position in space in his muscles.

LANGUAGE

What does all this doing have to do with talking? All these directions must be experienced with the child's body and with moving objects in space before the position in space words can have any meaning. It's easy to see the purpose in words when your toddler first says "up, up" and gestures with outstretched arms. These first directional words "up, up" have a concrete and specific meaning. The toddler has as yet no concept of the word "up" with its many connotations. With many experiences and with you nearby to label the actions, your toddler will begin to understand position in space concepts and their words. The process is gradual and will take all your child's preschool years.

Two- and Three-Year-Olds: Your Child Finds Words for the World

The two-year-old appears in better control of his body than the toddler; the three-year-old is a symphony in motion compared to the first creeping and staggering steps of an under-two-year-old. At ages two and three your child is beginning to "get it all together," practicing over and over and gaining a sense of his own abilities.

Your two-year-old is a stickler for ritual, and his philosophy of "everything in the right place" will either improve your housekeeping standards or drive you up the wall. He's learned the order of things in his world and will insist on consistency: slippers must be put under the bed, toy rabbit placed on top of the blanket, not under. This rigidity about the order of things is a sign of the emerging thinker. Your child at three will be less compulsive about the position of things in space and more interested in other people.

BODY

As locomotive skills increase, your two- or three-year-old will be able to think while moving. He will be able to move through a toy-strewn playroom, his mind controlling his body, stepping "over" or squeezing "between." Two- and three-year-olds are also competent enough to play tricks with their bodies. They can tiptoe, walk backward a few steps, or look through their own legs at the world upside down. All of these changes in perspective are just plain fun. Bend over and look at your child upside down and watch his expression. Although two- and three-year-olds can manage getting about with relative ease, they have no idea of their body's space needs. They misjudge and get stuck in tight places. Being only a year or two out of infancy when they had no idea that they existed as separate people, they now have some sense of themselves, as individuals but not a firm grasp on the space their body takes up. Experienced nursery school teachers are aware of this and often use mats for individual resting areas and rug squares or taped spots for group activities. Without these guidelines story time would end up like rush hour on a subway. Having become competent at getting about, a three-year-old can observe and imitate other people's positions in space. If imitation is flattery you'll be flattered when your three-year-old practices your posture, facial expressions, and some of your activities. Imitate his movements and see what happens. Older children are an endless source of interest, and this can have odd results. One of our preschoolers mimicked an older brother just recovering from a broken leg and added a limp to his walk too. Your three-year-old may get himself way beyond his own abilities imitating the next-door five-year-old's jungle gym expertise. You may have to bring him down and remind him that three rungs are great for three-year-olds and that he can climb to the top when he's five.

Your two- or three-year-old can wash his own hands after playing outside or before dinner. He is an avid water-play advocate and is also obsessed with "doing it himself." Hand washing fits the bill perfectly for the tactile pleasure of soap and water, the need to feel "big," as well as the mastery of a position in space challenge. Washing hands involves mind and muscle in considering in and out, on and off, over and under, inside and out, and back and front. His efforts won't pass surgical inspection, but that's not what matters. Management of other body parts is not as easily mastered. Your two- or three-year-old may try to blow his nose in imitation, but the "ins and outs" of sniffing and blowing confuse him. Skills vary in a number of other body-care tasks. Mouth-and bottom-wiping skills may also lack finesse.

You may notice a hand preference in your two- or three-year-old. By this age some children are clearly right- or left-handed in all things. However, mixed hand dominance is still quite common in children this age and is no cause for concern.

CLOTHING

Dressing oneself at age two or three is one great three-dimensional puzzle. Undressing is the thing children do best, but dressing skills are slowly improving. Two-year-olds can put on shoes and hats and sometimes pants. Three-year-olds can manage putting socks on and occasionally shirts or dresses. Fronts and backs of clothing may still be a mystery to three-year-olds. Mittens are possible, but fingers in gloves are so complicated you have to physically manipulate your child's fingers one by one from the outside. In nursery school three-year-olds may learn the "magic way" of putting on a jacket or coat by placing the garment on the floor, label near their toes, thrusting both arms in, winging the coat over the head—and presto, it's on. This complicated method leads to independence. Some clever individual invented this system knowing that the position in space skills of children and adults differ. Our adult method of putting on a coat requires us to manage the space behind us and that's just too hard for two- and three-year-olds.

FOOD

Feeding oneself is not managed in a day. Be gradual about reducing the thickness of custards and puddings to be managed, or introducing a fork after the spoon is a usual tool. Let your child graduate to glass and china plates after he has mastered holding a cup and eating from plastic plates. Watch your child and you'll realize how much practice it takes before he can handle the whole routine with ease. He must sit up at the table, select the right tool, use it properly, keep the food in the plate and the plate on the table, and keep the food in his mouth while chewing. He must select the right amount (not too much) and get into the rhythm of feeding and eating. Remember your first lobster or artichoke —a strange eating experience—and how you had to watch other people, imitate, and practice before you felt any grace eating these foods. Your two- or three-year-old is like that, not quite skilled enough for his grandmother's dinner table unless she's tolerant and remembers ages and stages.

TOYS AND ACTIVITIES

Nesting toys, puzzles, blocks, dolls and stuffed animals, drawing equipment, wagons, books, bean bags, beads, water, and sand are all favorite toys at this age. All have to do with the management of space: making things happen by controlling their movements, getting together what belongs together, and pulling apart what will come apart. Sometimes a "terrible two" pulls apart what belongs together too!

In doing puzzles some children have a greater sense of shape, size, and space than others. One child will pound puzzle pieces to fit them in spaces and another will be able to rotate a piece in his mind before picking it up and know just where it will fit. Building blocks teach the "up and down," "beside," "between," "over and under," and "top and bottom" of objects. The "doing" is the important thing. Your child is experiencing the position in space concepts by moving objects about in space just as he began to comprehend "in and out," "over and under" by managing his body in space.

Your two- or three-year-old is just beginning to pretend. His doll baby or teddy bear will be carted about and positioned a hundred different ways. Physically this is a giant step, because it was not so long ago that walking took all your toddler's concentration, and now your child is beginning to imitate what he has experienced. Teddy will be wrapped in a blanket and tucked in bed. The positioning of bear to blanket is difficult for a two-year-old. Although a three-year-old can handle bear wrapping, the complication of dressing a doll in baby clothes will have to wait a year or so.

Two- and three-year-olds love to put crayon, pencil, or brush to paper and see a line develop as the result of their efforts. A two-year-old is only mildly surprised when he draws with the wooden end, not the graphite tip of a pencil, and ends up with no results. He'll ponder a moment and try again with the other end. Even coordinating two hands so the paper stays still while the pencil writes on it is an achievement at this age. Drawing on large paper bags, cardboard boxes, or newspapers is satisfying, as the paper is less apt to wander away.

Wagons and trikes, favorite toys for two- or three-year-olds, are maneuvered up and down, over and under, forward and backward. Admire your child's persistence and perseverance as he learns to push and pull or to coordinate feet in trike pumping. Every new slope or curb is a challenge in spatial mastery as well as in the management of both self and object, so both don't end "upside down" in the gutter! Comment to your child on his new skills. Pushing a wagon backward takes a whole new set of directional arrangements. Remember how confused you were backing a car for the first time. The motor "doing" will continue even if you never say a word, but giving him the words as he performs the actions will give him the concepts he will need eventually in school.

Aside from the interest in seeing pictures in books, your child will like to practice turning pages. At eighteen months books were "read" upside down and pages were turned in clumps. Now your child knows "right side up" and can manage thinner, paper pages.

Bean bags are good toys for two- and three-year-olds because they are tossable but stay put. Balls are fun to roll to someone, but their bounce makes them unpredictable. For dropping and eventually throwing, your two- or three-year-old will enjoy bean bags and a container to throw them into, the bigger and closer the better for beginners. Cardboard boxes and laundry baskets are good choices. For quiet games during baby sister's nap, bean bags can be dropped in front of or in back of the easy chair, or tossed onto the bed or sofa.

Stringing beads and pounding pegs or roofing nails require eye–hand coordination, and the process produces results that say to the child, "Look what I can do." At first the manipulation of "in and out," "through," and "next to" of stringing beads is awesome. Each bead is a major obstacle and the end result may be a row of three. As skills increase so does the pleasure, and your three-year-old may string a whole set, undo them, and begin again, feeling good about himself and his abilities. Pounding pegs and nails is much the same. Changing the position in space of one peg or roofing nail from up to down gives a two- or three-year-old a sense of victory. For your young child the process is the significant feature. Years later the pounding bench will be ignored and your child will want his hammering to make something.

Water and sand, classic preschool toys, are perfect for two- and three-year-olds to experience position in space. The formless state of both water and sand makes them choice materials for hauling, dumping, and arranging. A trip to the beach or backyard sandbox will be an attraction with containers of sand to haul "here and there," fill from "bottom to top," and spoon "into and out of." Water play in the kitchen sink with a collection of safe containers will happily amuse your child while he explores the "ins and outs" and "ups and downs" of position in space. For a position in space surprise, give him a sieve or funnel. The first time he fills this new container he will be shocked to see the water or sand pour out the other end.

INDOORS AND OUTDOORS

Eight- and nine-year-olds love to "sleep over." The teens are the slumber-party years, but two- and three-year-olds like to "sleep around." They seem to get bored with their own beds or cribs and enjoy changes of scene. One mother of a large family we know never knew who would be in whose bed but felt assured when all the beds were full. If you can, feel loose about this temporary aberration—we guarantee it will be brief, giving way to the pride of possession in one's own room and bed. Let your child sleep under his crib for nap time or move his bed beside a bureau where he can reach the toys on top. Young children consider furniture part of their conquest of space. Try to respect your child's exercise in problem solving, though it'll be an annoyance to your housekeeping. If you are inspired to do a spring cleaning, let your two- or three-year-old get a feel of the new space arrangements by moving over, under, around, and through a furniture obstacle course. If you've no enthusiasm for spring cleaning, find a furniture showroom and pretend to consider a new sofa!

The mastery of space is most obvious outdoors in the growing capability of two- and three-year-olds. You'll see your child succeed in climbing up ladders and sliding down slides, crawling through culverts and swinging high, first from your pushing, then from his pumping. Jumping off small steps or ledges is fun for two- or three-year-olds. Notice their exaggerated crouches and tottering two-footed landings. Some position in space games that are fun:

- Jumping over small obstacles (the size of a Jello box)
- Jumping off a single step
- Walking along a board six or more inches wide, elevated four inches off the ground by a block or brick. Your two- or three-year-old will consider this a mighty challenge, and as you watch him walk with the caution of a tightrope walker on the high wire you will realize that indeed it is. Hold out a hand at first to help him balance and gain confidence.
- Rolling down hills and trying to roll up
- Following directions like the army sergeant's "Hup, two, three, four, column left," but making it a simpler "up" and "down" for a two-year-old, "into" and "out of" for a three-year-old
- Jumping and flopping on an old mattress
- Splashing in bath or pool, noticing how the toys sink and float. Join the parent–child swim class at the "Y" and sink and float together.

Children have different abilities and approaches to large-muscle activities. Some cautious children need time to warm up to new challenges. Other more impetuous tots embrace new tasks with abandon and need reminders to "take care." Some two- and three-year-olds are agile and lithe as gymnasts while others plod along, seeming to trip over their own feet. Each child needs different challenges and needs to feel good about his achievements. Success to the gymnast may mean a quick scamper to the top of the jungle gym, while success to the less coordinated child may mean being able to jump over a little puddle. Be aware of your responses to his successes. You may be an all-star athlete or a Sunday spectator, but your child is his own special person with his particular talents. At one time or another a change in position in space may frighten any child. Descending open stairs without risers, swinging too high, or seesawing may terrify a two-year-old. Fear of heights may panic a three-year-old atop a slide or a jungle gym. Respect your child's fears as well as his abilities. Don't tell him there is "nothing to be afraid of." He is afraid. Recall your shaky knees on the high dive when you haven't tried it for years or your first ski lesson as an adult when the instructor tells you the big downhill slope is a snap. It's all a matter of perspective.

LANGUAGE

Your two- or three-year-old can be a ready valet or houseboy if requested. He loves feeling needed and capable, and although his speech is limited, his understanding is not. He will be able to find your pipe "on top of" the hall table or let the dog "out." He can get the newspaper at the "front" door and carry it "into" the kitchen. Your three-year-old will ask "Where?" and be able to understand your answer. Your child is getting a sense of location even though his own use of words is slow. Just as in the beginning use of color or size words, your child uses position in space words inappropriately, aware that they are words for locations of things yet applying them incorrectly.

Children have some amusing language quirks along the way. They often learn half of a pair of opposite words and apply the meaning of both words to that one word. One of us taught a class in which children were throwing bean bags into a large basket. As one child increased his challenge walking backward farther and farther from the basket, he muttered, "I'm getting near." Near meant both "near" and "far" to him; one word served temporarily for both directions.

Your talking will help your child pair the proper words and ideas. Your words for his actions will help him have a precise vocabulary, applying the right word to the right action. At this stage, even though your child is beginning to conceptualize "over and under," "here and there," he will only apply them one by one to simple concrete situations. He responds best to specific instructions such as "Park your truck under the bed," or "Put your blocks in this box," rather than, "Let's clean 'up' your room." With his slight grip on the language of position in space, your child responds best to body language in moments of ambivalence. "Come here" seems to dare a two-year-old to run away and "come down" from the jungle gym spurs a tired three-year-old to climb higher. A young child can't be reached by words alone, so pick him up, position him on your hip, and jog in to lunch.

Four- and Five-Year-Olds: Your Child Begins to Order His World

Four- and five-year-old bodies are "position in space words in action," running up slides, tumbling, turning, and leaping. As their motor skills grow by leaps and bounds, four- and five-year-olds set out to master space with their bodies, creating challenges as they go along. In less active moments they conquer space by building with blocks, boxes, or

furniture. You can sit back and watch, able to stay at a distance enjoying the agility, strength, and creativity of your child. From time to time your child will want you as an audience to applaud his latest motor feat or manual creation, but mostly he'll want to share his explorations with children near his own age. You'll monitor safety, as the derring-do of a four-year-old or the competitiveness of a five-year-old can lead to efforts beyond his capabilities, but you will be able to pursue your own activities most of the time with eye or ear attuned to his pursuits. Children measure their competence at this age not by what they know but by what they can do—hopping, skipping, swing pumping, or shoe tying.

BODY

Because having friends and bragging are both features to four-year-olds, your child will test his body limb by limb and position by position to see if he can do things the "best" or the "most." Five-year-olds, having tested themselves at four, may use their skills in group projects or more conservative achievements. Four- and five-year-olds will enjoy trying spatial activities:

- Walking up and down stairs without holding on
- Hopping on one foot and skipping
- Attempting head stands and cartwheels
- Turning somersaults
- Whirling and twirling
- Hanging upside down
- Jumping forward and backward
- Swing pumping

Because of his new-found body skills your child will enjoy the classic body control games "Mother May I?" (described in Chapter 3), hopscotch, freeze tag, beginning jump rope, follow the leader, obstacle courses (of his own or your devising), "Simon Says," Hide And Seek, Blind Man's Bluff, and King of the Mountain. The games will run in fads, two or three weeks of one game, then another.

New body skills are not only used for motor stunts and showing off, they are practiced in practical ways. Four- and five-year-olds can brush their teeth and comb their hair. They will listen solemnly to the dentist's admonition to brush up and down, in and out, and be able to remember and follow the instructions.

If your child is in kindergarten at five he may be expected to know his left hand from his right. This is not an easy job. Even at six years your child may write in the air with a pretend pencil to make sure which is his writing hand before he dares label it "left" or "right." The teacher will require that many tasks (drawing, cutting, pasting) be done from left to right in order to establish the left to right progression for reading. You can help your child by occasionally labeling his left and right hands and feet for him as he does familiar activities. By age four or five the vast majority of children have firmly established left or right hand and foot dominance for writing, eating, and kicking. If your child is left-handed you'll want to get him left-handed scissors and see that his drawing and eating space accommodate his pen and utensil style.

Four- and five-year-olds' grip on direction is such that they can barely remember their own left and right, let alone execute tasks such as setting a table with glass on the right, fork on the left. Piaget set up clever experiments with scenes and dolls, and asked children to show what the person or doll sitting across from them saw, a view which would reverse left and right placement. Not until age seven could children take a perspective other than their own. No matter how narrow your table, your child will have to go around setting each place from his own position standing in front of the mat. In a practical way this hardly seems a serious handicap—one could always circle the table—but this same ability to abstract the perspective of another person applies to seeing things the way the other person does, standing in another's shoes and looking at that person's view. Table setting and empathy will progress with maturity.

There has been a recent increase in movement and dance programs as well as interest in gymnastics and the martial arts. All these activities focus on the handling of one's body in space. There is recognition of the connection between a sense of competence and a sense of being able to manage one's body well. Four- and five-year-olds are doing just that day in and day out as they learn to make their bodies do the bidding of their minds, as they test the limits of their own capabilities, as they relate their bodies to other things and other people. Four- and five-year-olds have a terrible time standing in an orderly line. They don't yet have an awareness of the space behind them and often infringe on space rightfully the next child's. Children differ in their ability to manage their bodies and in perceiving how much space their bodies need. Even for a child with spatial skills the child at the head of the line holding the doorknob is in the only fixed position. Children eventually learn both their own spatial needs and the positions they must take to allow for the needs of other people. Adults who have acquired this sense can walk across a crowded lobby and into an elevator holding themselves apart from other people and predict the space the next arrival may need. A class of four- and five-year-olds will bump and jostle before they acquire this cognitive skill.

Because they can only view themselves and the space they utilize by looking in front of them, children are fascinated by the three-way mirrors in clothing stores. You may be able to select a new wardrobe while your child views the back of himself, which he has never had a look at. Children's frontal perspective is confirmed by the fact that children almost never draw a person in profile until they are seven or eight years old. If they attempt a profile it has two eyes on one side à la Picasso. The perception of the whole self from all sides and angles and that representation in thought or drawing is a gradual development. The baby rotates and studies a toy to get a picture of its whole. In a sense a four- or five-year-old is getting the same picture of his own body by his activities in space.

Four-year-olds are intensely curious about what goes on inside their own bodies. They like to feel bones and joints, test each others' muscles, and look at pictures of inner organs. Outside of other people's bodies are studied and insides of their own bodies reflected upon. Inside products that come out are of special fascination. A four-year-old's discussions of nose drippings, vomit, blood, and bathroom products would turn the stomach of a surgeon. He is ready to understand some sex education and delights to think of himself riding about inside his mother before he was born. A five-year-old emerges from this lusty phase more self-conscious and even modest.

CLOTHES

If they have been encouraged to practice, four- and five-year-olds are old hands at basic dressing and undressing skills. They can quickly put on or pull off a pair of pants or put arms and head through shirt and sweater openings. A four- or five-year-old will be capable of learning to manage these tasks:

- Starting the zipper of his own jacket by inserting the zipper foot in the catch
- Buttoning. The finger dexterity and spatial mastery of buttoning take practice. Big sweater buttons are easier than little shirt buttons. Many a row is finished before your child realizes that there's a buttonhole left over and he must begin again to match hole and button from top to bottom.
- Snapping snaps and hooking hooks
- Buckling. Pull-down elastic pants will be out and the high style of big belts and buckles will make the space mastery of belt loops, buckles, and belts worth the effort.
- Putting on gloves
- Lacing and tying shoes

Teaching your child to lace and tie his shoes is a preview to teaching him to drive. There are driver's education classes but no schools for shoe tying. This ancient art is handed down from generation to generation. Trying to describe the intricacies of shoe lace entwining in words

as your child follows through on the actions will give you some idea of the number of space words your child understands.

Hangers and hooks will no longer totally baffle your child and he may be able to get the right portions of clothes onto the right parts of hooks and hangers. Motivation will be high when he first learns, and if hooks and hangers are low you may have permanent household help.

FOOD

Because they can handle most table food with ease, the ritual of four- and five-year-olds' eating now includes experiments with the "method of attack":

- Licking the filling between peanut butter crackers and sandwich cookies after carefully prying them open
- Eating the icing off the top of a cupcake
- Eating foods one by one off the plate and insisting the meat not touch the potatoes
- Peeling hard-boiled eggs, sometimes getting so carried away they peel right into the yolk
- Carefully working their way through layered cakes and parfaits
- Asking for an egg "over easy" or "sunny side up," and attacking it with precision
- Loving club sandwiches, an adventure in positions in space
- Asking for "pineapple upside down cake." The idea and name are as interesting to them as the taste.

TOYS AND ACTIVITIES

The growing independence and sociability of four- and five-year-olds mean more independence for you. You will be supervising near enough to prevent bloodshed but not close enough to get into the arguments. Alone or with friends your child will be inventive if you provide him with a collection of materials: lengths of rope, wood, blocks, pencils, crayons, dough, paper, and scissors, as well as recycled treasures such as egg cartons or Styrofoam. Your child's increased span of concentration may mean hours at his own amusements. A few new recycled items and a suggestion are all most children need to launch into projects. Make sure you have the following available:

- Blocks, small or large, from milk cartons to cardboard boxes. Big blocks mean houses and forts, little blocks the manipulation in miniature of the spaces your child has seen full size.
- Balls of all sizes. Learning to roll, throw, catch, and bounce are goals for four- and five-year-olds. Increased coordination means a child could make a game of throwing a ball into a big trash basket or rolling a ball to topple a milk carton "bowling pin."
- Rope to jump over or to use to tie things. A rope and pulley over a tree branch will occupy your child for hours. Your child will haul the same bucketful, dump it, fill it, and hoist it up again for the sheer pleasure of controlling the ascent and descent of the bucket.
- Pasting materials. Watching children learn to paste gives you an idea of their puzzlement over location. Most beginners put the paste on top of the picture to be pasted and stare in surprise when it doesn't end up sticking.
- Drawing material. By drawing pictures your child will learn about the relationship of one thing to another: the trees to the earth, the roof to the

house. As your child nears five years his drawing will become more realistic, copies of what he sees: the sun in the sky, flowers in the grass.

- Cutting supplies. This complex spatial skill takes several years to master. A sequence of skills is in Chapter 4 on shape.
- Writing materials. Pencil in hand, most four- or five-year-olds scratch out marks they call letters. Sometimes their efforts are copies of actual letters. At this age most children reverse or rotate some of their letters. Knowing the shape of a letter comes first and mastering its position follows. The position of d, b, p, or q defines the letter; the shapes are identical. Even in first grade some reversed letters are normal, and children need lines to help position the letters. On unlined paper words wander up and down and off the page. Even after your child has managed to get individual letters in proper direction and position he'll have to manage the spaces between letters and words in years to come.
- Sewing supplies. Give your child big needles and heavy thread to push through stiff cloth and don't expect any sewing accomplishments—just fun.

If your child is not a handicraft or "sit in one place" type some more active play will save the day:

- Make a playhouse with sheet over the card table to play under
- Imitate movements of a rabbit, crab, monkey, snake, fish, or kangaroo, and try new ways to move through space. If you weary of the large motions, suggest the stationary life of a clam or the tiny movements of a slow beetle.
- Pantomime body action. He can start with familiar drinking and eating actions and move on to firefighter or painter. Remembering and imitating the sequence of body actions is a hard task. Let older brother guess the topic.
- Dance to records, holding and waving flags or scarves

INDOORS AND OUTDOORS

No matter what level his actual skill, think of your child as a family helper. As you give him his first of many bed-making, table-setting, and dog-feeding lessons, remember you are training his mind. When he tucks under a sheet, carries a bowl full of water without spilling it, or places a spoon next to the knife, he is exercising position in space skills and his problem-solving abilities. If you give him a chance to arrange things you may find he has a sense of design, an aesthetic sense of the pleasing relationship of things in space.

However crude his early efforts, practice will increase his skill and you will have fewer household tasks. The bane of household chores is their repetition, so try to vary your job list. The novelty and the challenge is what will keep your child interested. Taking out the trash or

putting away the canned groceries is a flattering responsibility to a four-
or five-year-old who may earn the praise of an older brother or sister
who has long since grown bored with the job. Remind yourself of the
old adage, "Variety is the spice of life" and let your child do the following:

- Design his clothes-drawer format and put away his own clean laundry
- Sweep the stairs with whisk broom or brush, a new way to see the stairs
  he's just mastered on foot
- Line up his shoes under his bed or in his closet
- Put clean towels on the bathroom racks
- Arrange the cookies on a platter or sandwiches on a plate, then pass them
  around
- Carry glasses of drinks to guests, a serious and important task

You'll realize how many spatial words your child can understand when
you can send him scurrying under the bed to find a book you dropped
or outdoors to see who's coming. And you'll realize the words he doesn't
quite comprehend when you tell him it's beside the chair and he looks in
front.

If you have a friend with bunk beds or trundle beds the novelty will
delight your four- or five-year-old. "Spending the night over" begins at
this age if you live in a neighborhood where the child who changes his
mind when it gets dark can trot right back home. If you haven't a bunk
bed the novelty of a mattress on the floor will change his view of sleep
space.

At four or five years your child will have enough experience and
sense of direction to be trusted on short errands away from home. He
will go to the neighbor a few doors down to play and find his way back
with ease. Depending on your child's temperament and your neighborhood you may trust him to do errands at a short distance. Perhaps
because of his growing sense of self and basic security about his home,
this is an age when some children "run away" on purpose. The child is
often found nearby because "I'm not allowed to cross the street!" Although a child of four or five knows the way to familiar places and
home again, he will be seven or more before he is able to represent his
route by drawing a map. Drawing a map is a higher level of conceptualization than the motor and visual memory of the route.

Swinging is a favorite pastime. Four- and five-year-olds go higher and
higher in defiance of normal positions in space. Having some firm sense
of the normal relationship of body to ground must make the change
exhilarating for them. They experiment swinging belly-down on the

swing seat facing the ground, standing up, or twisting the ropes until they whirl when released.

You don't have to buy the department store's best or trot to the nearest tot lot to satisfy your four- or five-year-old's gymnastic yearnings. If you have gotten in the scrounging habit and have a bit of a backyard, a collection of tires, planks, discarded phone company spools (as big as a picnic table), a sawed-off rung ladder, and barrels may create a playground more imaginative and varied than either the city or a department store could manage. You'll have to let your landscape standards lapse in the same way you let your housekeeping standards slide. The flexibility of the collection of discards will mean endless creative rearrangements of space. Besides using these play materials for balancing, climbing, and jumping, your child will turn this collection into stores, fire stations, hospitals, and schools. A few added props will add zest to the array: a length of worn hose to play firefighter, a blanket for a hospital, cans and boxes for the store.

Water in tubs, hoses, pitchers, and buckets is a universally appealing toy. With a big tub, all you need are a few pieces of clear plastic hose (hardware store variety), pitchers, cans, and so forth. Your child will give a day's performance as a mad chemist at work. He will pour and repour until the water runs out. Put the whole collection over a piece of lawn which needs more watering. If your child has a moderate amount of self-restraint and your yard is fairly large, let him play with a hose. You can turn the water on low and provide a nozzle to control and change the spray. You may find water play will last longer than anything else your child has ever enjoyed. He may do any of the following:

- Create a target and aim at it. Put on your bathing suit and be the target.
- Draw with water in the air, creating momentary water arcs and cascades. Fountains are of endless fascination to children; with the hose he can make and control his own.
- Fill a tub and collect an array to sink and float (bottle caps, corks, Ivory soap, sponges, jar lids, plastic bowls, walnut shells). Your child will be interested in the position of things in the water and in what sinks or floats, but it will be years before he has an understanding of why.

As you travel about town your four- or five-year-old will be fascinated by the backs of things he's used to viewing from the front—the back of stores, a restaurant, or the school. Give him time to look and think because he's putting his whole world together and getting a scheme of things piece by piece.

If your child has special position in space skills or is just plain interested, go to: a horse show to watch horse and rider jump, trot, and gallop in harmony; a high school track and field event to see pole vaulting and hurdle jumping; a diving competition at a neighborhood pool; or a gymnastic exhibition.

LANGUAGE

Your child will acquire spatial words from having you apply these words to his own positions and the positions of objects he manipulates. He will learn the words of location, direction, and distance slowly over several preschool years. Position in space words are prepositions, parts of speech which come into a child's language at about three years of age. The locational words "in," "on," and "out" seem to be the easiest for a child to grasp because they are stable and exact. You are either "in" or "out"; there is no gray area. Words like "near" and "far" or "between" imply a relationship of one or more objects or people to each other. This relationship varies, and the relativity is hard for children to conceptualize. A child just over one year might say "up," using the word like a noun meaning, "Put me in that place in your arms," but the prepositional use of "I'm going up the stairs" would be a three- or four-year-old's utterance. Body actions and interactions with objects, plus your labeling each spatial relationship, require many repetitions before your child will absorb the concepts. Your child must experience "between" in the game of piling hands, in putting the filling "between" his bread slices, and in standing in line "between" two friends. These concrete experiences are necessary before your child can handle the abstraction of such difficult concepts as the number 2 positioned "between" number 1 and number 3. The doing has given him the feeling of "between" either with his own body or with a number.

Once children have a grasp on positional words they will enjoy classifying with these words. You and your child can think of categories as you drive from home to the school or the day-care center:

- Animals and their houses above or below the ground. What about bats and opossums who sleep unside down?
- Vegetables that grow above or below ground level—apples and potatoes, peas and peanuts. What about plants of which you eat the top or the bottom—rhubarb and carrots—or the inside and not the outside—pineapples and coconuts.
- Transportation above, on, and below the ground. Did you think of car lifts, elevators, escalators, gliders, parachutes, subways, and double-decker buses?

Where would a Ferris wheel or a roller coaster fit in? Notice the above and below of bridges and cloverleaf. Think of submarines and ferries.

- Clothes that go on the front or back of you, the bottom or top of you, the middle. If your child is visually imaginative and you're both feeling silly, think of bottom things on top places—socks on ears and shoes on hair.
- Things that belong inside or outside. What if you kept sugar outdoors or used your umbrella indoors?
- Indoor workers and outdoor workers. Did your child thing of the road-building crew or house builders who create their own indoors? Who works in high places and low places? Roofers and telephone repairpersons, street crews in manholes and subways.
- Sports—which would you rather try, mountain climbing or snorkeling?

Just as you are terribly impressed with your child's advanced vocabulary you will occasionally realize how many ramifications there are to the simplest words and how much your child still has to learn. One of us waited hours in the doctor's office with our child when the nurse patiently explained, "The doctor is tied up in the operating room." Our five-year-old mused, "I wonder why he is tied up and why don't they untie him?" If you want to stretch your mind, look up any of the position words in a good dictionary and see the multiplicity of meaning they have in the English language. In five years a child acquires enough positional word meanings to follow a teacher's practical instructions most of the time, but the sophisticated or idiomatic meanings follow later.

Chapter 8

"Some Like It Hot, Some Like It Cold"
How a Child Learns About Temperature

A CHILD FIRST KNOWS TEMPERATURE when his own body feels hot or cold. Later he touches or tastes his way through the world of toasty-warm blankets or chilly ice cream. The concepts of temperature, weight, speed, and volume are only understood in the most basic way in the preschool years. The subtleties and gradations are not understood at all. Abstraction of measurement requires mathematical concepts that a child won't grasp until he's well along in grade school. The early years of a child's life are meant for experiencing. Hot won't have a meaning to your child until he has felt it; the word combined with the experience will give him a grasp of the concept. The gradations on the thermometer can wait until grade school.

As a matter of health and safety you will keep your child's temperature environment reasonably steady for the first several years. Climates differ and different body types have different temperature tolerances, but you will bundle your baby against the cold and shelter him from the sun. You will make the decisions about what he wears because he has no prior experience of the vagaries of weather. As he matures intellectually he can apply temperature concepts. With experience he will develop judgments: what clothes are appropriate to wear in what weather, how soon to come in on a cold day. Your child's judgment about what is hot and what is cold will be affected by the climate he lives in and his own temperature preferences. Warm to an Alaskan is not warm to a Floridian. A chubby cherub may float all afternoon in a pool while his skinny friend shivers. Your child may bask in the sun long after you feel faint with the heat or he may love a crisp winter's day when you are ready for the fire. Individual differences make life more interesting.

The climate of the sealed, centrally heated and air-conditioned building may be well suited to the temperature needs of small children. You are spared the whining of a hot or cold child. Yet a steady temperature is boring. In its rhythm and variation nature is more exciting. So whatever your local weather is, temperate or tropical, as your child gets older and sturdier give him the feel of what it's like to be hot and cold. The experiences of the early years will enrich his images in later years when he reads of far-off lands and climates.

Temperature words have emotional connotations evoked from experience: the warm memories of snuggling close to your parents, the cool of the breeze on a hot summer day, the pleasures of finding a sunny spot in the living room, or the cool feeling after swimming. A child who has felt the catch in his breath on a very cold day will feel the invading cold as he reads Jack London's "To Build a Fire." A child who has felt warm, muggy air around an indoor pool can imagine the moisture's decay when he reads about a tropical rain forest. Give your child memories of crisp winter air or the heat of the summer pavement, the warmth of the earth in spring or the coolness of well water.

TEMPERATURE CONCEPT WORDS

Least Difficult	*More Difficult*	*Most Difficult*
hot—cold	warm—cool	high—low
		melt—freeze

The Infant: Birth to Eight Months or Crawling Age
You Bring the World to Your Infant

BODY

Infants' "thermostats" don't have the same control that those of adults have. The smaller the infant the more subject he is to changes in outside temperature. Infants can become cranky from using their energies to keep warm or fretful from too much heat. You have to maintain as steady a heat as you can for your infant by being aware of his reaction to change. As your child puts on weight and matures, his temperature mechanism will become more regulated; but at first you make the decisions. A close snuggle on a cold day or a bare wiggle in the breeze on a hot day will give your infant some of his first happy temperature experiences.

CLOTHING

In bygone years there were rules of thumb about clothing and seasons. In temperate climates cottons came out in April, wools emerged in November. Babies were garbed in sweaters or sunsuits according to season. The handy rules of thumb have undergone a change with the advent of air conditioning and energy conservation. The new emphasis on individuality has made people realize that everyone responds to heat and cold differently, and dress has changed accordingly. One baby may sit serenely in a sweater while another would be damp-haired from the same amount of covering. Whether indoors or outdoors, change the clothes to suit your child's own body temperature. Being aware of the immaturity of your infant's temperature control will make you wary of exposing him to extremes. Keep in mind the following. New fabrics mean that a warm baby need not be buried in layers so dense that his movement is restricted; on a really cold day several light layers will be warmer than one heavier one. A sleep suit warmed on the radiator or heat vent can start a cool night off right. (Watch out for hot zippers or snaps.) Plastic pants are pressure cookers on hot days, trapping heat inside. A diaper or nothing at all will keep your baby comfortable. Air-conditioned grocery stores require baby's sweater or blanket.

FOOD

Traditionally, infant's food and drink have been warmed. Adults test milk by shaking a drop or two on the inside of the skin of their wrist. Infants, like adults, often vary in their preferences for warm and cold food. Try your infant out with some of each. Even if you think warm is his preference try an occasional cool to liven up his life and expose him to the variety of the world. A cool drink on a hot day will lower his body temperature just as it does yours. A fruit-juice Popsicle may hit the spot on a hot day. Save the Popsicle or ice cream for some evening when you have the time to study his expression. That first lick of a cold substance will bring a puzzled then pleased expression. The look is worth recording!

BATH

Infants often react with wails to baths. The reason may be the sudden change of temperature. You take a warm baby's clothes off, he suddenly chills, then into the warm water he goes and out to chill again. The rapid changes are unpleasant. Bathe your infant in a warm room, blanket him until he reaches the bath or even lower him in a flannel blanket that's ready for the laundry. Also put his shampoo bottle in the bath to warm the shampoo before you use it. Baths or sponging can cool him on a hot day, especially if you let him dry in the air.

TOYS AND ACTIVITIES

A teething toy put in the refrigerator is a comfort to sore gums. You can cool a traditional rubber or plastic teether or give him a frozen carrot, bagel, or biscuit to gnaw on. For miserable teething days an ice cube wrapped in a dish towel (secured in place by a rubber band) will be an ideal teether. He'll learn the bliss of cool.

LANGUAGE

Hot and cold, warm and cool will be experienced in food, clothes, and changes of climate, but your infant won't understand any temperature words.

The Baby on the Move: Crawling Age to Twenty-Four Months Your Crawler/Toddler Goes to the World

Crawlers and toddlers have a new relationship with temperature. They can get themselves into trouble because of their intense curiosity, their urge to handle the objects in their world, and their lack of judgment and experience. "Hot, hot" becomes a matter of safety, a warning of danger as your child approaches lightbulbs, the stove, the fire, pots and pans, lighted cigarettes. Cold doesn't have the same safety implications except for touching metals just out of a deep freeze.

A baby's body, clothes, food, bath, and toys will all give him experiences with hot and cold. A crawler/toddler won't have any conception of when he is hot or cold. You will have to decide what your child needs to wear, how hot to heat his food, what temperature to make his bath. He might stroll into the snow in his sunsuit or happily eat hot cereal cold. He might plunge into a too hot or too cold bath and yell in protest. You are in charge of his temperature and his environment. He will experience all the variations you provide and gradually learn the conventions of what's meant to be hot and what's meant to be cold. He'll be surprised that his truck is hot if it's out in the sun in the summer. His explorations will alert you to the dangers of stove and freezer. You'll start a ten-year habit of aiming pot handles in toward the back of the stove, not out where your child can reach them. You'll put ice trays where small hands can't stick to them.

LANGUAGE

The roving crawler or toddler may learn the word "hot" quickly as you warn him of the kitchen stove. In spite of parental caution, most babies touch something hot and the experience makes the word immediately real. Many parents try to engineer a more cautious encounter by slowly guiding a child's hand toward a hot cup until he feels the warmth, then a quick finger touch as the parent says "hot." "Hot" is grasped before "cold." Hot, like "no," is a word of caution and prohibition. The experience of "hot" has given the word force. When your child says "cold" he may say it with an exaggerated cold shiver.

Two- and Three-Year-Olds: Your Child Finds Words for the World

BODY

Two- and three-year-olds are physically sturdy enough to enjoy some variety of temperature. They delight in hot baths and snuggles in the covers. They enjoy a shiver of chill when they lick ice-cream cones. Their bodies are mature enough to withstand romps in the snow or a few hours at the beach. They plunge into changes of temperature with enthusiasm.

CLOTHING

At two or three years most children don't have any judgment about what clothes are appropriate for what temperature. They simply haven't been around in the world long enough. You will learn your child's body needs and bundle or strip him according to your anticipation of his day. He'll find out from you to keep his hands in his pockets if you have forgotten mittens or it suddenly turns cold. If a cold breeze comes up he'll scurry under your coat, discovering two can be warmer than one.

FOOD

Let your child feel the food from the shelf and refrigerator—a cold fish or apple, a package of frozen food, or the tomato from the sunny window ledge. Let him test his soup with his finger or touch his glass before he sips. Feeling the chill of a refrigerated item or testing his food with his fingers will make him aware of the variety of food temperatures. The parent who encourages explorations of this sort is promoting thinking and encouraging independence and responsibility in the child.

INDOORS AND OUTDOORS

Two- and three-year-olds, like cats and dogs, will find the cozy and cool spots in your house. They curl up on a sunny spot on the rug or stretch out near the air-conditioning vent to cool.

Outdoors your child will have many temperature experiences:

- Snow: two- and three-year-olds' walking gaits are sure enough to romp and fall down, roll and slide
- Sand: your child can enjoy the beach and the water if you watch carefully. Even the backyard or park sandbox will have warm sand to run between fingers and toes.
- A cool brook: walking in a creek or stream will shock his toes
- A swimming pool: the backyard wading pool will be tepid and a big pool chilly. Different body types have very different tolerances for the chill of a pool.
- A shady tree or porch on a hot summer day
- A beach umbrella: put it up in the backyard for a cool place to read a story

LANGUAGE

Two- and three-year-olds can understand and use "hot" and "cold" as words and will heed your warnings, approaching objects with caution if you label them "hot" or "cold." The relativity of "warm" or "cool" will have less meaning.

Four- and Five-Year-Olds: Your Child Begins to Order His World

Getting to know the world means thinking about and talking about all sorts of things. Four- and five-year-olds are fascinated by the color of a cardinal, the shape of a tulip, the taste of a papaya, or the temperature of a snowball. They are interested in everything around them and soak up information like sponges. Your child will continue to sort and categorize his experiences, and temperature will be one more quality to consider.

BODY

Reflective four- and five-year-olds are not only interested in the texture, size, shape, and color of their various body parts, they also are aware and interested in their body temperature. They are beginning to recognize a range of feelings vaguely classified as hot or cold. Some children are more sensitive to temperature changes than others and will tell you they are hot after a run in the sun or cold when getting out of the bath. Other children are nearly oblivious to body temperature and seem not to notice even the rages of a fever. Various body types—the well-padded and the lean—have definite reactions to temperature. You and your child may not see eye-to-eye on what's hot and what's cold, so

within the range of common sense respect his preferences. Your child will be interested in the following:

- Feeling his warm breath on his hands or seeing it on the cold windowpane
- Touching his nose after coming in from play on a cold day
- Feeling the heat of a sunburn with his hands
- Finding his warm body spots—under arm, inside mouth, between legs, between toes. Your child will be interested in his temperature being taken, and if calm and not wiggly may graduate from rectal to temperature taking under armpit or tongue.

A change of body temperature causes various reactions. Notice with your child: goose bumps from chills; blue lips after a cold swim; sweating in the sun; shivering in a cold wind; flushed face from exertion; and the sting on fingers and toes after a romp in the snow. People have mannerisms and body postures related to temperature. Pantomime gestures and see if your four- or five-year-old can guess whether the gesture suggests a hot or cold day. Some ideas are: You can hunch shoulders, clutch crossed arms to chest, blow on fingers, curl in a ball, sprawl out and pant, rub hands together, or hop up and down.

CLOTHING

Your child's body type and individual preferences will determine his clothing and covering needs. A treat for a chunky four- or five-year-old may be sleeping in the nude on a summer night, while a slender child might love the downy feel of a sleeping bag on a chilly evening. Let your child begin to make some of his own weather-related clothing decisions. The thermometer won't help him at this stage; instead suggest he go outside to "feel" the temperature, then come back in and decide whether to wear long or short sleeves. You can make all the decisions in your child's life or allow him the opportunity to think for himself. Decision making takes practice like any other skill, and weighing the alternatives between wearing a heavy or light jacket may prepare your child for the more difficult decisions of later life.

FOOD

Children four and five years old still view objects in the world in static states. They see beginnings and ends but have little notion of the process between. They accept transformation of color (bread to toast), size (kernels to popped corn), and shape (butter melting) as magical and natural phenomena. Your four- or five-year-old needs many opportunities to observe change to help him in his understanding. Cooking experiences allow him to be an active participant in the process. Your child will enjoy making ice cream, applesauce, and Jello.

Four- and five-year-olds can tolerate some extremes of temperature in their food. Their "hot" oatmeal or cocoa is somewhere between the temperature range of an infant's tolerance and an adult's. They are responsible enough to manage hot soup and iced drinks, but you must still be temperature-wary and warn your child of the dangers of some heat-retaining foods, such as the inside of french fries, melted cheese on top of pizza, and the sugary tops of cinnamon buns.

The handling of food with a variety of temperatures will give your child firsthand experience in the stiff and firm, the oozy and running, and a clearer understanding of temperature's effect on things. Your goal is not to produce a miniature gourmet with a taste for vichyssoise, but a thinking child with an understanding and appreciation for the variety in life. Try simple activities in which you spread peanut butter on hot toast or bread, put whipped cream on chocolate milk or hot cocoa, put sugar on hot or cold cereal. These contrasts will cause your child to notice the different effects heat and cold have on substances.

BATH

Four- and five-year-olds luxuriate in the tub like Romans at the public baths. Cleanliness is not the feature; relaxation and recreation are what the bath is all about. Toy boats and bubbles are still fun, but your child is beginning to branch out and enjoy more unusual experiences. Give your child temperature surprises:

- A warm shower followed by a cold, brisk, refreshing sprinkle
- A cool bath on a hot day when you can't go swimming
- Putting some ice cubes in his hot bath. The rapid melting process will intrigue your child. It will start him thinking about temperature as he watches the ice cubes melt.

TOYS AND ACTIVITIES

Playing outside will have an effect on your child's understanding of temperature. The sun and shade, warm and cool, will change the quality of play and play materials. Snowmen or sand castles will be the results of varying conditions. Warm days may produce slower-paced activities —water sloshing and hole digging. Crisp fall days may promote trike races and leaf-piling contests. Play materials left outside will demonstrate the effects of temperature on objects. Your child will notice the following:

- The burn or freeze of a metal trike seat that has been in the sun or snow
- Gooey play dough and melted crayons from sitting in the sun
- Frosty or toasty metal slides or swing seats, depending on the season
- A layer of ice on the top of a pail of water left out in freezing temperature or a warmed pail of water left out in the hot sun

Your child will enjoy playing out of doors, experiencing the temperature whatever the season.

For summer fun try some of these:

• A mini-car wash. Line up all the trikes and kiddie cars and arm your child with buckets and sponges.

• A doll and doll clothes washing sessions. Plastic dishpans make good doll tubs and a clothesline strung from bush to bush extends the play. If you are an automatic drier user, your child will marvel at solar power.
• Mud pies. Rock raisins and stick candles add to the fun.
• Fans, hand held for do-it-yourself air conditioning
• Swings. The back-and-forth movement will create a breeze.
• Sleeping out under the stars. Your child will notice the later it is, the cooler it is.
• Water play with the hose. Your child may notice that the water coming out of the hose is first warm, then cold.

For winter fun try snowballs put in your freezer for a day without snow; an invigorating jog together to the mailbox or the end of the block;

snowmen and snowwomen creations; shoveling snow to warm up; or bringing in an icicle to watch it melt.

INDOORS AND OUTDOORS

Most four- and five-year-olds have a healthy respect for the dangers of stoves, campfires, irons, and toasters. Some children at this age are attracted to matches, so keep an eye out for loose match packs around your house that might tempt your child. To channel this interest let your child help you by blowing out candles, collecting tinder for the fireplace and twisting newspapers for kindling. A temperature treasure hunt indoors will stretch your child's thinking about cold and hot beyond the two- and three-year-old's concept of "hot, hot, don't touch." He will notice the more subtle degrees of temperature in his search. Some cold spots might be cold water spigots; bathroom fixtures: toilet, sink, tub; refrigerator or freezer; the basement floor; ceramic tiles; marble; window glass; or the nose of a dog. Some warm spots might be a stove front; the pilot light area of a gas stove; a radio or television turned on; a spot of sunlight on the floor; the motor area of a refrigerator; a drier turned on; windows in the sunlight; the dog or cat.

Your child will rejoice in the first snowfall of the winter and the first warm spring day. The changing scene delights him. Take walks together in each season to feel the temperature and understand its effects. Notice in the summer:

- Berries ripening in the sun
- A walk on the beach and in the forest—which is cooler?
- A dog panting to cool off or digging a hole to lie in
- Walks are cooler in the morning and evening than at noon—why?
- How hot your feet get after a walk on a hot day
- Flowers blooming

Notice in the fall:

- Flocks of birds flying south
- Squirrels gathering nuts for the winter
- Cooler days
- Leaves falling

Notice in the winter:

- The "smoke" as warm breath meets cold air
- The sting of cold on cheeks and nose
- Bare branches

- Furry dogs and short-haired dogs in sweaters
- Smoke from fireplace chimneys

Notice in the spring:

- Some days are cool, some are warm
- Leaves unfurling
- Buds and bulbs beginning. (In early spring bring in some forsythia or apple blossoms to force indoors.)
- Birds singing
- Nests for keeping eggs safe and warm

LANGUAGE

The words "hot and cold" and "warm and cool" will be a part of your four- and five-year-old's speaking vocabulary if he has heard you use the words to describe his experiences—a hot day and a cold drink, a warm muffin and a cool breeze. The temperature concepts words "high" and "low" and "melt" and "freeze" will not be as clearly understood. Your child will be aware that the temperature of his body or the air can be measured, but the exactness of number will leave him "cold." His grasp of measurement will be limited to understanding that on a thermometer the higher the hotter, the lower the colder. Ninety degrees Fahrenheit or 32 degrees Celsius will come in time, but in the meanwhile your child will be laying a foundation for future concepts. The concept words "melt" and "freeze" will be understood in much the same way. Dripping ice cream cones on a summer day and making Popsicles at home will provide the experiences, but the scientific explanations will have to wait.

Experiences with temperature and the ability to use words to describe these experiences make it possible for a child to think about cold things and hot things in their absence. Your four- or five-year-old will be using temperature to order his world. Encourage this intellectual classifying. With your child think about the following:

- What are some hot and cold weather clothes? (sandals, sunsuit, shorts, boots, mittens, scarf)
- What are some hot and cold weather sports? (baseball, golf, boating, sledding, skiing, skating)
- What are some sport surprises? (tennis and swimming in winter; ice skating in summer)
- What are some cold and warm weather foods? (hot chocolate, hearty soups, warm breads, salads, sherbets, gelatins)

- What are some hot and cold occupations? (lifeguard, dry cleaner, welder, baker, ski instructor, snowplow driver)
- What are some animals that live where it is hot or cold? (lions, tigers, monkeys, polar bears, seals, and walruses) Your child is getting his first of many geography lessons. He doesn't yet know about the arctic or the tropics but he is beginning to know that there are different climates with different kinds of animals.
- What are some plants that like warm sun or cool shade? (roses, tomatoes, sunflowers, ferns, and mosses)
- What are some foods that are stored where it is cold or at room temperature? (ice cream, frozen orange juice, meat, crackers, bananas, flour)

Chapter 9

"See Saw, Margery Daw"
How a Child Learns
About Weight

YOUNG CHILDREN can grasp only the most rudimentary notion of weight. Their first experiences consist of managing their own body weight. The two-year-old dragging a big chair to reach a forbidden shelf has a sense of what is heavy in the strain of his muscles. For him "light" is what he can lift and "heavy" is what he must drag or shove. Surprises await him when he discovers that size does not necessarily indicate weight as he first thought. He finds he can carry the large cardboard box that his arms will barely go around, but the bowling ball won't budge off the floor. After many experiences, the young child begins to understand that weight is relative: Daddy can move the garbage pail although he cannot.

There are very few concept words for weight, since the more exacting measurements of weight involve numbers and concepts beyond a young child's understanding.

WEIGHT CONCEPT WORDS

Least Difficult	*More Difficult*	*Most Difficult*
heavy	light	balance

The Infant: Birth to Eight Months or Crawling Age
You Bring the World to Your Infant

BODY

Newborn infants, like astronauts who have just returned from outer space, must adjust to their own weight. They have spent nine "weight-

[174]

less" months in the womb. Your infant's first weight experiences are all centered upon controlling his own body weight. Lifting and managing each body part is a gradual and slow process. Over several months he will learn to control his own heavy head, turn over, and sit up. He must balance the weight of his upper body for sitting. When his sitting balance is good enough to manage without his hands, his hands will be free to play with toys.

TOYS AND ACTIVITIES

Watch your infant as he readies to pick up a toy. Before he has had experience he will approach objects making inappropriate efforts for the weight. Too much pull will send a light toy flying; too little will leave a heavy one sitting. Toys for infants should be small enough for hands and light enough to lift but your infant will begin to enjoy some weight variations in his toys by picking up sponges (light); an apple (heavy); a yarn ball (light); an empty plastic bottle (light); and a water-filled plastic bottle (heavy).

LANGUAGE

The concept words won't have a meaning to an infant, but he'll have begun to make his first judgments about weight with his muscles.

The Baby on the Move: Crawling Age to Twenty-Four Months Your Crawler/Toddler Goes to the World

BODY

Your roving baby has become adept at handling his own body weight. His mobility will mean you are also mobile—maybe losing a few pounds. As you trot about you'll observe your child's progression of postural changes, a series like the charts of evolution from apes to primitive humans, from a four-limbed creep to an erect walk. The stages are these:

- Creeping, transferring weight from stomach and chest to forearms
- Crawling, hands and knees taking the weight
- Pulling up, getting his legs used to carrying weight
- Taking his first steps, holding your hand. You have to stabilize him as the sudden shifts of his body weight will throw him off balance.
- Toddling by himself. You will have to baby-proof your house, checking the

stability of lamps, bookcases, tables, flowerpots, and telephones. He'll grab at nearby objects to keep from falling over and they may not take his weight.
• Trotting capably, managing his body weight alone

As the ability to walk unaided increases, your child will pause and crouch to pick up a toy. The first crouch may be a rude ending for a surprised, seated toddler, but at this age your toddler will cheerfully rise and stagger on from a tumble which would put you in traction. The ability to lean forward and pick up rather than crouch is the next stage.

LANGUAGE

The concept words "heavy," "light," and "balance" will not be used by a crawler or toddler and probably will be barely, if at all, understood. As your child masters the weight of his own body he readies himself for the weights of the world.

Two- and Three-Year-Olds: Your Child Finds Words for the World

In the mind of a two- or three-year-old weight and size are one—the bigger something is, the more it weighs. Your child's view of weight will also include the shape of the object. Piaget conducted experiments with a clay ball to determine what effect change of shape would have on children's view of weight. He took a round ball of clay, and as the children watched he rolled the same ball in a sausage shape. Even though the children had not seen any clay taken away they always answered that the long thin sausage weighed less than the original ball it was made from. They believed their eyes: the sausage looked lighter. You can't change your child's view of the world, but understanding the way his mind works makes your life together more interesting.

BODY

Your child has progressed from a helpless infant unable to control his top-heavy body to an upright person capable of supporting and moving his own body weight. Considering his weight gain of twenty pounds or so it's a good thing you don't still have to lug your child about. His movements are becoming less awkward, more precise. Two-year-olds, like high-wire cyclists, use their arms held away from their bodies for stability. Three-year-olds can walk or run about without using arms to balance. Tiptoe balancing is a new achievement at two or three, and you will find your house quieter when it's practiced.

BATH

Your two- or three-year-old water baby will enjoy weight experiments in the tub. He won't comprehend the properties of sink and float materials nor contrast the reactions of heavy and light substances, but he will have lots of fun and build a backlog of experiences to draw upon when he is older. Let him use the bath toys in Chapter 7 (position in space) to make "weighty" discoveries.

TOYS AND ACTIVITIES

Two-year-olds still use their hands as a pair, picking up and carrying with both hands acting together. Three-year-olds are more able to use their hands separately. Both two- and three-year-olds need toys to push and lift. Your child will relish experiences in weight:

- Shoe boxes with taped lids for light building blocks
- Cardboard boxes to push and pull about with a friend or toy as the rider. Make a hole partway down one side and put a rope through to make pulling easier.
- A little suitcase, flight bag, or knapsack to carry things in
- Ping-Pong balls, a weight surprise
- Balancing on a swing
- Balancing on a square board centered on a brick. He'll tip and totter.
- Balancing on a balance beam made of a board (see Chapter 7)

INDOORS AND OUTDOORS

Two- and three-year-olds enjoy the feel of weight in objects as they tug, pull, haul, and carry things about. It makes them feel independent and strong. Carrying big things they consider heavy makes them feel grown-up and important. Give your child the opportunity to handle and lift things that are both heavy and light. Some ideas for lifting or carrying:

- A wastebasket to the trash barrel
- Leaves to the compost pile
- A log for the fire
- A grocery bag from the store. Have the checker pack a bag or two with light things (potato chips, paper towels) so your child can carry it into the house.
- A laundry bundle on the way to the washer. Remember your child can't carry and climb stairs.
- A puppy or baby. Your child will have a special feeling of responsibility if he can lift up a pet with your supervision. You'll have to place a baby for his holding and really hold on too, but he'll feel awed by the privilege.

LANGUAGE

Heavy is important! A two- or three-year-old will call attention to his strength as he picks up an object. He'll probably mispronounce and overemphasize the word "hea . . . by!" letting you know what he can do. If you are wise you will be awed by his feats, for like an ant carrying a giant crumb his strength is impressive and his self-esteem growing. His measure of success is in what his body can do for him, and you. "Light" and "balance" won't interest him much as concept words, but "heavy" will be part of his vocabulary and a measure of his success in life.

Four- and Five-Year-Olds: Your Child Begins to Order His World

Four- and five-year-olds' judgments about weight have to do with what they see or feel. With no abstract notion of ounces and pounds your child will measure weight in the pull of his muscles. The scales in the doctor's office, the grocery store, and the post office will give your child the idea that weight is recorded in numbers, but the numbers beyond ten will not be understood.

The thinking of four- or five-year-olds takes an interesting turn. They think that the bigger an object is the heavier it will be, yet many experiences will contradict that rule. Piaget's research on children's conception of weight reveals that they judge weight by what they see. Young children are unable to deal with the abstractions of weight until they are almost ten years old. At that time they can see weight and size as qualities, separate and independent of each other, and they can abstract the idea of a pound as a stable measure. They will understand how an object can be heavy and small, or large and light. Before that, your child is a good victim for the old joke "which is heavier, a pound of feathers or a pound of lead?" His answer is based on feel or sight. If he has an idea of lead as a compact heavy substance and has handled a feather his answer would be "lead." If you could bundle up a big pound package of feathers and a small one of lead, his answer would be "feathers." What he had felt or seen would carry the day; the abstraction of a pound would be meaningless faced with the evidence of his own perceptions. If he were familiar with balances and the lead and feather bundles balanced he would be confounded. The discrepancies between what children expect and what happens stimulates their thought. Your child's experience and the contradictions he encounters will set the stage for his further understanding of the world around him.

BODY

Four- and five-year-olds can handle their bodies with great efficiency. Hands no longer work only as a pair. Their independent hands can feel two different weights, one in each hand. At this age the use of his hands parallels the use of his mind. Your child can now take in and compare two things at once. In earlier years his concentration on one object made him ignore the second. One toy was abandoned when a new one attracted him. Not only can he use his hands independently, but his two-footed jumps become hops on one foot. As four- and five-year-olds try out their bodies they balance on one foot and get a sense of how far they can lean out before they topple over. Body contact, rolling, wrestling, running, and tumbling with friends give four- and five-year-olds the feel of their own and their friends' weights. Seesaws mystify but are mastered. Growing cooperation with friends opens up new vistas. Two can pick up what one cannot. The laws of physics are discovered in the pulley, the lever, even in the postural adjustments as your child learns to push or pull heavy things across the floor. All in all, as body movements become more refined so does judgment about weights.

FOOD

Four- and five-year-olds may be a bit bored with food basics and will liken some grown-up gourmet touches. Tea parties and friends for lunch call for some decorative details. The surprise of foods that float will add to your child's concept of weight. To please your budding gourmet offer some of these:

- Croutons, oyster crackers, popped corn, or carrot rings that will float on soup. What else can your child dream up?
- Whipped cream or marshmallows on cocoa
- Ice cream or sherbet floats

TOYS AND ACTIVITIES

Through his play your child will have many experiences of weight and balance:

- Pressing flowers under books
- Building with blocks. He'll make shaky and sturdy mansions and castles.
- Hammering. The up and down motion requires your child to manage the weight and balance of the hammer's head.
- Dropping water balloons
- Pushing boxes and wagons on inclines and hills
- Hauling wet and dry sand
- Throwing beach balls, Nerf balls, tennis balls, and Superballs. A bowling ball will be a weight surprise.
- Balancing in a hammock (harder than it looks)
- Pulling in a tug-of-war, the loser feeling the ultimate experience of weight
- Trying out scooters, bikes, roller skates, and ice skates. Each new vehicle or article of footgear requires a new set of body orientations. Just as the tightrope walker uses the assist of outstretched arms, your skater will use his arms to adjust his weight as he lurches. Scooters and bikes require hand and foot balance, everything tucked in close to the body.

Experiences of weightlessness (or almost so) will puzzle and delight your child:

- Walking around a big inner tube
- Jumping on a trampoline or the "Moonbounce" at a school fair
- Floating in the water. A child must be of a certain size and body weight before he can float enough to swim.
- Throwing paper and balsa airplanes, tossing of Frisbees and sailing paper plates
- Throwing a balloon up in the air and catching it
- Letting go of a helium balloon
- Catching a bubble or a milkwood fluff
- Flying kites (with your help)
- Dropping "parachutes"—a Tinker Toy or spool tied to a cloth square makes a parachute
- Feeling a pumice stone, which looks heavy but is light like a sponge

OUTDOORS

If you let your child help in the yard he will have many experiences of light and heavy:

- Catching a light flake of snow and shoveling a few heavy shovelfuls
- Catching a floating leaf and hauling a heavy load of leaves in a wheelbarrow
- Putting rocks on flying picnic napkins and paper plates
- Carrying a heavy basket to the picnic and a light one home

Or farther away from home:

- Seeing steamrollers, hoists, garbage trucks, cranes, and wrecking balls in action rolling, crushing, lifting, and crashing
- Seeing heavy airplanes, then watching them fly off
- Floating in a plastic raft, a canoe, or a rowboat, then dropping anchor
- Picking up stones and watching someone skip them along the water
- Watching lumbering elephants and darting birds

LANGUAGE

Your child will talk about the big heavy things he's lifted in as deep a voice as he can muster. Heavy impresses him. Light will interest him in reality but will rarely enter his vocabulary. Balance is a word he will understand but is a word most children never use. These words will be another set of qualifiers, other physical attributes of the objects in his world. Together you can play weight thinking games. Can you name heavy things and light things? Would you rather carry cotton balls or rocks, toothpicks or logs? Could I sit on you, could Grandpa sit on me? What are heavy jobs? He'll be asking you questions such as *"why* do airplanes fly and balloons float?" You may find your concept of weight isn't at the level Piaget says ten- to twelve-year-olds can achieve. Either hit the books or leave it to his high school physics teacher for the answers.

Chapter 10

"Jack Be Nimble, Jack Be Quick"
How a Child Learns About Speed

THE THREE-YEAR-OLD whizzing across the lawn feels he's "faster than a speeding bullet." Footraces and toy car races, rolling balls and marbles give basic experiences that set the stage for an understanding of speed. The preschooler will grasp the extremes of "fast" and "slow" in terms of his own pace. The complex understanding of speed as a product of distance and time is beyond a child's comprehension until he is in upper elementary school. Like temperature, weight, and volume, more precise measure of speed is dependent upon an understanding of numbers.

SPEED CONCEPT WORDS

Least Difficult	More Difficult	Most Difficult
fast	slow	quick

The Infant: Birth to Eight Months or Crawling Age
You Bring the World to Your Infant

Becoming a parent has the effect of putting on the brakes, at least temporarily. The birth process forces you to slow down. Whether you are a new mother or a new father the miracle of birth causes you to pause and reflect upon your new role and your new infant. This snail's pace helps you get to know each other.

All infants spend the first few months gradually becoming accustomed to the world. They need a slow pace and a quiet, peaceful welcoming, not a new environment full of bright lights, loud sounds, cold drafts, or sudden jerky movements. The way you handle your infant gives him a sense of the world. He will feel your pace. If you move him from place to place in a leisurely, gentle manner he will react positively to his new world, but if you briskly pluck him up and plop him down with an anxious-to-get-it-over-with attitude he will sense that too. Take advantage of these early months, slacken your speed, relax, and enjoy your infant as you care for him.

Watching a dance in slow motion would be the ideal entertainment for an infant. His eye tracking skills are just beginning. Be aware of your infant's visual skills as he follows you, looks at the toy you hold out for him, or watches the mobile over his crib. Adjust your speed to his. If you keep up your normal, quick adult movements, your infant will be lost in the blur of activity. As your infant's eye tracking skills increase he will pick up speed but still not at an adult's rate. When eye–hand coordination begins your infant will again need objects that slow down or stay put.

Individual infants have differing inner speeds. Though all infants are slower than adults, some infants seem to function in high gear and some in low. Some infants nurse in five minutes and some need forty-five. Some babies have trouble slowing down for sleep and others have trouble getting revved-up for action. Recognizing your infant's inner speed will help you understand some of his reactions to the world.

LANGUAGE

Your infant enjoys the sound of your voice, but even more he enjoys your response to his voice. Slow down and give him time to coo back. Adapt to his speeds and let him set the pace.

The Baby on the Move: Crawling Age to Twenty-Four Months
Your Crawler/Toddler Goes to the World

The pace picks up! When your child is in motion your own gait quickens, you have more to oversee and more to tidy up. In the development of independence crawlers and toddlers have an interesting relationship with the person who cares for them. Independence is achieved by bouncing off the adult they depend on. It is as if parent and child were connected by a giant rubber band. When the parent moves from room to room the child follows, keeping the parent in sight. When the child moves the parent follows, seeing to the child's safety.

The parent who is used to running from room to room rapidly getting tasks done will leave a wailing child behind; the child can't move that fast and needs to keep the connection. Many parents find they need to scoop their child up and move him to a new location rather than slow their own rate. Other more sedentary parents or those who read or write at home may find their pace too slow for their explorer. The sedentary parent may have to move from room to room so his crawler or toddler has new objects or else his child will explore an unwilling parent.

BODY

The several different body types seem to have different speeds. The light, wiry child may climb to the top of the stairs in a flash, while a plump, relaxed child may hesitate on the first step. The match of temperaments has to do with a recognition of what speed parent and child find best. If both move at the same speed there is no problem. If both are in motion at different paces the unsettling effect can result in a child who is anxious and insecure from being left behind or one who is restless and bored. Most parents have to slow their walking pace to accommodate the speed of a crawler or toddler. Slowing down allows time to watch your child's encounters with the world. The slowed pace doesn't last long and the child who feels that his speed is respected is free to begin to move out more and more on his own. He knows that when he needs to come back, his moorings will be there. By the time your child is four or five you can relax while he wears himself out in the neighbor's yard, if you've matched your pace to his for his first few years.

You will have become familiar with your own pace in relation to his. No one can spend an hour in a grocery store or park without seeing children dragged along by parents. The child's undragged arm waggles fruitlessly in the direction of what interested him, now receding into the distance. If you have time and your pace is slow take him along. If you have an hour to buy birthday presents for his three siblings leave him with a sitter. Respect for each other's paces is respect for each other.

LANGUAGE

Your crawler or toddler won't have any notion of the words "fast" and "slow" but he'll feel the motion in his bones. Fast will be a backpacked jog with you in the park or a ride on the back of your bike with the wind ruffling his hair. Slow will be any time he has to wait!

Two- and Three-Year-Olds: Your Child Finds Words for the World

Two- and three-year-olds are established as body types and personalities. You have a firm idea of how long it will take your child to get from one place to another and how fast you'll have to move if he goes where you think he's heading. You can even predict what might interest him and slow him up on the way.

Two-year-olds love rituals; in eating or hand washing they can be incredibly slow. You can feed them and wash their hands, taking away an area of competence, or you can use the time when they're engrossed to do something of your own.

CLOTHING

Two-year-olds can't dress themselves, but three-year-olds are earnest and precise (after their fashion) and can take ages getting dressed. You can stuff your child into his clothes day in and day out, but if he doesn't practice he won't pick up any speed in the process. If you find you're always saying "faster, quick, hurry" like a bettor at a greyhound track, it's time to reassess. Perhaps on day-care days it's your turn and on weekends it's his.

BATH

You may view the bath as a time to get your child clean; he will view it as playtime. He has the attitude of a visitor at a hot spring spa: warm water rests the body and soul. Fast has no place in the bath routine. Give him all the time he needs by assigning the most slowed-down adult in the house to the bath detail or plan your most slowed-down activity for that routine. Perhaps the mending would qualify, but the daily paper has more appeal.

TOYS AND ACTIVITIES

Toys that lead to speed are great favorites for two- and three-year-olds. Kiddie cars and trikes are pushed faster and faster for the joy of controlling the speed. Some children are naturally reckless and set off downhill on tricycle or sled uncaring about the results. Others are anxious when the motion gets out of control. The texture of the land to be traversed can frustrate the speeder; the drag resistance of the bumpy road or the grassy slope makes for huffing, puffing, and pushing. Bare floors and sidewalks are ideal for a heady charge into space. For cautious types the rough road is restful; they can carefully manage to move but without the fear of going out of control.

Music is ideal for speed experiences. When the beat and the child's pace match, the "patter of little feet" spells joy. Put on a record or two and find out if your child is a jazzer or waltzer. Some children have a feel for rhythm and even at two or three will vary their rhythm to match the music's beat. Join your child and do a few of your favorite dance steps as you hold him in your arms. He will squeal in delight. If you play an instrument give him some fast and slow melodies and watch him respond in body action. If you're loose let him bang on his favorite pot or drum and you move to the rhythm he beats. You and he may create a dance Balanchine never dreamed of!

The game of chase is an all-time favorite of two- and three-year-olds. Part of the fun is getting caught. A hug and a kiss and they're off again. You can get caught too if you slow down or zag when zigging would have let you escape. The wise parent plays tag interspersed with cuddles. It's a happy time because now your child is old enough to initiate some hugs too. The chasing extends to everything that moves up ahead —pigeons in the park, ducks near the pond, chickens in the barnyard, and poor put-upon Fido. The tolerant dogs of the world learn to lie low and not be noticed so they don't have to be chased.

LANGUAGE

You may have graduated from an Evelyn Wood speed-reading program but it will do you no good if you are reading to your two- or three-year-old. Just as you slow down your speaking speed when talking to a young child, you need to slow down your reading speed. It must match his rate of comprehension. Your two- or three-year-old will enjoy simple books about familiar subjects. He is not ready for long narration read at top speed.

As you talk together you and your two-year-old child will be communicating—he in short sentences of two or three words, and you in a slowed-down version of your normal speech. Your subject matter when you speak to your child will be those objects and actions which interest him. You will hear yourself emphasizing key words to catch his attention, and you'll listen intently to catch his sentences and squeeze out the full meaning of his three words. Three-year-olds often go through a period of stammering when their minds race faster than their utterances can follow. The advice is to stop what you're doing, pay attention, and listen. Don't aggravate the situation by hurrying a stammering child with your inattentiveness. Your child may use the label "fast," "slow," or "quick" for things he sees, but you'll use them more often than he will by trying to speed him up or slow him down. The words you use won't alter his pace much, so save "fast" as praise when his pace is just what you wanted, "quick" for times when you hurry together to pick up the toys before a happy outing, and "slow" for the moments when you both feel happily lazy.

Four- and Five-Year-Olds: Your Child Begins to Order His World

Some people are always in a hurry and some spend a lifetime waiting for others. The ability to speed up and slow down allows you to get to places on time, and to get the job done. Your four- or five-year-old will begin to slow down and speed up depending on the need. He will quickly hurry through lunch to sample the new dessert or dawdle through the meal if the mood strikes him. He can dress in a flash if a friend is waiting to play or take an hour undressing for bed.

You still need to be aware of the pace of your child's day; a day full of frenzied activities produces a child wound tight as a top, a day with quiet slow-paced activities produces a child itching for some friskier play. If your child is in school the pace of the day will take care of itself. After a busy, fast-paced morning with a group your child may need quieter, slow-paced play alone in the afternoon. If your child is not going to nursery school you need to see to it that the pace of his day is varied.

BODY

The trot of the two-year-old and the gallop of the three-year-old is fading in the distance now. Four- and five-year-olds love the feel of speed, but also enjoy slower-paced play. Toddlers dash about until they nearly drop or until you drop them into bed for rest and relaxation. Four- and five-year-olds are developing their own sense of speed in movement and activities. If your child is a slower-paced individual you may need to spur him on to get a feeling of speed by jogging together to get the paper or racing him to the front door. If your child seems like quicksilver, never stopping, you need to lure him into slower-paced activities such as looking at a book or baking cookies together. Some fast-paced children can't slow themselves down, nor can you rein them in for long. They have special needs and require special handling. It is difficult being a child who is constantly on the run; it is also a challenge for the parents. If you suspect your four- or five-year-old has an unusual motor drive for his age, check your view with your child's teacher, if he has one, and get your pediatrician's advice. A school setting is often

frustrating for a child who needs to move, and for his school success he needs a team backing him. The pace may be a medical problem labeled hyperactivity, and part of the cure may be recognizing an individual child's physical needs.

The superhero has great appeal to most four- and five-year-olds. They believe the ability to run, fly, and conquer is related to speed. For them, speed is power. In every preschool class at Halloween there are half a dozen Superman and Wonder Woman costumes. Playground games center around jumping and running to the rescue with capes flying. Both imaginative play and body control are typical of four- and five-year-olds. They are able to slow down, stop, and speed up again when moving. They like the challenge of changing speed on command. Your four- and five-year-old will enjoy performing these feats:

- Running up and down a hill as fast as he can go
- Inching up and down a hill as slow as he can go
- Skipping and hopping fast and slow
- Balancing on a swing on his tummy, dragging a hand along the ground in tortoise time
- Whizzing down the slide forward and fast or creeping down backward and slow
- Catching and kicking balls. Four- and five-year-olds will still track best with slow-moving balls, but some children have advanced coordination of eyes, hands, and feet, and are ready for the fast ball league.

Most four- and five-year-olds are able to run fast enough to feel out of breath or to get stitches in their sides. They are proud of their new running skills and consider these minor inconveniences to be badges of courage and speed.

CLOTHING

Four- and five-year-olds are able to handle the basics in dressing and undressing. Speed adds a challenge. When you are desperate for action ask your child how fast he can get into pajamas or out of a wet bathing suit. He will be slower with new dressing skills such as buttoning, buckling, and tying.

TOYS AND ACTIVITIES

A child's inner speedometer has an effect on the types of toys and kinds of play he enjoys. The devil-may-care speedier child likes the rough and tumble active play that involves his total body and produces instant results. He enjoys running, jumping, and scampering; building large block constructions quickly; vigorous clay pounding; and tricycle races. Even a puzzle challenge is measured by speed: "Did you see how fast I did that?" The slower, more deliberate child likes play that requires precision. He enjoys small blocks or construction sets to make buildings of intricate pattern; paper, pencil, and scissors for coloring, cutting, and pasting; and miniature toys for dollhouses, villages, and farms. For this child a puzzle challenge is measured by the degree of difficulty and the accuracy with which the puzzle is done. The slow child often sets very high standards for himself and is a perfectionist.

Most children enjoy the drama of a toy race even if they are playing alone, racing "the red one against the blue one." Children of this age have no real understanding of speed and its relationship to time and distance, but they know who crossed the finish line first. Piaget's experiments have shown that true understanding of speed occurs at about ten years of age. All sorts of speed experiences precede this comprehension. Any gradual slope or incline provides a good track for racing toys:

- A safe driveway
- A mud or grass bank outdoors
- A plank and a brick (or book) to produce a slant. He'll discover the steeper the slant, the faster the race.
- A large piece of sturdy cardboard to rest on a step, creating a ramp

Anything that is "crashable" is "raceable." Your child can think up his own racers or try these:

- Balls of various sizes and weights. Guess which one will win the race— Nerf or basketball, jacks ball or Ping-Pong ball.
- Toy cars and trucks
- Shoe boxes with doll or stuffed animal passengers
- Old shoes with leather soles
- Bread pans and brownie pans

INDOORS AND OUTDOORS

Your four- and five-year-old is interested in the speeds of things in the world. He is noticing the blender's fast and slow; the hair dryer's fast and slow; the many speeds of the mixer; and the hand-powered egg-beater speeds from fast to slow.

Pouring liquids will give your child a sense of the relationship of texture and temperature to speed. Many opportunities in the kitchen will help your child understand that thin and warm liquids travel faster than thick and cold ones. Let your child experiment:

- Pouring honey and syrup on pancakes. Have a race to see which pours faster, a spoonful of honey or a spoonful of syrup.
- Pouring hot or cold chocolate syrup on ice cream. Which is faster?
- Pouring a thick milkshake and a thin milkshake into glasses

Your four- and five-year-old will be using his eyes and ears to determine the speed of things. He won't be clocking miles per hour, but he will be getting an idea of the variations of speed. He will comprehend fast and slow and have a notion that there is some acceleration or deceleration in between. Things that move from one place to another will be studied:

- The range of speeds in a horse's motion, from a slow clip-clop walk to a thundering gallop
- The urgent pace of emergency vehicles on the run; the flashing lights and wailing sirens warning of impending speed
- The slow, steady pace of a barge or tugboat and the swift movement of a speedboat or sailboat with full sails
- The chug-chug of an antique car engine and the tire squeal of a speeding car on a turn
- The excitement of a chase—the dog chasing the cat, the cat chasing a bird

The forces of nature and their changeable speeds will attract a four- and five-year-old's attention:

- The speed of water from a waterwheel, dam, or waterfall
- The speed of wind. He can see a brisk wind as tree branches bend and sway or feel the slower puffs of air as he throws a beach ball or flies a kite.
- The pitter-patter of an occasional drizzle or the rushing downpour of steady rain, sleet, or hail
- The slow drift of snowflakes at the beginning of a snowfall or the pell-mell fury of a blizzard

Your four- and five-year-old will be experimenting with the speed of things in the great out-of-doors:

- Racing the family dog
- Racing with a friend. A three-legged race or spoon race would be exciting too.
- Playing "Pooh sticks." The classic game favored by Pooh Bear and Christopher Robin requires a bridge. Drop sticks on one side and rush to the other side to see which stick comes out first. If you have a stream without a little bridge you can still play the game. Drop sticks in the water at one special tree or rock and have the finish line be another tree or rock farther downstream.
- Seeing a race. See if your town has a horse, motorcycle, dogsled, soapbox derby, high school track and field, frog, turtle, or worm race. Cheer for the fastest; cheer for the slowest!

LANGUAGE

Four- and five-year-olds will use the words "fast," "slow," and "quick" in their everyday speech. The concept words add a touch of drama to their explorations and descriptions. You will also notice that your child is capable of understanding your normal flow of speech. You rarely have to slow down to make yourself understood as you did for the toddler or two- or three-year-old. Your child can now process what he hears easily and will be able to repeat poems, songs, jingles, and advertisements. His own expressive speech is marked by an increase of speed. For some language enrichment think of fast animals (rabbit, ostrich, jaguar) and slow animals (tortoise, snail); fast-moving toys (skateboard, toboggan) and slow-moving toys (pogo stick, kite). Have your child identify words that describe fast and slow movements. Do "whizz" and "dart" mean fast or slow? Do "dawdle" and "poke" mean fast or slow? Your child is beginning to expand his vocabulary if he hears you use different words to describe the same concept. To the child who is ready to combine two concepts you can say: "Move quickly like a tiny ant," "Move slowly like a big bear," "Move slowly down on hands and knees," or "Move quickly up on your toes."

Even if your child has a fair understanding of the concepts "fast," "slow," and "quick," the world must at times seem a puzzlement. What in the mind of four- and five-year-olds are "fast foods" or "fast colors"? And what does "this watch runs slow" mean? A world of hamburgers, colors, and clocks jogging along on little legs may pop into his imaginative brain.

Chapter 11

"Take a Cup and Fill It Up"
How a Child Learns About Volume

*H*AVE YOU EVER REFEREED the parceling out of equal amounts of juice to two four-year-olds? Unless the juice is going evenly into identical glasses you have a fight on your hands. You can't convince the child with the low, wide glass that he has the same amount as the child with the "fuller looking," taller, thinner glass. Children can't understand the subtleties of volume until they are almost through grade school. However, even the baby can grasp the gross comparisons of full and empty. The young child enjoys many, many experiences of pouring from one container to another, emptying, filling, and overflowing! These experiences will ready him for the understanding of the complexities of quantity.

VOLUME CONCEPT WORDS

Least Difficult	*More Difficult*	*Most Difficult*
full—empty	half	use of standard units of measure: measuring cups, measuring spoons, etc.

The Infant: Birth to Eight Months or Crawling Age
You Bring the World to Your Infant

One of our babies enjoyed the independence of holding his own bottle, but at the first gulp of air he would fling the bottle in any direc-

[194]

tion. For young children, volume is an absolute: something is full or empty, there is no in-between. The independent six-month-old holding his bottle gets no clues from feeling a weight change or seeing the liquid gradually reduced. His sense of empty is instantaneous when his sucking produces air. An infant's experience with volume is limited to this single episode of "empty." Many more opportunities await him in the months and years ahead.

The Baby on the Move: Crawling Age to Twenty-Four Months
Your Crawler/Toddler Goes to the World

The chronicle of a child learning to drink from a cup is an essay on a baby's judgment about volume. Left on his own with a fairly full cup the one-year-old would give it a two-handed grasp, raise it, and deftly toss the contents onto his own shocked face. With milk dripping from eyelashes and out of ears your child has had his first "full" and "empty" milk disaster. There will be many more, but as you and he learn together you will ration his supply ounce by ounce and he will learn just the right tip of the cup to the lip. Even when your child has become adept at drinking from his own special cup he'll have to relearn if you give him a smaller, wider, or taller cup and the usual supply of milk. The new level will throw him. He will tilt at his usual angle but this time the milk will slosh in his face or fall short of his lip because he has failed to make the necessary adjustments. After a few such experiences your baby will learn to peek into the cup to get an initial gauge of how much milk is inside before he starts drinking. By age fifteen months most children learn to drink deftly from a variety of cups, adapting their lift to different liquid levels. About this time you will cheer to your child's merry words "more" and "all gone," his initial version of announcing the state of "empty."

When your child learns to pick up and throw down (at about one year) and has a notion of the permanency of an object, he begins his career of "dump and fill." He'll empty his playpen, his crib, his bowl, and any container he can pick up. He'll also love filling them up again, filling until they hold no more. Your child is beginning to conceptualize volume as he stuffs teddy bears into trash baskets. Both his teddy bear and the trash basket maintain the same shape whether together or apart, but the relationship of container and contained is completely different for liquid volume. Any fluid substance such as water, mud, or sand changes shape to fit its container. In the baby's mind the liquid and the container are not seen as separate. The two are seen as one. One of our

196/ Growing Wisdom, Growing Wonder

friends claimed she regularly bought two quarts of milk for the children and one for the floor! Keep your sense of humor and a handy sponge; your child is on his way to judgments that will make for a drier floor.

Two- and Three-Year-Olds: Your Child Finds Words for the World

Two- and three-year-olds' natural enthusiasm for sand, water, and mud give them much experience with volume. Given a collection of cans and bowls, pitchers and spoons, these substances will hold your child's attention longer than any other playthings he has. This doesn't mean your child can arrive at any conclusions about volume as a geometric abstraction. He is just getting a bit more subtle about judging when to slow the pouring to prevent an overflow! This "school skill" is called estimation, and in a basic way he is starting on that kind of thinking.

TOYS AND ACTIVITIES

Your household helper will be proud if you honor his new skill of judgment and put aside a little pitcher (syrup size) for him to use for simple tasks:

- Watering your plants. He'll be happy making twenty-five trips from faucet to fern, carefully watching his pitcher so it won't spill. Show him how high to fill it and put a mark there.
- Filling the dog's or cat's bowl
- Pouring his own milk or juice at mealtimes. For your own sake make sure his little pitcher holds no more than the cup or glass he is to pour it into. As he gets more adept let him pour your water.

LANGUAGE

Your child will use the words "empty" and "full" to describe the states of "not-a-drop left" or brimming over. "Empty" will be said with the pride of a job well done when he seeks your praise for eating or drinking it all up. "Full" may be said declaratively as an apology for spilling.

Four- and Five-Year-Olds: Your Child Begins to Order His World

When it comes to judging volume, four- and five-year-olds believe their eyes, not logic. Piaget conducted many experiments involving liquids and their relationship to containers. His studies with children show that young children are perception bound: what they see is what they understand. Even with careful pouring and watching, a four- or five-year-old can't believe that the same amounts poured in a low, wide container and into a tall, thin container are identical. His pondering tells him that he began with the same amount and should end with the

same amount, but his eyes see a great disparity—the taller, thinner container really looks as if it has more and "the eyes" at this stage of development have it. Even as adults we are teased into thinking the yard of ale is more than a mugful and the tall, thin tropical cooler has more than the low tumbler.

Parents who have not even read Piaget have this same sense of their young child's notion of volume when they put the tiny bit of ice cream that's left in a small bowl to make it appear as if it is a generous amount.

Four- and five-year-olds not only use height as the absolute measure of amount, they become very exacting in their observations and line up glasses or containers side by side to check the liquid level. Water play and cooking activities with see-through plastic containers will give your child many opportunities to pour, measure, and observe what is happening. He will get satisfaction from these simple activities:

• Dividing a can of juice into two glasses for himself and a friend. His growing sense of fair play will cause him to line up the glasses to make sure each contains the same amount.

- Pouring rice, dried beans, water, or anything else safe and pourable into a variety of containers. This idea is part of the Montessori practical life curriculum and is a favorite with young children. They find the transferring back and forth from one container to another both a challenge and a pleasure. Equip your child with a tray, an assortment of plastic containers, and some pourable substance. When he tires of this activity you can recycle the beans into soup.
- Cooking cakes, Jello, oatmeal, or grits. All require measuring. Let your child be your assistant; turn on the faucet and measure out the cup of water. He will know "full" and "empty," but will only see "half" as part of a whole. If your recipe calls for half a cup of sugar, have him fill the one-cup measure half full. Using a half-cup measuring cup would confuse his tentative fix on the concepts "full," "empty," and "half full."
- Playing with water in the tub or kitchen sink, your child will busily pour and rearrange liquids. Unbreakable containers and funnels will extend his thinking about what fits into what. A mesh vegetable bag hung over the tub faucet will hold his supplies until the next session.

LANGUAGE

Volume is the most difficult of the qualifying concepts to learn. A young child must be able to understand many variables, such as the size and shape of the container and the amount to be contained. The many abstractions cannot be comprehended until a child is about twelve years old. Your child will understand the concepts of "full," "empty," and "half," and use the words to describe amounts. Seven years later all his pouring experience will pay off when he can understand the volume of a cylinder or a cone.

Chapter 12

"Sugar and Spice, and Everything Nice" How a Child Learns About Taste and Smell

THROUGH TASTE AND SMELL EXPERIENCES children learn a great deal about their world. Your child's taste and smell world will be what you expose him to. He could grow up eating only artificial flavors, processed and packaged foods. He would probably be healthy and intelligent but he would have missed some of the experiences that make everyday life richer and more varied. The taste experiences of children lead to their taste preferences as adults. Compare the dullness of the "meat-and-potato person" to the followers of Julia Child and the Galloping Gourmet. The wok buyers and taco makers are having more fun! Natural foods with their flavors intact are coming back. Artificial flavors and seasonings have become suspect as the cause of allergies.

Be sensitive to the smells of each season. In our culture we live in a world of air fresheners and deodorants. Smell and odor have gotten a "bad name," yet smells bring back some of our strongest memories: lilacs in the spring, sea air in the summer, burning leaves in the fall, hickory smoke in the winter's fire. Children need to experience the pleasures of the smells of the world from bakery shop to flower garden, from pine woods to pungent mushrooms. Bake bread and squeeze oranges with your child. The tastes and smells will blend into a happy memory. Together learn more about the world through noticing tastes and smells each day.

TASTE AND SMELL CONCEPT WORDS

Least Difficult	*More Difficult*	*Most Difficult*
good—bad	sweet—sour	salty
		bitter
		spicy

Other taste and smell words come from specific taste or smell experiences, for example, minty, piney, and fruity.

The Infant: Birth to Eight Months or Crawling Age
You Bring the World to Your Infant

The senses of taste and smell are well developed in newborn infants. A baby a few hours old can use his sense of smell to find nourishment. Tiny infants turn away from foul odors and prefer sweet tastes above others. Think about your infant's taste and smell environment. Is it always air from an air conditioner and stale cigarette smoke or is it occasionally a breeze across a flower bed or carriage slumber under a pine tree? You must introduce him to whatever variety he has in his first few months; he can't go anywhere by himself.

BODY

Baby lotions and powders sweeten a baby's smell, masking burped milk odor and generally enhancing the smell of a clean baby. Liven up your infant's smell life:

- Put bars of lightly scented soap in his clothes or bed sheet drawers
- Use an occasional fresh, line-dried sheet or towel instead of a packaged air freshener scent from the drier
- Place a sachet, potpourri, or pomander ball on a table near his crib, out of reach but within smelling distance
- Put a flower near his feeding table
- Put his carriage or stroller in a garden or under a blooming bush or tree. Watch for bees (safety) and butterflies (delight).

FOOD

Just think that every new food you introduce to your child will be his first taste of that food in his whole life. When he's ready for cereals, fruits, and vegetables, look into the ways they can be bought or prepared. With seven children between us neither of us has ever been able to make ourselves taste baby food in jars. The smell seems totally lost in the pureeing and processing. More than thirty years ago there was a study of babies' nutritional needs. The babies were given a large variety of pureed natural food substances in little dishes. They could dip fingers in and eat what they liked. The results were fascinating. The babies went on food jags but over a period of weeks they ate a balanced diet. You certainly can't offer twenty substances a meal, but by pureeing some of the fresh foods you eat you can give your infant many taste adventures. Get to know your infant's cereal, fruit, and vegetable preferences, and respect them. Provide his nourishment with foods he enjoys. You can choose your own diet but your baby is dependent on you to honor his interests. From time to time try a tiny taste of a less favored food; maybe his taste will have changed.

LANGUAGE

Your infant can't talk about his taste or smell likes and dislikes but he will communicate eloquently with open or pursed lips, licks or tongue thrusts, smiles or spit bubbles, and head turning. No kind words from you about the flavor will affect his body language!

The Baby on the Move: Crawling Age to Twenty-Four Months
Your Crawler/Toddler Goes to the World

Taste and smell will encourage crawlers and toddlers in their explorations but not in ways you'd expect. Eight to twenty-four months is a prime age for consuming poisonous substances. Your toddler may munch his way through a cigarette butt and sip pine-scented toilet cleaner if they are within his reach. He'll find rotted crumbs on his crawls under the kitchen table and relish them more than the day they were served as part of fresh food. You can't rely on taste or smell to warn your baby. You have to put poisons out of reach and survey his route for anything unsafe to nibble. Taste testing everything, edible or not, is the order of the day.

BODY

Long before toilet training you'll notice that most babies are either oblivious or perfectly pleased with the smell of urine or feces. To your child, his body products and their odor are a marvel of his own creation. Don't get your adult revulsions at the smell mixed up with his emotions about his body products. Even the most fastidious adult can usually manage to change his own child's diaper without wincing, though he'd gag at another baby's diaper.

FOOD

The crawler/toddler period is a period of food fetishes. You'll have to think about your own attitude toward food and handle your child's diet as casually as you can. The sooner he feeds himself the less you and he will tangle over food. Twenty-five years ago the baby books were full of

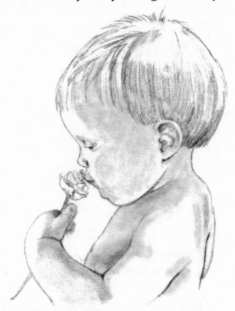

baby menus, special platters laboriously prepared, eye-appealing baby dinners. After half an hour of making mock chicken legs out of baby veal you'd feel ready to choke your child if he didn't eat it. Don't fall into traps, getting crises over who's boss mixed up with three meals a day. Put out easy-to-pick-up, nourishing food in small amounts and chat with your baby as he eats. Look at the long run, how much he's eaten in a month, not in a meal. Food jags are outgrown just like shoes, so bear with them. If your baby eats with you let him have small samples of whatever you eat; if he eats alone let him see your dinner as you cook it so he can try a nibble of any new substances. He may like them. The grass is always greener, so eventually he'll clamor for a taste of whatever you eat. When your roving child gets hungry between meals make snacks—apples, cheese, raisins, or toast—something that counts as food in case the next meal is shunned. He may need fueling a lot more often than you do.

OUTDOORS

Whether in stroller or afoot your crawler/toddler will find tastes and smells along the way. In the city it may be the smell from the local bakery or sidewalk flowers on display. In the country it may be fresh-cut grass and honeysuckle. A toddler's approach to smell bears the same brand of enthusiasm as his approach to most everything: he almost climbs into flowers, sniffing like a puppy. He is as likely to snort as sniff, but he will be pleased with what he smells. Pause from time to time to smell things, and lead your baby to them. Smells need not be perfumy. The faint rot of moist pine woods or fallen apples and the tang of road tar can be pleasant.

LANGUAGE

Your crawler or toddler will not know the words "sweet" or "sour" but he'll name some of the foods that have these tastes. Children have more sweet taste buds than adults and will clamor for goodies with sugar. The cake Mother used to bake won't taste the same when you are grown even if you use the same recipe because your taste buds have changed. Even your definition of "sweet" changes. Each family works out its own treat and snack list, but your child will early learn names of the sweets he likes. "Sour" probably won't be in his vocabulary but the wonderfully eloquent screwed-up face at tasting sour will speak louder than words. Taste and smell classifications are controversial even to the experts. They argue whether there are four or twelve categories, and then try to settle what goes into each category. You and your child needn't worry about classifications, just taste and sniff along together, expanding each other's palates and worlds.

Two- and Three-Year-Olds: Your Child Finds Words for the World

Two- or three-year-olds often join the adult dinner table, eating what you eat. They have opinions, preferences, and rigidities about taste, but dish by dish they become more daring. Remembered smells will recall past experiences. That damp wooly smell will send them looking for the wet dog, the perfumy smell of shaving cream will announce that Daddy is up, and the scent from the oven will send up a cry of "Cookies!"

FOOD

Two- or three-year-olds can be good company on short outings. Trips to the market can be taste and smell adventures. Make the shopping trips a shared responsibility as your child looks out for bananas or limes. Let him select, buy, and eat a banana or nibble a piece of cheese during your shopping. You'll be better prepared to run the gauntlet of candies and gum which projects into the checkout lines at every supermarket. His active participation in your shopping will make his trip more expansive than a view of the gumball machine.

Two- and three-year-olds are fairly conservative about food, scorning new flavors and smiling at the same old standbys day after day. Adventurous eating grows gradually and thrives in an atmosphere where your child can taste but is not forced to "eat-it-all-up." Let him choose new foods at the grocery store for you to prepare and give him some samples from your menu. You may be eating hamburger when he does but he'll be curious about the blue cheese and Bermuda onions topping yours.

Now and again let him have some old-fashioned taste treats, almost surefire successes for young children:

- Cinnamon toast tidbits. Butter his toast strip and let him sprinkle on his own cinnamon sugar.
- Gingerbread, or if you're energetic, gingerbread boy and girl cookies. He can put raisin or chocolate-bit buttons on top.
- Lemons squeezed into lemonade. The skin oils are released as you squeeze, increasing the smell.
- A tiny pie made of scraps of your crust or a mini-cake baked in an empty egg-shell half. His tiny cake will be ready long before the big one is cooked. It's hard to wait when the smell is so good! (Peel off the eggshell like a cupcake paper.)

OUTDOORS

The sense of smell was once much more useful than it is today. Primitive humans used smell to find food and warn of danger. Smell has fallen into disrepute, possibly because our noses have been dulled by pollution and anesthetized by the antiseptic world. The smells we smell most are those put in housecleaning powders and fluids to mask the smells of dirt. Even incense is unreal in its perfumed intensity, so from time to time give your child the experience of natural smells in the outdoors. If you live in the city see what the park has to offer, or drive to a "pick-your-own" farm and gather apples, grapes, strawberries, cherries, or peaches—and eat some on the spot! Find one apple tree and smell it as it blooms in the spring or is wet from a summer shower. Find one rose blooming in June.

Even though you may not be a nature buff or a natural-food freak, let your child know every now and then where natural foods grow and what they taste like. Stop some summer day by the side of the road and pick and eat blackberries. Whatever your locale, keep an eye out for persimmons, blueberries, walnuts, or hickory nuts. If you fish, drop a line for a crab or bass, and take it home and cook it. Your child may only taste one tiny bite but the flavor will be different from anything he's ever tasted. Even the city windowsill can support a pot of your child's own parsley, chives, or mint. If you use it leaf by leaf it will adorn many a menu. If you live in the country, smell will be a part of your child's life from barnyard to herb garden.

LANGUAGE

At two or three years your child will communicate in simple ways about the smells and tastes he likes and dislikes. He'll let you know his likes by a smile of acceptance and his dislikes by a shake of the head in rejection. If you watch carefully you may find his likes and dislikes don't match yours. One man's meat is another man's poison. Horse manure may be a normal smell to the rider, almost perfume to the gardener, but a shock to the city dweller. The heavy scent of a gardenia may choke one child and charm another. Don't try to set up your child's classifications, just delight in the diversity of his reactions and his growing vocabulary. What interests him is what he and you will taste, smell, and talk about. Soon he will remember and talk about the minty, piney, and fruity tastes and smells you and he have shared. His vocabulary will grow with his expanding experiences.

Four- and Five-Year-Olds: Your Child Begins to Order His World

Four- and five-year-olds are adventurous and social. They are into other people's houses and yards, and bring home tales of what other people eat for lunch or grow in their gardens. Now is the time to move away from peanut butter and jelly, adding an occasional taste and smell experience to the other new adventures in your child's life. You don't have to join the "Fruit of the Month Club" or work your way through the ethnic restaurants in your town. Dust off your cookbook and experiment with new tastes together. Take a walk and sniff as you go, enjoying the smells of each locale and season. Your child's taste and smell adventures with you will set the stage for a fuller life.

BODY

Children have their own sweet smell. They have no need of the packaged scents found in children's toiletries or scented bubble baths. Let

your child get to know and appreciate the pure odors of the world. For some fragrant experiences:

- Put a drop of peppermint oil behind his ear as perfume
- Place a clover or rose petal on his pillow to insure sweet dreams
- Make a sachet or pomander ball together to hang in his closet
- Crush a mint or rosemary leaf from the garden for a pleasant scent
- Hide a balsam pillow in his shirt drawer for a surprise

FOOD

Your child's food preferences will be based on his individual likes and dislikes as well as on the family menus. A bite of moussaka, cannelloni, tortilla, or sour dough rye will be the beginning of many taste experiences. Most of us have fond memories of childhood tastes and smells. Remember, you are creating your child's memories for the future. Let him be an active family member participating in food preparation. He will enjoy putting:

- Cloves in the ham
- A bay leaf in the stew
- Cinnamon on custard
- A vanilla bean in the sugar to make vanilla sugar
- Pepper in the salad; nutmeg in the cookies. (If you use a grinder for peppercorns and a grater for the nutmeg seeds it will be more fun and more aromatic too.)
- Parsley on the meat platter. Let him taste the garnish.
- Lemon and mint in your iced tea
- Vinegar in the salad dressing
- A cinnamon stick in hot cider
- Caraway seeds, raisins, nuts, anise seeds, or cranberries in bread dough
- Any herbs or spices in ethnic foods such as oregano in Italian recipes, curry in Indian dishes, dill in Scandinavian foods

Play a game with your child when you are cooking and baking; let him guess what you are cooking. Can he smell roast beef, brownies, popcorn, gingerbread, hard-boiled eggs, bacon, spaghetti sauce, banana bread, and his favorite cookies baking? Let your child's taste buds help him identify foods. Have your child close his eyes and give him a sip or bite. Can he tell what it is? You might try a pickle (sweet or sour), celery (leaves and stalk taste different), a piece of honeycomb or maple sugar for a special sweet treat, watermelon, mint tea, orangeade, and peanut butter.

Smell and taste affect each other and appearance can affect taste. For mysterious adventures have your child try to taste these same foods while he is holding his nose or give him a bit of salt and sugar, and see if he can tell which is which. Like the martini drinker who insists on an olive in his drink, four- and five-year-olds are beginning to notice that certain food tastes complement each other:

- Cookies and milk
- Bacon and eggs

- Mustard and catsup on hamburgers and hot dogs
- Bread and butter
- Crackers and cheese
- Peanut butter and jelly
- The surprise contrast of sweet and sour in salad dressings, and some Chinese foods
- A concoction your child thinks up, such as eggs and catsup

Temperature has an effect on food. Heat releases food odors and changes the texture and taste. With an increase in temperature, sweet and sour tastes become stronger, and salty and bitter become weaker. Four- and five-year-olds begin to have preferences for the taste of cooked or raw foods. Ask your child which he prefers the taste of:

- Raw or cooked carrots
- Cole slaw or sauerkraut
- Strawberries or strawberry jam
- Raw apples or baked apples
- Raw vegetables or cooked vegetables

Learning about foods is a way of learning about the world. Explore with your child the tastes and smells of the more exotic foods in the grocery store. Buying a piece of ginger root or a plantain will extend your child's thinking beyond the taste alone. He will begin learning about other cultures and nations. Limit your exotic purchases to a sample size so that if you dislike the taste it won't be a big financial loss. If you like the new smells and tastes you can always buy more. Try Chinese cabbage; buckwheat honey; bean sprouts; persimmons, kiwi fruit, kumquats, litchi nuts, or mangoes. Let the grocery shelves tempt your palate for the tastes you have not tried. Point out the chocolate-covered bees or the bird's nest soup. There are some foods you can laugh about and talk about, but don't have to try.

INDOORS AND OUTDOORS

The world's smells are another interest to four- and five-year-olds. They will be the first to notice the fragrance of the hyacinth or the stench of the skunk. Some odors such as tar or gasoline are offensive to one child and pleasant to another. See if your child likes these smells:

- A new car or house. The odors of fresh paint, varnish, new wood, and plastic are distinctive.
- A swimming pool
- Clean laundry

- Pine bark or cocoa chip mulch
- Concord grapes
- Sassafras
- Evergreens
- A campfire
- Freshly turned earth
- The sea
- The world after a rainstorm

Just as your child is beginning to know what you're baking or cooking by the smell, he will begin to get a sense of location by the odors he encounters. Four- and five-year-olds have no geographical understanding, but if they've been there before their sense of smell tells them they are nearing the beach, the mountains, or a big industrial area. They have no sense of direction, but they can find the burger place or the pizza parlor by smell alone. Your child will be able to identify a long list of place smells. He will be cataloguing the odors of familiar places:

- The doctor's and the dentist's offices
- The pet shop and zoo
- His friend's house
- The gym where you jog or play basketball
- Public bathrooms
- The barbershop
- The lumberyard
- The dry cleaner's
- The library
- The movies
- The bakery
- The florist
- A stable
- The shoe store
- The hardware store
- His school
- His church, synagogue, or other place of worship

When your child is with you on shopping expeditions he will want to pause to sniff the aromas at the spice deparment, the perfume counter, and the soap display. Giggle together at scented pens, stationery, socks, toilet paper, "scratch and sniff" books, and T-shirts!

Four- and five-year-olds are mature enough and knowledgeable enough to have a sense of danger when it comes to taste and smell. They will taste and warn you of sour milk or alert you to a baby or puppy accident on your new rug. They can also notice the smell of scorching, smoke, and gas. Respect your child's cautions and review your household safety procedures.

LANGUAGE

Four- and five-year olds are graphic in their language. They use the strongest words possible to convey meaning or describe feelings. "What stinks?" is a typical expression. Your child won't necessarily use the concept words "good" and "bad" to describe smells and tastes, but he will understand the meaning. His words will probably be "yummy" or "yucky," or some other slang phrase to describe "good" and "bad." You keep using the more conventional concept words for taste, but accept his version. After all, he has the idea.

The indelicate smells and fragrant scents of the world interest four- and five-year-olds. Your child will be honored that you are willing to discuss "smells" with him. Four-year-old minds may need some elevating beyond bathroom and body smells, but most four- and five-year-olds are busy classifying the good along with the bad. Together think about some of these odors:

- People smells. What does Grandmother smell like (lavender), Grandfather (pipe tobacco), Daddy after tennis (old socks)? Don't be surprised if your child likes people who smell nice and is wary of people with bad breath or tobacco smells. He is more sensitive to odors than you are.
- Holiday smells. What tastes or smells do you associate with Halloween (pungent burning jack-o-lantern), Thanksgiving (turkey and pumpkin pie), Christmas (evergreens and candy canes), Passover (a seder with a sample of bitter herbs), Fourth of July (punks and sparklers)?
- Animals and their ability to smell. Big noses usually mean superb sniffing skills. Which animal do you think is the better sniffer, an elephant or a gorilla? Your child will be interested to know that mother animals and babies can find each other in a crowd by scent alone. Special animal sniffing talents will be fascinating to your child: the foxhound and bird-dog, the truffle-seeking pig, the nectar-seeking bee, the honey-seeking bear. Can you think of animals who are not able to smell? (whales and porpoises)
- Good smells (food baking, flowers, a baby) and bad smells (garbage pail, Limburger cheese, the indoor monkey house)
- Good tastes and bad tastes are personal. Compare your absolute favorites and biggest dislikes.
- Sweet tastes (jam, syrup, ice cream), sour tastes (vinegar, lemon, yogurt), salty tastes (pretzels, bacon, french fries), and bitter tastes (liver, green peppers, olives).
- Jobs that require a special taste and smell talent. They will be interesting

to your child if he is especially sensitive to odors and tastes himself. Tell him about tea tasters, wine tasters, perfume makers, and creative chefs.

- Things that have no odors. Can you name five things?
- Combining concepts. What is green and sour? (a lime) Green and bitter? (spinach)
- Taste and smell words applied to people: the sweet old lady, the sourpuss, the bitter old man

If in your household taste and smell are another one of life's adventures, mealtime atmosphere will be pleasant and conversation will range far and wide.

Chapter 13

"Early to Bed and Early to Rise"
How a Child Learns
About Time

CHILDREN HAVE NO UNDERSTANDING of clock time as we know it until they are seven or eight years old. Time is one of the most abstract of qualities. The clock and the calendar as measurements of time are preceded by many basic experiences. The young child develops a sense of time through the order of his day. He measures time in relation to the events in his own life: lunch, bedtime, day, and night. Anyone who has ever wrestled with a preschooler's grip on "today" as "yesterday's tomorrow" knows how difficult time is to comprehend. A child who has a meaningful concept of "before and after," "begin and end" has a sense of time in contrast to the Mickey-Mouse-watch wearer who cannot read the dial or make any sense of thirty minutes after the hour. Children can develop a sense of time, an understanding of sequences in the preschool years, but watches and calendars have no meaning until grade school.

TIME CONCEPT WORDS

Least Difficult	More Difficult	Most Difficult
stop—go	start—finish	begin—end
	now—not now	until—then
	before—after	at the same time
day—night	morning—afternoon	later
	today	yesterday—tomorrow
	first, next, last	first, second, third

short (time)—long (time)	names of:
	weekdays
	weekend
	seasons
	months

The Infant: Birth to Eight Months or Crawling Age
You Bring the World to Your Infant

Newborn infants and their parents exist in a timeless world. There are no events which distinguish night from day, morning from afternoon, yesterday from today. The first weeks at home are a blur with parents and babies floating in and out between feedings and changings. New babies are need-oriented, not time-oriented. A hunger pang or a cold, wet diaper demands attention at twelve midnight or twelve noon. Slowly, eating and sleeping needs become more and more predictable. A schedule of daily events begins to order the household. After the first month together you will find yourself in your bathrobe less and less, and you will be dressing your infant in daytime outfits to show him off and in nighttime sleepers to keep him warm. You should be cheered by this attention to wardrobe detail; it means that you and your infant are emerging from a timeless never-never land and are in agreement as to what is day and what is night, when it is nap time and when it is meal-time.

By three months of age your baby will be reasonably settled into a routine and family life will be getting back to normal. You and your infant have adapted to each other. Parents who once were "night people" are slowly becoming "morning people," and infants are lengthening their nighttime stretches. Time was when infants were kept on schedule and fed exactly on the appointed hour regardless of need. The pendulum then shifted to feeding on demand, leaving both parent and child without moorings. Today the approach most pediatricians favor is one of balance. Flexibility is stressed within a structure. Too rigid or too loose a schedule frustrates both parent and child. Respond to your infant's needs and timing. He will want to play, but not when he is overcome with fatigue. He will want a frolic in the bath, but not when he is ravenous. At the same time you can give your child a sense of your time frame. Have playtime sessions when your infant is contented and alert, but during daylight hours. At nighttime feedings, attend to the basics of filling his tummy and drying his bottom, then tuck him back into bed with a goodnight kiss. Your approach will help him know what to expect.

Infants don't like reruns. Research has shown that babies get bored with the same visual or auditory stimulation. A sound or a design repeated a few times is exciting, but sooner or later the thrill disappears and the baby turns off his attention. This boredom is an important stage in an infant's intellectual development. It signals the beginning of a developing memory. The ability to recall events and remember objects is essential for thinking and surviving in the world, and the infant has begun on these necessary skills. Your infant will anticipate feeding when he sees the bottle or will raise his arms to be picked up when he sees you enter the room. He will gradually know that his jacket means an outing and that a bark means that Rover is near. Daily routine helps your infant anticipate the future.

LANGUAGE

An infant's time orientation is limited to a few expectations of events to come. Your baby's concept of time is just beginning to develop and the words "stop and go" or "day and night" have no real meaning. Keep talking; in a few months he will understand "night-night" and "bye-bye," words that describe specific events in time.

The Baby on the Move: Crawling Age to Twenty-Four Months Your Crawler/Toddler Goes to the World

Babies "on the move" live every moment to the fullest with no glance to the past or eye to the future. Your crawler/toddler's active exploration of the world involves him in the present with his attention devoted to everyday happenings. Your child's growing memory helps him understand the permanency of objects in the world. He can recall events for a short period of time. He must remember single events before he can have a feel for the sequence of one event following another.

The idea of time as a fixed position is beginning to make some sense to your child. The events of his day are starting to form a pattern for him. His temporal 'gauge is still pretty rough, but during the months ahead lunch time, bath time, story time, and bedtime will all be differentiated. At first your child will think of time as a "place": bath time means "in the bath," bedtime "in the bed." This notion is perfectly reasonable because a young child deals best with the concrete. The understanding of time as a specific place gradually develops into time as a specific event. Knowing that it is 8:15 P.M. on Tuesday, the twenty-fifth of June, is nothing compared with understanding the abstraction that events are sequenced with a specific relationship to each other. Your child's play with toys gives him concrete experiences with one thing in relation to another. Stopping and starting, putting one shoe under the bed, then the other, give him practical experience with ordering things. Ordering objects prepares your child for ordering events.

Structuring your child's day in some consistent manner that suits you both is not just wise management, it is a necessary requirement for your child's developing sense of time. A routine is comforting in its sameness; its regularity gives your child a feeling of positions. Bath time comes "after" supper time; "first" shoes go on, "next" we ride the elevator, "then" we go to the park.

Your crawler/toddler may seem like a paradox when he can remember a silly game that you played yesterday, but not his own grandmother whom he saw last month. His memory is not selective, just growing, and events in the not too distant past are easier to remember. It's good to keep this thought in mind when you leave your one-year-old baby with a sitter for a few days while you enjoy a short, well-earned vacation. Upon your return home you expect a happy reunion of hugs and kisses, but your baby may only respond with a blank stare. Your baby isn't playing "hard to get," he is simply forgetful. A period of familiar sounds, sights, and gestures will soon bring back the past and your reunion is only slightly delayed.

LANGUAGE

As he approaches two years of age your child may have an idea of "stop," "go," "day," "night," and "now." He comprehends "now" because that personifies his very existence. "Not now" is of no interest. He cannot cope with the abstract idea or the concrete experience of waiting. Accept the fact and your life with a toddler will be smoother.

Talk to your baby about the here and now. His language ability will reflect his interest in the world. He wants words for the important people and objects in his world. Temporal words like "go," "now," and "today" will only have meaning after "Mommy," "Daddy," "milk," and "cookie" are understood and spoken.

Two- and Three-Year-Olds: Your Child Finds Words for the World

Time for two- and three-year-olds is a fixed point, a starting and stopping of activities. "Night" comes "after" "story time" and a cuddle; "day" begins at breakfast. Children under age two live only in the present, but two- and three-year-olds are beginning to talk about the past. "Yesterday" was when you all went on a picnic. The exact label may not be correct, it may have been last week, but your child is start-

ing to order events in his life. The future still has no meaning for your two- or three-year-old. He links time with events: the arrival of the garbage truck or the ride on the bus. The abstraction of the future has nothing for him to latch onto.

BODY

Two- or three-year-olds are able to wait a little bit. Their emotional responses are dependent upon their body needs. They are less "on the move," or maybe they just pause more between comings and goings. The passage of time is a difficult concept to comprehend and young children are not able to wrestle with the notion. Growth, especially of their own bodies, helps them get a feeling for "now" and "not now," "before" and "after." New baby teeth as well as growing hair and nails will be of passing interest to your child.

Toilet training will depend upon your child's concept of time. Readiness to handle toileting means not only a physical maturation and emotional interest in being grown-up, but having an intellectual grasp of the temporal concepts "stop" and "go," "start" and "finish," "before" and "after." Two- and three-year-olds will take this big step toward maturity.

INDOORS AND OUTDOORS

Snow to a two-year-old seems wondrous. His memory is pretty much tied to happenings in the recent past, so he can't remember his first season of snow a year ago. Seeing him have his first experiences is one of the joys of watching a child grow. His enthusiasm and wonder can't help but touch you.

A young child perceives time in much the same way as he perceives speed, volume, and temperature. The beginning and end points are significant, but the in-between can hardly be fathomed. A two-year-old will enjoy helping you plant seeds or bulbs for the fun of it. The harvest in the future will be enjoyed in the same way, but the relationship between the two events won't be understood. Two-year-olds don't make good farmers or gardeners but they are happy planters and reapers. Three-year-olds can enjoy watching things grow if the wait isn't too long. Growing bean sprouts is a good starter for three-year-olds because it's speedy and they can see the beginning seed and end sprout together, something which helps dispel some of the mystery of the in-between process. If your three-year-old enjoys his first "green thumb" adventure give him some more sprout seeds to try. Enjoy his mung or alfalfa sprouts in salads and sandwiches.

Many two- and three-year-olds fear the dark. The combination of their developing imagination and the dark night often causes sleeping problems. Use a night light in your child's room and occasionally explore the night together. Getting to know the shadows, sounds, and smells of the night often help in dispelling fears. It's worth an occasional late bedtime to see fireflies or the lights of the city glowing, and to hear crickets or night street sounds.

LANGUAGE

"Pretty soon," "in a minute," "after supper," "finish your soup," are all familiar time concept words to a two- or three-year-old. Your child won't know if a "minute" is two seconds or two hundred seconds long, but he will understand that it means "Hang in here, I'm coming." Concept words such as "not now," or "a long time," or "tomorrow" make no sense at all to a two- or three-year-old. A "long time" can mean anything from two minutes to a week if your child is waiting.

A two-year-old has a growing memory and can recall the "forbidden" from day to day. Even though he remembers your prohibition, temptation is often too great, and a two-year-old will approach the ashtray or television saying "no, no" to himself as he fingers the "untouchables."

A three-year-old uses time words in the same way that he uses color words or numbers. "Last year" may mean "last week" just as a "blue sweater" may really be "green." He knows there is a group of words to describe certain qualities, but the particulars escape him. Your three-year-old may also like the novelty of the word "when" and use it frequently. He will ask "when" he is going to the playground and "when" the sitter is coming. He isn't ready for a timetable, but take heart, your child is aware enough to anticipate events.

Your two- or three-year-old will continue to gauge time by the events of his day. You keep up the dialogue by telling your child what's ahead, what you're doing, and what's been done. Your talking will give him a feel for the sequence of time and the appropriate use of time concept words. Keep your chitchat timely. Your two- or three-year-old is interested in current events, not the new baby due in six months or the house you used to live in. History and futurity have no appeal for this age group.

Four- and Five-Year-Olds: Your Child Begins to Order His World

Four- and five-year-olds pay attention and remember things for longer and longer periods of time. They have the beginning of a sense of time in the way they can follow a daily routine. They know what comes before and after: a bath before dinner, a rest after lunch. They can think and talk about things which happened last week or will happen tomorrow. They can talk about objects remembered.

The measurement of time by clocks and watches, weeks and months,

dates and calendars will still be well beyond their comprehension. They may recognize these time notations as part of the bric-a-brac of the adult world, but understanding time as a continuum historically or even seeing how minutes, hours, days, weeks, months, and years relate will be conceptually years ahead. Your child's first sequences of events will be personal and the sense of time will gradually move from the present to the more remote. At four and five your child's most remote concern may be what you're planning for dessert or what he wants for his birthday. He's still unable mentally to conceive of faraway lands and long ago times; he has much to learn about his own.

PEOPLE

In a wonderfully egocentric way your child feels that time began when he was born. In the same way that an infant has no sense of objects existing unless he holds them or looks at them, your four-year-old can't conceive of the people in his life existing except in relation to him. A classic child's question when looking at his parents' wedding pictures is "What was I doing when you were married?" Grandmother or Mother are seen as always gray-haired or grown, their earlier existences as another mother–child pair disbelieved. Gradually, as a child learns to hold more than one idea, more than one concept at a time, he can see you as mother and daughter, himself as son and someday father. All these conceptions evolve with time.

It has been said that time is the most precious gift a parent can give a child. Yet it must be time in the right doses and in the proper balance for both adult and child. The time you have to give to your child will depend on the other demands in your life. Giving your child too much of your time will take away his own initiative. Four- and five-year-olds can wait, they don't need food, attention, or you instantly. Their own sense of time is such that they have a rough gauge of "in a minute" or "after a while" (if you use them accurately), and they should be able to respect your time a bit. A study by Burton White at Harvard University showed that the most competent children were those who had a word, a moment, a comment off and on with parents and then set about their own business. Parents who sat down with their child and selected and directed their play weren't helping their child develop independence and self-reliance. You and your child can work out your relationship. You can give him time and attention in small doses: a smile, a suggestion, or word of praise from you will help your child develop on his own. He'll bask in your approval but won't be locked into having you as his constant pal or playmate.

BODY

Children often judge time by the vigor of their bodies' action. They think that time moves faster when they are busy, like the expression, "Time flies when you're having fun." Even adults get the same feeling: My goodness, is it that late? I was so busy." The hours will seem longer to you when your child is not happily occupied in vigorous or quiet play. Help your child organize his time judiciously, spending his energy over a whole day's schedule, not just in a few hours' involvement.

Parents and children alike have body clocks, the metabolic rate that makes them "morning people" or "night people." Sometimes parent and child are out of phase. Get to know your best times and your child's best times and plan around them. The sinking spell he always has before supper may not be the moment for his haircut or your trip to the grocery. You may have to try for an afternoon kindergarten session if you're both fuzzy until noon.

The growth of his own body is a good way for a child to begin to understand the passage of more remote time. Gift shops sell fancy charts but many families put marks up the kitchen door frame with heights and ages noted beside. Four- and five-year-olds don't understand the numbers but by backing your child up to the chart you can indicate growth by touching the place on his own body which shows him how tall he was at age two.

CLOTHING

Trying on his baby clothes is a good way for your child to grasp the passage of time as well as his change in size. In order to envision time a child must understand a sequence, the notion of a series of things following each other in an orderly fashion. To dress himself your child must establish an order—socks go on before shoes, boots after. It's not as simple as it seems. If his feet are dressed before his body he'll have a hard time putting on his pants. Learning the sequence is a matter of practice. One day your child will don his mittens then stop short when he has no hands to zip his jacket! The more responsibility he can have for establishing a workable sequence of his own the quicker he'll learn. It is said we learn by our mistakes!

FOOD

Through cooking and eating your child can understand the duration of time. The more your child can participate, the better grasp he'll have on the orderly sequence of food preparation. As anyone who tries to put on a first dinner for guests knows, making everything come out at the same time takes an orchestration of preparation and cooking. Don't give your four- or five-year-old the job of fixing dinner, but let him help. Shaping a hamburger, opening the buns, setting the table while the hamburgers cook, getting out the catsup, and sitting down to savor the results provides a lesson in sequence no fast-food chain instant hamburger could provide. "Instant foods" are just that, a sort of denial of time; so when you do have time let your child share in making dinner from start to finish. He'll also be proud if you let him help make a pie from apples to finished product. If he's picked the apples the time frame is even longer. Sometimes cooking disasters can be great learning experiences. If you don't pay attention or set a timer, food cooked too long can be burned, ruined, or tasteless. Your child will get a sense that there was a right and measurable time interval which was exceeded.

TOYS AND ACTIVITIES

As your child's attention span and memory lengthen and his friendships expand, his play becomes more elaborate. Games and imaginative
play have beginnings, middles, and ends; plans are made and are carried out. A lengthened attention span means play lasts longer; your
child will need time to carry out his schemes. A game not finished today
will be picked up again tomorrow and completed. You'll have to leave
block houses standing half-completed and bear with a camp-out in the
dining room for three rainy afternoons. Though he cannot read a clock,
your child will begin to clamor for time enough to do things. You'll
hear cries of "Oh no, *not* lunch. Not now, we're not finished!" In the
first few years you were the manager of his time. Now you have to move
away and let your child get a feel for managing time himself. Some
parents find this hard and program their children so that all their time is
structured and filled. The schedule and the clock manage the child and
in the overstimulation of his day the child never has time to be bored.
Giving your child time to himself without any plan gives him a chance
to develop his own creative outlets. It takes time to be creative. If you
let your child discover "slow" time as well as "fast" he will gradually
develop not only a pace of his own but a balanced sense of time, time he
can manage for himself. This sense of time is one he'll need in a few
years when he'll have to allow enough time to finish his homework
before bedtime. Some people never develop an accurate sense of time
and aren't able to gauge an activity to be completed in a time frame.
Your child needs a chance to make these judgments long before he can
read a clock. Anyway, a clock won't help if the sense of time is lacking.

For the days when you haven't the temperament to let your child take
his time, the abstraction of time devices, a watch, a clock, and the
kitchen timer will help you get him into your time frame. Though children can't tell time they are aware of its control over their lives: school's
opening and closing, the rush to the grocery before it closes, and the
school bus schedule are all part of your comings and goings with him.
These times control you and in the same way your child learns to accept
that "it's time to pick up your block," or "it's time to wash your hands."
"It's time to . . ." works like magic when "I want you to . . ." might cause
a tantrum. If you have some trying times of the day, use the ring of the
timer rather than your voice, saying, "When the bell rings it's time to . . ."
The timer is an impersonal arbiter most children find easy to obey.

Many toys and play activities lead to time concepts. Your child will learn from these:

- Sequences he develops in pretend house play. Babies fuss, are fed, changed, and bedded. Firefighters douse fires and have dinner. He will recapitulate the time sequences in his own life.
- Sequences in drawing, cutting, and pasting
- Stop and go of table and outdoor games
- Sequences of doll, car, and puppet play
- Rhythm of music. Knowing when to clap and how long to hold a note are time experiences.

OUTDOORS

Four- and five-year-olds get a sense of the passage of time in the observed growth of plants and animals, in dawn and day, dusk and night. They begin to get a sense of the passage of seasons in their experiences out-of-doors. The cycles of nature are still pretty overwhelming, so share with your child simple single experiences he can understand. In your community let him watch the passage of time in the following areas.

Buildings A building going up day by day, a sequence he couldn't imagine from seeing a finished building.

Birds Birds building nests, fetching worms for baby birds, and flying off for winter.

Bugs Larvae become cocoons, then butterflies.

Beasts Parent and baby pets. Caring for growing pets—tadpoles, hamsters, kittens, and puppies—can give him a feel for time and growth.

Flowers Look at one tree or branch. This approach is just right for a four- or five-year-old observing the cycle of nature. Pick a tree in your yard or park and look at it each day, seeing the changes in spring and fall as buds turn to leaves or leaves fall from branches. Also observe morning glories, day lilies, or moon flowers grow and bloom.

Take a walk at night and see what you can see. Take the same walk in the daytime. Have lemonade by the full moon and talk about the day. Together watch sunsets and at least one sunrise. The whole world seems different in the stillness.

LANGUAGE

Time is so conceptually abstract that it takes both experiences and talk about the experiences to get the abstract concept in order. There are many chances during a day for parent and child to talk about the sequences of activities which mean time to a child. Together talk about some of these:

- The day's events just past. Let your child remember what he did before lunch and after dinner.
- Yesterday's events. You may have to jog his memory with a hint.
- Tomorrow's plans. Where will you go on your day off?
- His next birthday. A birthday is the stellar event of the year to a four- or five-year old. "You can come to my birthday party" or "I won't invite you to my birthday party" are the social weapons at this age. Your child will like to talk about who he'll invite and what they'll eat, even if the birthday is ten months away.
- Holidays. Your child will remember recent holidays and look forward to the next. Children sequence holidays before they sequence months.
- Books you've read together. Your child is now old enough to remember and retell the story in sequence. A five-year-old with picture book in hand can tell a story to a two-year-old brother.
- His babyhood. With a few pictures you can tell him tales of himself, the sequence of his own life with himself as the hero.
- Seasons. If the seasons are distinctive in your climate he will like to remember and look forward to snow, swimming, digging the garden, and raking leaves.
- Events in pantomime. Imitate tooth brushing or knee scrubbing and see if he gets the message. Pantomime is a wonderful way to sequence events. Think together what comes first, second, third.
- Night and day activities. Name some night animals.
- Cause and effect: "If you do this what will happen then?" Every cause and effect leads to thinking about sequences in time. Think about the concrete: "One more block on the tower. Will it fall down?" Or the abstract: "If you leave the door open what would happen? Would the cat get out?"

Four- and five-year-olds enjoy listening to a whole book and have enough memory to enjoy a story read a chapter a night. Give your child the job of telling what happened last night so you'll know where to start. Make up stories together starting "Once upon a time. . . ." Let him talk about the sequences in pictures, such as those in the Sunday comics.

Considering adults' difficulties with time (jet lag, resetting the clock forward or backward for daylight saving, the confusion of losing a day crossing the international dateline), children learn a great deal about this abstraction in their early years. Their knowledge is woven into their practical lives, so when numbers and calendars come later they are the final touches, not rote memory order imposed without understanding. Your child may use the names of the days of the week out of sequence, even state that things happen at 15 o'clock. He will mix up these specific time words but will accurately use general time words such as "now," "later," or "today" if you have used them with him.

It is fun to be able to stop talking about teddy's toes or truck wheels (the everyday objects of your child's day) as you did with your two-year-old, and be able to talk about ideas and plan a bit for tomorrow. Your child is growing up.

Chapter 14

"One, Two, Buckle My Shoe"
How a Child Learns
About Number

CLIMBING UP THE STAIRS a three-year-old chants, "one, two, three, five, ten, eleven." The listening parent wonders whether to be proud or concerned. Parents think of numbers as the beginning of math, but math doesn't begin with numbers for preschool children. Numbers are the end point, the abstract symbol, the name for the groups of things children have carried and nibbled, sat upon and played with for years. To think of numbers as a beginning would be like teaching an infant letters before you talk words to him. A sense of number develops very slowly. Children begin learning their math from objects in the world about them: a cookie in each hand, a shoe on each foot. Long before a child can solve a math problem he must have matched and sorted many objects. All his handling of objects gives him a sense that "three" is more than "two" because his block pile is taller or his hand won't hold one more cookie. A child filling two boxes with blocks or setting a table for four people is "doing math"; he is filling in the background concepts that make numbers as symbols useful to him later. Number concepts (like color, shape, or size) are tools for identifying and organizing the world. Concepts of size, shape, and position in space must grow along with your child's sense of number before he can do math in school. He must grasp the relativity of "big" and "little" before he can sequence numbers small to large. He must recognize curved and straight lines before he can identify number symbols. He must have positioned his own body "between" before he can conceive of 8 as between 7 and 9.

Parents can feel quite calm if they realize that including zero there are only ten different numerals which combine and recombine in math. Any child can learn these ten basic numbers when he's ready, but the feeling for the use of numbers comes through doing, with blocks and play dough, with crackers and jelly beans. Understanding is based on do-it-yourself experiences. Parents don't have to know math; they just need to give a child lots of objects to sort and handle. It's unlikely that your child will have a grasp of numbers more than "five" until kindergarten; then the teacher can take over. Learning by doing gives your child a firm number sense, a far cry from the rote memory recital of one, two, three, four, five.

NUMBER CONCEPT WORDS

Least Difficult	More Difficult	Most Difficult
more		less—most
some	all	
	many—few	several
	nothing	zero
none	both—pair	double
	half—whole	part
	equal	not equal
	almost	nearly
1, 2, 3, 4, 5	6, 7, 8, 9, 10	first, second, third

Number concepts in practice include money and groupings, as in flock, herd, and dozen.

The Infant: Birth to Eight Months or Crawling Age
You Bring the World to Your Infant

To know the world outside, an infant must first get to know himself. An infant can't establish a sense of number until he has established a sense of himself as a creature separate from the world around him. His exploring eyes, mouth, hands, and feet give him a conception of himself in relation to other things and people. He gradually acquires the idea of one thing separate from another yet relating to it. Thus his understanding of number proceeds from the basic beginning, seeing himself as "number one."

The Baby on the Move: Crawling Age to Twenty-Four Months
Your Crawler/Toddler Goes to the World

A toddler doesn't know any numbers but he begins to know a number of things and that's the beginning of his sense of number. A sense of number is built bit by bit as he handles many materials: cereals and cookies, buttons and bows. It's a long way to the number symbol 5 carefully drawn with a primary pencil and used in math problems, but the symbol won't have any meaning without the experiences that precede it. An eight-month-old banging a spoon in each hand, a fourteen-month-old putting one block on top of another, an eighteen-month-old taking two socks off two feet are all on the way. One cracker in each hand is a satisfying sense of equal. One cracker in each hand and no hand to pick up a third is a rough experience of odd and even. Dumping and filling, the happy occupation of a toddler, give a background for full and empty sets. Relating objects one to another—trucks and cars, cups and saucers, spoons and forks, identical blocks—are early groupings, the ordering of the world that is expressed in numbers in later years. A toddler's incessant call for "more" will establish series of cookies, cars, and blocks. Sock pulling, car pushing, walking, wiggling, testing, piling up, and tearing down will give him the background, the sense of number, he will need before he can handle the number labels 1, 2, 3, 4, 5. Your child's practical experiences with size, shape, position in space, indeed with every concept area, are more necessary to his future math skills than counting. His math discoveries will come through his play, lining up and parceling out; you don't have to worry if neither you nor he says numbers. "More" and "all," "many" and "both," the words you use for quantity, are more important at this age than numbers he can't conceptualize.

Two- and Three-Year-Olds: Your Child Finds Words for the World

A typical two-year-old's birthday party gives an idea of a two-year-old's grasp of number. You've just given a birthday party for your two-year-old and six friends. Hallmark provided the decor, there were enough goodies for everyone—and it was a disaster from beginning to end. Four out of the six friends wailed; the presents started a battle; the food went uneaten. One mother took her sniffling child home with icing in her hair and teeth marks on her wrist. What went wrong? There is an old-fashioned formula for birthday parties: include the same number of children as your child's age during the preschool years. The two-year-old should have had just one friend. Why? What does a birthday party have to do with a two-year-old's grasp of number? Developmentally, two-year-olds are at the point of comprehending things one at a time. They can handle one concept at a time, one friend at a time. As there is for the birthday party, there is rule of thumb for math. Children can understand and use numbers one less than their age until they are four. Between four and six years they learn to comprehend and use numbers through ten. Most parents would respond, "But my child can count to five already." Counting isn't the same as understanding and using numbers. Send a three-year-old who can count through five upstairs to bring down "five" buttons out of a box of "fifteen." You may get "three" or "nine." If you send him for two, a number he can grasp, his trip will be successful.

BODY

For a child, number begins with his own body parts. Two- and three-year-olds study all those matching parts of their own bodies, the pairs of hands, feet, ears, eyes, arms, and legs, and are amused at the solos— belly button and nose. Your child's number discovery will come through a sock on each foot; a mitten on each hand; a shoe on each foot (or most likely pulled off!); trying to hop on one foot; hanging his coat on a hook; putting two legs in one pants leg; pairing shoes and socks; and holding up two or three fingers to show his age.

FOOD

Two- and three-year-olds are very serious about kitchen responsibilities. It is a weighty matter to put one cupcake paper in each muffin-tin hole. Give your child time to check them out laboriously row after row, making sure they are filled. This task goes by the fancy name of one-to-one correspondence in math circles, and it is basic in handling numbers. For more practice let your child perform these tasks:

- Give the dog one biscuit
- Stick one finger through a cookie with a hole in the middle
- Take out one hot dog and one roll
- Put one straw (or two) in each glass
- Place a square of cheese on each cracker
- Loop pretzels over as many fingers as he can
- Put bread in the toaster slots
- Put one or two croutons in each soup bowl
- Put a raisin on each cookie

TOYS AND ACTIVITIES

Matching container and contained is a favorite activity for a two- and three-year-old. You can give your child household toys to satisfy his urge to fit things into other things:

- A shoe box garage for every toy car or a shoe box bed for every doll
- A twenty-four-bottle beer carton and a bucket of old tennis, golf, or Ping-Pong balls
- An old wooden or metal milk case and empty plastic or cardboard milk cartons to fit in
- A six-pack case and old plastic cups or soup cans
- Grocery store throwaway cheese ball or fruit-shipping container and balls to settle into each hole
- Pots and pans with lids to match
- Egg cartons and old bottle caps for each depression

INDOORS AND OUTDOORS

Two- and three-year-olds are in their small way very organized. Once your child has learned that the salt and pepper go together on the kitchen table he may insist you always put them "right there." Cater to his sense of order and organization, which is his way of mastering the world about him. Let him help you organize:

- Setting the table "one for Mommy, one for Daddy"
- Putting a napkin out for each napkin ring
- Putting the cups and saucers together, piling the plates (if you have plastic china or a careful child)
- Putting an empty bottle in each six-pack carton hole
- Carrying one clean towel to each bathroom
- Putting out a coaster for each glass in the living room
- Putting a pillow on each chair
- Fetching his shoes and the baby's so you can go for a walk

Let him help you find things that belong together and put them where they belong: toothpaste and toothbrushes; combs and brushes; knives and forks (let him put away the dull table knives); and pairs of shoes, socks, mittens.

Two- and three-year-olds bring their growing sense of order to the outer world, noticing things that belong together, such as mother and baby animals, a flower to put in a vase, and a letter to put in a mail slot. They get a sense of "many" from seeing the infinite quantity in nature: raindrops, falling leaves, snowflakes, and sandpiles.

LANGUAGE

The concept words from the chapters on size, shape, and position in space are far more basic than number names for two- and three-year-olds. A two- or three-year-old will often use number labels inaccurately. He may say he has five candies when he has two or ten. He has the label in the right area but he is applying it wrong. When he does count accurately he touches the objects as he counts them. Your child will have a grasp of "more" and "some," "none," "one," and "two" if he has trotted about on his two feet, picked up and put down with his two hands, and studied his matching eyes and ears. He'll fetch you one apple from a bowl and shrewdly ask you for two cookies when you'd planned to offer one.

Four- and Five-Year-Olds: Your Child Begins to Order His World

Four- and five-year-olds are interested in and impressed by numbers. Your child will know your next-door neighbor has three bathrooms and the dog down the street just had six puppies. These declarations are not

always accurate numerically, but the use of numbers makes him feel grown-up. Your child's boasting is based at times on fact, "I have two brothers," and at times on fantasy, "We toasted a hundred marshmallows." Keep in mind that a young child's use of low numbers is more likely to be correct. The rule of thumb for numbers is that four-year-olds understand numbers through four, and five-year-olds through ten. This is the norm, but like all other concept areas understanding develops at an individual rate. One child may know "four" at age four, inside, outside, and backward, while another child hasn't grasped the concept of "four" until age six. Just as there are children who can sing on key at three or ride a bike at four, there are children who are gifted in their use of number. They will go through the same progression, the handling and arranging of objects before abstraction, but at a faster pace.

How can parents help a child develop number concepts? Your child will need the same kinds of experiences at age four whether he is still struggling with the idea of a sock for each foot or debating how to divide the breakfast bacon evenly. He needs opportunities to handle and sort all kinds of things. He needs objects to order in a series from fewest to most. He needs materials to arrange and rearrange, adding to piles and taking away from groups. He needs opportunities to use what he has learned in a way that is useful and pleasing to himself and others. The "aha!" of understanding numbers is spontaneous and independent in a child. Your role is not to "teach" numbers, but to tolerate the mess of pine cones in the hall and sailboats in the bath.

BODY

Four- and five-year-olds have a sense of their body as a whole and also of their various body parts. They know that certain body parts come in pairs (arms, legs, eyes, and ears) and that hair strands and eyelashes can't even be counted. The matching bodies of identical twins or triplets are especially interesting to four- and five-year-olds. Your child will enjoy looking at, thinking about, and talking about bodies in relation to number. Ask him questions:

- How many belly buttons he has
- How many teeth his baby sister has
- How many dimples are on his chin or freckles on his nose
- How many body parts he has that come in twos (Did you think of cheeks, elbows, nostrils?)

In bygone days first grade teachers demanded, "Figure in your head." The ability to add two plus two without using fingers was considered the epitome of first grade mathematical skills. Today the emphasis of "new math" is on understanding, not rote memory, so "counters" such as beans, sticks, or fingers are considered perfectly acceptable. Your child will instinctively use his fingers (or toes) to count or figure out a problem.

CLOTHING

Any trim or frill on clothing that can be counted will be special to a four- or five-year-old. Your child will count pockets, buttons, or polka dots. "Pair" is a number word that four- and five-year-olds love. They grasp the "twoness" quickly and relish the ways we use the concept. Have your child think of things you wear that come in pairs, such as pants, shoes, socks, and mittens. Your child's logic may lead him to question some of the rules of convention. A "pair of pants" means one pair, but a pair of sweaters means two sweaters. We say "a pair of stockings" because there is a covering for each leg, but we say a "pair of pajamas" because there are two pieces—a top and bottom. Getting to know the world sure takes time. Just when your child thinks he has it, somebody changes the rules!

FOOD

The abstraction and relativity of numbers makes it difficult for young children to comprehend the concept. A four- or five-year-old still judges things by how they appear to him. To him a tall canister of cookies has more cookies than a shorter, wider one because it looks that way. You couldn't convince him by counting that both cookie containers have the same amount. A child focuses on one aspect of the set and makes an estimate of number based on a single quality of height, width, or length. A young child's notion of number, like his concept of volume or size, is based on concrete impressions: "more" equals bigger, taller, longer, or bulkier. With maturity and experience a child is able to consider more than one quality at a time. Until then remember that your child believes what he sees, and his group of raisins, blueberries, or sunflower seeds will seem "unequal" to yours unless they are arranged in the same way.

Gradually a young child experiences some of the more subtle aspects of number. His sorting and counting, arranging and rearranging will lead him to puzzling discoveries. While munching on a cookie it may dawn on your child that he is eating "one" cookie and that it is his "second" cookie and that it is the last from a plate of "five" cookies. One cookie has three number names at once. This realization is quite a step. It means your child is aware that number is not inherent in an object but a tool for sorting and seriating. He is beginning to understand that a number has a dual nature. "Two" can signify an amount (two peaches in the bowl) or a position in a series (the second dip of ice cream on a triple-decker cone). In mathematical circles these uses of numbers are referred to as cardinal and ordinal numbers. The ability to make this theoretical distinction means your child is thinking about the same number in two different ways as he groups jelly beans and counts popcorn.

Your child may have a rough idea of "parts" of "whole" numbers. He is able to understand and estimate half of a stick of butter, half of an apple, or half a cup of milk. He is familiar with half of a watermelon and half of a stick of gum, but he cannot handle fractions other than half. Young children usually prefer to have a "whole" of anything rather than a part or piece, regardless of the size! Your child would rather have a whole tangerine than a half even if he never finishes more than half. Certain foods, like cookies, in the mind of a four- and five-year-old just can't be divided!

Numbers are basic to cooking whether you are putting ten lemons in the lemonade or one cup of sugar in the cake batter. Your child is a ready and willing helping hand, eager to use some of his new number skills. Try some cooking and eating fun:

- Baked potatoes. Your child can handle the job from start to finish, selecting a potato for each person in the family, then washing them, and putting them in the oven.
- Sandwiches made with two or three fillings: a ham and cheese, or a bacon, lettuce, and tomato
- A vegetable dish with two or three vegetables, such as succotash or rata-touille
- A salad with three kinds of fruit or three kinds of lettuce
- Rolls with one, two, or three parts. If you're not a bread baker give your child tubes of store-bought dough to shape into biscuits or rolls
- A relish tray. Let your child arrange carrots, celery, olives, and so forth, with enough so that each member of the family gets one of everything
- Eggs. Your child can be a waiter and take the breakfast orders, unless the Cub Scout den members are breakfast guests!
- Orange juice and coffee. Your child can measure and add the cups of cold water.
- A sandwich served in two, three, or four pieces. Let your child decide how many sections he wants and then give him a table knife to cut through soft bread. This task involves both a number and shape concept.
- Pancakes. Let your child choose one big pancake or five little ones.
- Cake baking. Your child will like making the decision between baking a two- or three-layer cake, or dozens of cupcakes. Pause to look in the bakery

shop window at the multi-tiered wedding cakes or eight-layer tortes. If there were fan clubs for bakers, four- and five-year-olds would join.
• Letting him take the same number of cookies or raisins as buttons on his coat or pockets on his pants.

TOYS AND ACTIVITIES

If you visit a classroom for four- or five-year-olds you will find all kinds of "materials" for learning about number: colored cubes, rods of various lengths, felt boards, puzzles, pegboards, geo-boards, card games, and board games. All of these toys and activities in schools are designed to help young children make discoveries about number. At home your child can do much the same thing and you don't need all that special equipment. Just begin collecting recycled materials that invite sorting, grouping, and counting, such as buttons, keys, corks, washers, colored plastic price tabs that come on plastic bread bags, paper clips, and clothespins. Every household has its own special brand of throwaways. Look for interesting "counters" that are by-products of your job or hobby. By handling groups of rubber bands, golf tees, or film spools, your child is developing an internal concept of number. Understanding the formal operations of addition and subtraction, multiplication and division in grade school is based on your child's manipulation of many objects in the preschool years. Your child won't gain an understanding of "five" from instruction or a workbook. He will begin to get a sense of "five" as he plays with bottle caps, arranging them in groups and patterns of three and two or four and one. At some point in his play the sameness of "five" in all its patterns will jump out at him and he will be as pleased as Einstein with his very own discovery. Continued arranging and rearranging, grouping and regrouping will bring further clarification. Your child will absorb each new experience and discovery into his concept of number.

Many standard games for young children require a sense of number: moving two spaces on the game board, counting the dots on the dice, recognizing number two on the "spinner," keeping score. Other games involving number for four- and five-year-olds are: dominoes, bingo, tic-tac-toe, hopscotch, "Simon Says," and musical chairs.

INDOORS AND OUTDOORS

Out in the big wide world four- and five-year-olds find that knowing numbers gives a new sense of power and control. Beginning in the preschool years pushing the elevator button is a child's privilege. Identifying animals and plants, road signs and vehicles gives the sheer intellectual pleasure of knowing more about the world. Collecting lists of things and information about them becomes a pleasure in itself. An awareness of number patterns helps in this identification. After the mastery of the usual and proper number of things, number surprises fascinate: the monocle, the unicycle, the double-decker bus, the three-legged stool. With your child, pause to reflect on numbers in the following.

Transportation   Try to find a sailboat with one or many sails (a catamaran is a boat surprise); two- and three-wheeled bicycles and tricycles; a bicycle built for two (with a baby seat it can carry three!); and a truck with four wheels or eight.

Buildings   Think about one-room buildings—a log cabin, a tent, a barn, a treehouse, an old-fashioned schoolhouse, a doghouse. Think about buildings with lots of rooms—office buildings, mansions, apartment houses, beehives, or purple martins' houses. Count together pickets in a gate, panes in a window, steps in a stair, chimneys, doors, or porches.

Birds   Find birds with two colors (a robin) or many (a peacock).

Bugs   Try to spot insects with six legs and spiders with eight; the centipede opens new horizons!

Beasts   At first the world is divided into two- and four-legged creatures, 'til along comes an octopus. Four- and five-year-olds will delight in these discoveries:

- One-hump and two-hump camels
- The number of stripes on a raccoon's tail or skunk's back
- The number of horns on a deer, cow, or unicorn
- The number of dots in the track of an animal's footprint—observing and counting the pattern helps identify the beast
- Seashore bivalves and the garden snail's single shell

Flowers   Pick out blossoms with one bloom on a stem—a tulip, a daffodil; or many—a lily of the valley, gladiolas. Find patterns of number of petals: try "she loves me, she loves me not" on more than daisies.

LANGUAGE

"What is your name?" and "How old are you?" are often the questions adults ask children. When four- and five-year-olds begin to have a feeling for the social banter and ask us these questions we are a bit taken aback. It takes a few more years of living before four- and five-year-olds realize the peculiarities of our social conventions—adults ask children their ages but not the other way around! Take their questions in your stride. Names and ages are important to a four- or five-year-old,

but your age is beyond his mental grasp. Your child knows four is older because he can see he is bigger than his toddler sister. He may remember that you are twenty-nine or thirty-nine, but not know which is older. He may even think that the baby sitter at nineteen is older than you. How nice!

Four- and five-year-olds probably can't explain verbally what they are discovering about number, but certain number words are becoming labels to attach to ideas. "Many," "few," "several," "nearly," and "almost" are rough estimates. "All," "nothing," "whole," "one," "none," "zero," "equal," and "not equal" are more precise quantity words. "Both," "pair," "single," and "double" are new words with specific number meaning. Four- and five-year-olds savor new words and delight in the unusual. Together think about words that combine with number to describe a quantity of food, such as a bunch of bananas or grapes, a head of lettuce, a loaf of bread, a double dip of ice cream, a pinch of salt, or a dozen eggs.

Animal groups that have specific names appeal to four- and five-year-olds. The exact number is unimportant, the cluster or set is what matters. Think with your child about animal groups such as a flock of birds, a herd of cattle, or a gaggle of geese (the alliteration of this group seems silly, but because of it he will long remember the set). Four- and five-year-olds love to count things. Counting to them, like skipping, is just plain fun. They don't have to have a place to go or a need to know how many. They skip and count for the pleasure of it. Your child will busily count everything from the cookies on the dessert plate to the spots on your tie. In the car keep your four- or five-year-old busy counting categories of things. Make your suggestions a bit on the unusual side so your child doesn't run out of numbers in the first five minutes of the game. With two children in the car, say that the first child who finds ten of something wins. Look for American flags, red trucks, or men with beards. Like all the lists in this book, our intent is just to get you started. Have your own ideas based on your particular locale.

Four- and five-year-olds are able to deal with ideas more and more. This growing ability means they can think about and talk about numbers of things without having to touch or see the objects. Play a memory game together before bedtime or when you are in a long line at the grocery checkout. Can you recall these numbers:

- Guests at a birthday party
- Babies in the neighborhood
- Trips to the zoo
- Telephones at a grandparent's house
- Pairs of shoes you own
- Toothbrushes in the toothbrush holder
- Pillows on the sofa

Chapter 15

"What a Good Boy Am I" and "Boys and Girls Come Out to Play" How a Child Learns About Feelings and Relationships

Picture two polite mothers sharing coffee while they give their two-year-olds a "social experience." One child lies atop his new truck screaming at the intruder, ready to sink his teeth into his new "friend" if necessary. The other child clings to his mother's knee, sloshing her coffee. Two well-meaning mothers wonder what's gone wrong. Planning social experiences for young children is often frustrating. A parent who understands children's emotional development can plan appropriate social experiences. Social and emotional growth are interdependent. Two-year-olds can't play together like five-year-olds, since they have neither the emotional maturity nor the practice of social skills. There are many levels of emotional and social development and successful experiences at one level lead to the next level. Parents can also help in children's growth by reinforcing social skills and talking about feelings. You can set the stage for success or failure. Life will not be without tantrums in the grocery store or fistfights in the car, but it can be smoother. If you understand the sequence of emotional and social growth you can help the toy snatcher become the team player, the wailer talk through his tears.

Understanding and handling emotions and relationships augments intellectual development. Acquiring a concept of feelings is difficult because feelings are intangible, more so than color, shape, or size. Emotional concepts are learned in the same way your child learns other concepts: by experiencing the feeling, by having you label his feeling, and by his symbolizing the feeling in word and thought himself. It's certainly harder to understand "mad" than "round," but after "mad"

[239]

has come along in its various guises and manifestations your child can learn to understand the feeling in himself and others.

Every chapter of *Growing Wisdom, Growing Wonder* emphasizes that your child develops self-esteem through his growing competence in every area, in your appreciation and acceptance of his individuality, and in his awareness of his place in and contribution to his family. Your child's growth in self-esteem will make him a happy social being expecting the best from those he meets. Your awareness of your child's physical and intellectual limitations drawn from each chapter will help you set the stage for happy relationships with others. As your child grows from babyhood to school age you will gradually move further and further away from his interactions with his peers. You will begin at arm's length, ready to protect babies from each other, and move to "within earshot," available only as a crisis arises. As his social life expands you'll have more time for your own too!

FEELINGS AND RELATIONSHIPS CONCEPT WORDS

Least Difficult	*More Difficult*	*Most Difficult*
want—need (as in "I need, I want")	easy—hard (as in "I can do it")	
my—mine	together—turns (as in take turns)	friend—share bad (as in feel
happy—sad	like, love, mad (anger)	bad, guilt)
afraid	funny (humor)	wish (fantasy)

Many of the social and emotional concept words are broader and more far-reaching than other concept words. Parents often do not think of either emotional or social concepts as a learned skill. They don't know how to talk about feelings or friendship. We have added an additional sequence chart to help you understand how a child develops emotionally and socially, and how you can help.

The Infant: Birth to Eight Months or Crawling Age
You Bring the World to Your Infant

You are your infant's world. You feed him when he is hungry, keep him warm or cool, soothe him when he is unhappy, give him interesting things to see, hear, and touch. You begin communicating to him with body language and spoken words from his first moments of life. You nourish him physically, emotionally, socially, and intellectually. A newborn infant needs one person caring for him who knows his needs and respects his individuality. You need to learn your infant's preference for sleeping on his tummy or back, being tucked into fuzzy or satiny blankets, nodding off with or without a lullabye, or being burped during or after feeding. These preferences are all signs of a developing personality, and no two babies are alike.

In the past the mother has traditionally been the caretaker, the first link to the outside world. It was his mother's face the baby first recognized and his mother's voice or touch that calmed. Today the structure of the family is changing. Fathers are sharing child care or taking over the rearing entirely, live-in mother's helpers, or infant day-care centers are also caring for young infants. There has been some research on the effects of this shift on the baby, but only time will tell. Needless to say, the mother is not the only one capable of rearing a child: nannies and grandmothers in certain societies have been "mothering" effectively for centuries. The secret of success seems to be one caring adult who is more or less always there, ready to burp a bubble or catch a smile, tuned in to one small person's earliest communications and communicating back. Gradually as the infant matures, he can relate to more than one person.

For the first two months an infant doesn't know who he is, where he is, or what he is. His reactions to the world are intense. He doesn't have specific feelings, just needs for food, warmth, and human contact. As his needs are met he begins to experience pleasant sensations: soft mel-

FEELINGS*

	Child	Parent
Birth ↓	Infant reacts to physical needs such as hunger, cold, and so forth. Infant's feelings involved with physical needs.	Parent talks to, cuddles, soothes, and meets infant's physical needs.
4 mon. ↓	Baby reacts emotionally to people and his surroundings. Smiles. Older baby wails at strangers.	Parent interacts with baby, talking, smiling, comforting, and so forth.
1 year ↓	Child becoming aware of self as separate from others.	Parent expresses pride in child's growth and praises him for new skills (feeding self, walking, talking).
2 years ↓	Child seeks adult help. Feelings expressed but not in words.	Parent supports child. Enjoys him, comforts him, and helps him solve problems.
3 years ↓	Child expresses feelings to others with actions, rarely words.	Parent recognizes child's feelings and says words for him, "You are mad" or "Tell Jimmy, 'no.' "
4 years ↓	Child sometimes expresses feelings verbally (talks instead of hitting or yelling). Child frequently expresses feelings verbally. Child shows sense of humor and sympathy to others.	Parent encourages verbal expression, "Tell him, don't hit him." Parent praises child's efforts. Parent enjoys humor and shares sympathy.
5 years ↓	Child has developed adequate self-esteem and control to respond appropriately to verbal expression of others.	Parent continues to praise child's effective efforts.

* This chart is an outline of two complex developmental sequences. The chapters must be read before this chart can be fully understood. The chart will then be helpful as a guide to children's emotional and social levels. By using the chart par-

RELATIONSHIPS

Child	Parent
Infant is not yet a socially responsive creature.	Parent relates to infant and waits for first social smile.
Baby plays alone with hands, rattle, and so forth. Smiles. Older baby plays with others (Peek-A-Boo).	Parent and baby interact. Give and take, sometimes initiated by baby, sometimes by parent.
Child has sense of self in family.	Parent includes child in family activities.
Child can play near another child, noticing him, but cannot manage much interaction (parallel play).	Parent exposes child to people outside family. If outsider is child the same age, provide similar or same toy for each. Minimize interaction.
Child can play briefly with one other child. Can wait to take turns if adult helps him wait (cooperative play).	Parent provides easily shared toys and supervises activity, supporting "turn taking."
Child can play briefly with one other child. Can take turns on his own (cooperative play). Child can play for a longer period of time with one or more children.	Parent nearby, but less actively involved. Parent may need to encourage sharing.
Child can be a cooperative group member.	Parent encourages child to be both a leader and a follower.

ents can make sure they are not expecting social behavior beyond a child's (or his playmates') emotional capabilities. The ages are approximate, as the child's progression depends on his experience and personality.

odies, warm snuggling, a full tummy. This is the beginning of a lifetime of feelings. Your infant will become more aware of the world day by day.

Your newborn's dependency at once overwhelms you and touches you. You wonder if you are up to the challenge and at the same time want to get on with it. A parent–child relationship forms a very special bond; it defies analysis and it cannot be put under the microscope. It just is. You are the one person who knows your child best; you are the person meant to introduce him to the world. You will be his first friend and first enemy. You are the first step in a long chain of relationships with other people.

Your infant's introduction to the world determines his emotional, social, and, in turn, intellectual approach to life. If his experiences are pleasant and positive he will continue to reach out for more. There are several classic studies of infants reared in institutional settings where their physical needs were met but where they were deprived of maternal caring. Babies who were cared for physically but without human interaction were slow or retarded in their intellectual and social development. In some tragic cases the babies failed to thrive physically. Recent studies of infants in institutions who were provided with emotionally interacting caretakers have shown exciting gains in the baby's initiative and intellectual approach. The effect of nurturing on development is clear.

For the infant in the first two or three months no one else exists except mother or her substitute. At about the third or fourth month the infant begins slowly, gradually to notice the other people in his world. His environment will have a direct effect on his emotional and social development. Your baby's environment depends on the number of siblings he has and your distance from relatives and neighbors. This environment, combined with your baby's individual reaction to the world and the world's response to him as an individual, will structure his feelings and relationships. For the first few months you will have to take it on faith that your infant's contentment is his emotional and social response to your caring efforts. At about three months he'll give you that first smile that will make all your effort seem worthwhile. He will respond to you with a smile that is reserved for you and only you. Your voice and face will trigger this reaction because you are special to him. His gummy grin will be all you need to keep up the good work and his smiles will make you smile back. In a month or so he will expand his intimate circle of friends. Watch for indications of his emotional and social growth:

- Quieting when you pick him up
- Enjoyment as you hold him
- Readiness to be with others
- Excitement when people are near. Note his waving arms and kicking feet; the action even speeds up as people get closer.
- Laughter in response to a tickle
- Vocalizing back to you or starting up a conversation meaning, "Pay attention to me"
- Smiling at strangers

The end of the infant period is marked by even greater growth. Notice the signs in your six-, seven-, or eight-month-old, such as his:

- Smug, contented look when he is part of the family activities. He looks around, smiles, and totally enjoys being part of the group.
- Smile to the friendly baby in the mirror (not recognition yet, just fascination)
- Instinctive understanding that adults and children differ. He will generally respond positively to children, may fear strange adults.
- Kiss
- Shouts for attention
- Panicked look as you leave his sight. This new aspect of dependency is hard to live with, but it means he is growing mentally and emotionally. You have to have had something or someone in order to experience loss.
- Sensitivity to "happy" and "angry" feelings and words. He has no understanding of the words, but he is beginning to know there is a difference.
- Pleasure in social games with adults or children (see infant section in other chapters for happy baby activities he and his circle of admirers can initiate.)

The Baby on the Move: Crawling Age to Twenty-Four Months
Your Crawler/Toddler Goes to the World

Your child's view of himself depends in part on your view of him. The crawler/toddler age brings frustration and inevitable conflict between parent and child. Your baby wants to move, to investigate, to explore. Whatever he wants he wants right away. You want him to eat, sleep, and stay still in ways and at times that don't necessarily suit him. He hasn't the memory to look back or the time sense to look ahead. He doesn't understand his own feelings and he certainly can't understand those of other people. He must learn to understand and control himself before he can successfully relate to his peers. He wants to be independent, yet he is still almost completely dependent on you. You frustrate him, yet he adores you. If you are going to guide him through this important age you must look through his eyes at the world, for he cannot look through yours. If you can understand how he feels you can support, guide, and be proud of his mighty accomplishments. His physical wanderings and struggles will tire you, but his intellectual and psychological growth will excite you. He's on his way to becoming his own person.

PEOPLE

One of the first signs of your importance to your child is the "stranger anxiety" he shows at just under one year. Children differ in the vigor of their fear of strangers. At under one year the reaction seems related to recognition and attachment to the people in your child's small circle. New faces are unknowns. During the second year most children use their parents as a launching pad, and gradually more "strangers" become friends. You are your child's launching and landing pad; he comes and goes from you. His mental health is tied to yours and even though he reacts to "strangers" you will probably want to get him used to a baby sitter or two so you can get away from him occasionally. If you are to serve as his stability you must keep your own perspective. Spending the day with a whining or tantrum-throwing child can make him seem ten feet tall in your mind. Getting away from him and then coming back makes you see him for the tiny tot he is, meager in experience, great in his need, and strong in his drives. You will set the boundaries for his urgent physical and emotional drives. He can't set them himself. To your child you are omnipotent, and he will love you and struggle with you for several years, moving back and forth from you physically and emotionally but always keeping you in sight. You are his resource because he is still totally dependent on you for everything that is important to him.

Traditionally mothers have been home with young children for the bulk of the day and fathers have come and gone, taking the responsibility of child rearing to a lesser degree. Times are changing and fathers are taking a much greater role, spending more time with and taking more responsibility for their children. If ever there is an age when two can parent better than one it's the crawler/toddler year when shared perspective and a shared sense of humor can help both parents see that the day's frustrations were really two steps forward and only one step back!

Siblings have a particular relationship at this age. If they are older they can be helpful, playing an endless variety of games, such as Peek-A-Boo, Pat-A-Cake, or Hand-And-Take-Back. An older child can make a baby laugh and gain a great sense of importance as he does so. On the other hand, a crawler/toddler who moves about into everything, quite lacking in judgment, is a threat to older children who care about their belongings and creations. You must protect the older child from the toddler's destructive wanderings if you are to preserve the friendship between him and his brother or sister.

"Friends" or "playmates" are a diversion at this age, but don't expect either friendship or play at any recognizable level. People are treated much like objects during the second year, and your child may find his friend's eyeball as interesting as the wheel on his truck. Crawlers and toddlers can't "play" together, but if you are within reach to protect them from each other one child does delight in seeing another child. They observe and imitate one another, although interaction is on the snatch and snatch back level. Children who see each other regularly seem to learn about each other and interact earlier than children with no exposure. Perhaps even more important, parents who see other children with their own realize the universality of the difficult aspects of the second year and get some sense that these struggles are temporary.

BODY

The physical drive of children differs from one body and personality type to another. The more vigorous and energetic your child is the more head-on encounters you are likely to have with him. It matters a lot that you are bigger than he is and can pick him up when the going gets rough. The wonderful thing about a child with a volatile temperament is the degree of the changes. At one moment you have a biting, kicking tantrum on your hands and the next a snuggle bunny covering you with wet doggy kisses. It's hard on your child to feel so strongly, but with you controlling him he will gradually learn to control himself. In a year you won't need to be an arm's length away when he is with another child; you'll move across the room or even around a corner as his self-control grows.

FOOD

Independence in feeding will mean one area you and your child don't have to struggle over. An eight-month-old can't feed himself, but by one year your child can do a good job if you provide the right food and resources. Because of the great ambiguity between independence and dependence there are days when your toddler will want you to feed him. Making an issue over this need is as foolish as making an issue over his "need to do it himself." We all have days when we'd like someone else to "cook the dinner" or "do the dishes," so respect his request when he wants to be fed. The urge toward control over his own life will keep his regression temporary. If you aren't fighting over who gets the spoon you can pleasantly chat with your child as he eats. At least he's in one place and this can be a social time.

In other chapters you will find many suggestions for humoring your child's food choices and promoting a positive feeling about his meals.

TOYS AND ACTIVITIES

You are no longer your child's whole world. He needs to move into the world of objects as well as people. During the second year the involvement in an intense exploration of objects and toys is an important intellectual step. A child who is so absorbed in people that he isn't interested in things is slowed in his development. As your child moves into exploration of the world of objects he may have a special plaything which comforts him at times of stress. It may be a worn teddy bear he has slept with, a blanket, or a doll. This object may be so important to him that he falls apart if he is put to bed or is taken away from home without it. He treats this comfort toy as if it were somewhere between a person and an object. It is a handy transition and should be respected for the importance it has to your child.

During his second year it becomes less easy to substitute one toy for another. Your child has begun to recognize his own belongings and to have favorites among them. He is not at all ready to share with someone of any age. Ownership comes before sharing, and if you protect his rights and possessive feelings he will share sooner than if you do not. Once a child feels very sure that his rights are protected and that he can have his own toys when he needs them, he can begin to "lease" them out briefly. If you insist that your child "share" his toys without regard to his feelings about the toy or the borrower, stop and ask yourself if you set the same high standards for yourself. When a "friend" who is known for bending fenders asks to borrow your new car, do you feel just like your hesitant child? Your child may be very wise not to trust his toddler friend. Toddlers often don't give things back. Your child's feelings about sharing his old favorite teddy bear or the new toy of the day need just as much respect as your feelings about sharing a new car. Gradually your child will want to share at least some of his toys, some of the time. At first the "game" is give and take and sometimes the giving doesn't last very long but, remember, it is a beginning, and like all other concepts, sharing grows imperceptibly. Different occasions demand different "toys." Put out easy toys for tired moments and involved toys for quiet times; put out many toys if two children are to share the premises.

INDOORS AND OUTDOORS

To avoid having an issue every moment of the day over where your child goes and what he touches, take a few hours and "baby-proof" your house. Put poisons and breakables safely up and away. Put pots, pans, and unbreakables down where your child can have the joy of opening doors and drawers and discovering them. Brace tables and cover electric outlets. Find a place in most rooms for a few baby amusements. Now you'll have hours of amusement yourself watching your child explore instead of a year of endless prohibition, "No, no! Don't touch!" He'll grow competent if you emphasize more "cans" than "cannots."

Going outdoors almost every day can make the year much pleasanter. The open spaces mean your toddler will wander farther away. He can still see you; no doors and hallways block his view. There's something wonderful about getting more than an arm's length away from your child. You can see him in a different light and view his progress with a perspective that close proximity denies you.

Play with other children is often more peaceful in a yard or park, away from someone's home turf and favorite possessions. Children may seem to take no notice of each other, but when you get home your eighteen-month-old may give a good imitation of an acquaintance's play. He remembers and he imitates, a feat of symbolism he couldn't have managed a few months ago.

Your relationship with your toddler will be a lot better if you don't expect him to keep pace with you. A stroller will be handy for going to and from the park, because although a toddler can walk to a destination, he is incapable of following someone else's pace. You have to follow his. It's not even a matter of physical capability, but his ability to judge, predict, and follow someone else's lead.

LANGUAGE

Your child's behavior expresses his feelings. Actions, not words, are his mode of communication. His nonverbal "conversations" are composed of smiles, hugs, and howls. Your child won't even know that he feels "mad," "sad," or "happy." He is just in the sway of powerful unnamed feelings. Your words won't reach him when he's overwhelmed, so keep saying, "You're 'mad' or 'sad' or 'afraid.' " It will be a long time before he can understand and use words when he has feelings, but your naming them is the first step.

Your child will not use any words with children other than siblings until he is two or three, and then only sparingly. He will speak through you for several years to come, for you are his interpreter; his words are hard for others to understand and have meanings only his intimates can fathom.

Two- and Three-Year-Olds: Your Child Finds Words for the World

The circle becomes larger and your child reaches out to relate to more and more people. His control over his feelings grows gradually as you support him in his growth. Nature has a way of taking care of parents' mental health because children's growth occurs in spurts. The rough times alternate with the plateaus for consolidation of progress. As a baby magazine article said twenty-five years ago, "The crying days are the growing days!" Some texts suggest the half-years are the difficult times. Other texts suggest that the even years are the trying ages and that the odd years are more relaxed. Your child won't follow anybody's norm but he *will* change from year to year. When he's growing nothing stays still, not even his feelings. Gradually your control of him will slacken and he will have learned to control himself. He will take his first giant steps during his third and fourth years.

PEOPLE

As your child begins to see himself as a creature apart, he reaches out to others: grandparents, neighbors, the grocer, strangers. He begins to separate himself from you when he's two by way of opposition to your ideas and plans. "No" is the cry that defines his person; "mine" is the cry that defines his possessions. When he's three the "I" of his ego-centrism will have become "we." He will spend more time trying to please you and less bucking you. You need to accept your two-year-old's feelings, but you will limit many of his actions. You will be pressing him to grow up in toilet training and in controlling some of his own behaviors. He will cooperate much of the time and you need to praise his progress toward civilization. When he digs in his heels he may throw a tantrum or express fears and anxieties because this struggle for power over himself threatens his security with all-important you. It's an exciting year in personality growth and the less you tangle the better off you both are. Give your child control and choice where it seems reasonable and be firm and decisive where you cannot. When you feel in control of him you can admire his "bossy" swagger. He's barely three feet tall, but he has carved out his own territory and by now part of it is in your heart. At three years of age he wants to please and is interested in helping and imitating you. If he's worked out the worst storms of separation he can be with you and away from you with much less stress than at two.

Two-year-olds with their ability to focus best on one thing at a time or one idea at a time, often do better with one parent at a time. So keep your family spirit but make routines of dressing, eating, bathing, and bedding a one-on-one situation. Even an occasional outing with one parent will work better for your child without the conflict of whose hand to hold or whose lap to sit on. Three-year-olds are able to relate to more than one parent or person at a time but still enjoy the closeness and the special feeling when sharing an activity with one parent. Two-year-olds with their rigidity and love for routine need the "bath person" always to do the bath and the "bed person" always to do the bed, but three-year-olds like an occasional job switch, noticing and appreciating the different styles and techniques of Mommy and Daddy.

Siblings either younger or older find two-year-olds exasperating and three-year-olds good companions. A two-year-old can't be trusted with a baby because he lacks self-control and feels jealous of anyone who interferes with his possessive feelings about toys or parents. Older children are usually intolerant of tiny two-year-old tyrants. Three-year-olds can be fine companions, often helpful and sweet to a baby and happy followers of older siblings. They are old enough to follow instructions and have a long enough attention span to "play games."

Five- or six-year-old children in the neighborhood can often play successfully with your two-year-old. They are big enough to awe him and haven't the backlog of rivalry that siblings have suffered. Two-year-olds playing together need a nearby adult to oversee. They are interested in each other although still too self-centered to share. Their best play is a kind labeled parallel play; they play side by side with identical toys, often imitating each other but rarely interacting. Interactions if they come could be a rage over a toy, a bite to settle possessions, or a body laid over a toy to define, "It's mine."

If three-year-olds have had experience playing near other children they are ready to cooperate for brief periods of time as long as the child they are playing with is on the same level and of the same generous spirit. Even with a child as young as two, it is easy for a teacher to tell if the child has had play experience with a sibling or friend. The child who has been around other children can devise strategies, substituting toys or pretending when there isn't enough to go around.

At two or three, children still can't understand feelings. Feelings are more abstract even than time or volume concepts, but your child will begin to notice the consequences of feeling in other people. When a playmate cries your child may frown or cry too. When you are sad or low your child may pat you lovingly or fetch his blanket and offer it to you. This is a tender moment; he is moving out of his own sphere toward other people.

Two- and three-year-olds sometimes have sinking spells and lapse back to earlier days, asking to be dressed or fed. If you support instead of bemoan his retreats, your child will struggle onward and upward to claim further independence. The certainty that you'll be there, no matter how far he goes, helps him cherish his new-found independence.

Besides real live playmates, the houses of two- and three-year-olds are often peopled with imaginary playmates. These mental representations are creatures your one-year-old could never have thought of or talked about. The world is still half-real, half-magic to your young child and it is quite common for a two- or three-year-old to have a friend or two conjured up out of his fantasy life. You will be admonished to "Set a place for Biggie, he's hungry" or "Don't sit on Lucas, he's in that chair." These characters often come with a full set of qualities, sometimes qualities your child would like to rid himself of. A "Biggie" in our household almost got left behind on vacation because in spite of scolding from his almost three-year-old master he kept "going in his pants." Just in time "Biggie" managed toilet training and we left his diapers behind as we did his master's. These creatures of imagination serve a useful purpose and fade away when their function is over. In our households we still cherish their memories for they betoken our children's struggles to grow up.

There are a number of crises that may enter any child's life: illness, hospitalization, a family death, divorce of parents. Each age reacts differently toward these crises; the reaction depends on the child's emotional and cognitive level. Separation from his parents or disturbance and change in his relationship with his parents is most difficult for a child to bear. Without past experience or a sense of the future a child does not interpret these events as an adult would. He only perceives the change in his own world. If the changes are bad and the adults around him are preoccupied or upset, in his egocentric view he assumes some action of his own must have brought about the distress in his parents. With time your child will learn to understand your feelings and their causes, but at two or three he can't even understand his own.

BODY

Growing awareness of himself as a separate person means a growing awareness of his own body and the bodies of other people. Toilet training is often accomplished not only to please you but in imitation of a parent or an older sibling.

Awareness of self and of others brings the first recognition of the difference in the anatomy of boys and girls, a beginning of several years of curiosity and wonder at the discovery of the differences. You will need to talk to your child about the differences in the sexes so your daughter won't assume she has lost something or your son fear that his penis might disappear. At two or three you have your first chance to tell your child how happy you are that you have a boy or a girl child.

Two- and three-year-olds may have a number of fears and anxieties about dirt, blood, noises, animals, the dark, or strangers. Your child cannot yet separate the real world from the world in his dreams, nightmares, and imagination. These fears and concerns are very real to him. One by one you must help him conquer the anxieties that are a normal part of growing up by accepting his fear, by reassuring him that you will help him, and by telling him that the time will come when he will no longer be afraid of these things. Fears are outgrown just as clothes are. Many two- or three-year-olds have a special concern about "dirt." They exaggerate cleanliness and won't get dirty in any way, even with paints and clay at nursery school. They are so recently toilet trained and are trying so hard to stay clean in this way that they overdo and overextend their tidiness. Don't dismay, the same child will be champion of mud-pie making at four. Body hurts and blood are particularly frightening to a two- or three-year-old. He thinks his whole self may flow out of the cut or hole in his finger or knee. This thought is not too illogical, for look what happens to a balloon or a stuffed animal when it gets a hole. The kisses you used to use to repair hurts are temporarily replaced by Band-

Aids. For a year you will probably have to cover his every wound with tape or bear his anxiety as he looks at his scratches and fears the worst. One of our children wore Band-Aids from upper lip to belly button for a few months, a small price to pay for a three-year-old's peace of mind. Many of the other fears of two- and three-year-olds have been mentioned in other chapters. Each fear must be resolved in the same way, with your understanding, your reassurance, and the passage of time.

Along with body consciousness comes use of the body as a source of pleasure or a tension outlet. Some children still suck their thumbs at age two, and at three most children explore their own genitals and masturbate. Just as in all other interests, your child will move on to other focuses in the world if you don't make a giant fuss over his normal expression or curiosity.

CLOTHING

The clothes won't "make the man" at two or three unless they are easy to pull on and off. Your child will urgently want to "do it myself" and this calls for a wardrobe of slacks with elastic and shirts without buttons. Perhaps all these clothes are less chic than zippered, buttoned, or hooked-and-eyed outfits, but the beauty is that your child can manage them. Clothes he can manage himself will make dressing another issue removed from the list of possible daily struggles and give him that "I can do it" ego boost. Easy to manage pants or skirts vastly accelerate toilet training too.

FOOD

For two- or three-year-olds mealtime can be a prime social time. Your child can manage to feed himself adequately and eat the same food as the rest of the family. When his hunger is abated he can talk well enough to be part of simple family conversations. When his mouth and hands are full he may even enjoy listening to other people talk.

TOYS AND ACTIVITIES

Play moves from the simple examination and manipulation of objects of the toddler stage to increasingly imaginative and symbolic play. A toddler drops blocks from his high chair or crib to see what happens; his play develops out of curiosity about the things in his world. A two- or three-year-old is beyond this primitive stage and begins to use toys in the way they were designed—blocks are used for building, not tossing, most of the time. Watch for this new level of development in your child's play. You will see dolls and animals that were crawled over or chewed upon in earlier months suddenly hugged, rocked, or tenderly tucked into bed. Your child's "pretend" will start with realistic models: a doll, a toy cup, or a toy telephone. The toy will suggest the play, and the symbolic representation of reality in your child's play will be brief. He will thrust the cup to baby for a quick sip and his telephone conversation will be limited to "Hello . . . good-bye." It may not seem like a big step to you, but in only two or three years your child is able to use toys as symbols for *real* babies, tea cups, or telephones and to comprehend their functions. As your child becomes experienced in this kind of play he will express more and more of his feelings and his notions about the social experiences he has had. For a child this kind of play is a way to experiment, to try new roles, to be in charge. For a parent this kind of play is a revelation. If you look and listen carefully you will learn a lot about your child's special feelings and ideas. As you observe your child at play you may notice that your child at one time or another may use a shell as a cup or a block as a telephone. Be proud of his creativity and ability to substitute; your child has reached another level of symbolic play where the representation of objects is even more abstract.

Two-year-olds seem to race ahead in their own level of play, but their play with others is not yet very developed. They need time and experience to help them grow socially, but you can help your two-year-old "play" with others by providing the appropriate materials. Two-year-olds play best with these:

- Fluid materials such as sand and water. These materials share easily because it's hard to define "yours" and "mine" in a pile of sand or puddle of water.
- Identical toys. One fire engine or one baby doll spells trouble for two two-year-olds. Either put away the solos or find two of something. If you're off to visit a friend take along your kiddy car or trike so each child is equipped. There will probably still be tussles over the red truck or blue truck, but having "one" for each child cuts down on the number of altercations.
- Many toys of one kind. With lots and lots of blocks, pebbles, or boxes everybody has enough. Two-year-olds can't count or estimate three or five pinecones or toy cars; as long as everybody has a pile to call his own it's OK.

Three-year-olds have a budding interest in other children and will be less focused on "my" toys. If your child has had exposure to other children he may even give his "friend" some of his toys in order to interest his friend in playing with him. Three-year-olds will work out simple schemes to play together: "Drive the truck to my house. I'll put blocks in your truck," or "Let's make a garage." The play is not very complicated or long lasting but it is the beginning of the sophisticated and imaginative play that groups of four- and five-year-olds will engage in.

INDOORS AND OUTDOORS

Many misconceptions still dominate your child's view of the world. In his first year your child learns that objects existed apart from his own action upon them. Armed with a sense of permanence of objects in the second year, he learns much about their attributes. Yet he still does not see the world as adults do. He endows objects and phenomena in the world with human qualities, believing that the happenings in his world are purposeful. The table he knocks against is seen as hitting him, the moon follows him as he walks at night. Whatever moves is thought to be "alive," be it a car or a tree in the wind. Gradually the world becomes less magical, more sensible and stable. When your child is two or three you will see him react again and again to things as if they too had feelings. He still sees himself as the center of the universe; even inanimate objects seem to him to have purposes which relate to him. As adults we revert to these primitive notions when in times of stress we hit the table we have just cracked an ankle on or kick our car when it "refuses" to start. Though we are not confused in reality, we feel at those moments as if the inanimate world is against us, and we retaliate. Your child does not understand these realities and many of his fears and reactions stem from the mystery of a universe whose motivations he does not understand.

Dreams and nightmares are often accepted as being real. Your child's thoughts and feelings seem powerful and overwhelming. It takes a long time to learn that just because you think angry thoughts, bad things don't happen—especially when sometimes they do! An angry child who hurts himself accidentally often assumes this is punishment for his bad feelings. You can't persuade your child to give up feelings and beliefs he is barely aware of, but he does need you at his side as he unravels the mysteries that surround him.

Part of the stability of the world for your child will be having a place in the family. This place is in part defined by the functions he can perform for the family. In *Childhood and Society** author Erik Erikson

* Erik H. Erikson, *Childhood and Society* (New York: W. W. Norton and Co., Inc., 1964).

describes an anthropologist's visit to an Indian village. An old grand-father asks a child of three to close a heavy door, a difficult task but one she is just capable of doing. Erikson reflects on an Indian culture where a child moves from stage to stage with expected achievement. The Indian boy's first bird kill is received with the same gravity and respect that his first hunted buffalo will be when he is grown. In the complexity of our culture it is difficult for a small child to feel that he is an important part of his family and gradually of society. Through his play, your child will try to re-create and understand the world around him, but he needs concrete ways to make contributions to his family. Throughout *Growing Wisdom, Growing Wonder* there are suggestions for household tasks in which your child can participate. If your child's cooking creation is an integral part of dinner, if his shoe fetching has actually helped you get on your way, if he can make the baby laugh while you get a package ready for the mail, then he will begin to sense that he is an essential part of his family. Performing tasks like these will increase your child's self-esteem. The two- or three-year-old who likes himself most of the time will go out into the world expecting to like other people.

LANGUAGE

Perhaps the most useful phrase to use with your two- or three-year-old is "I know how you feel." The more you can understand, define, and accept his feelings the more he can understand them himself. You will have to put the words in his mouth, verbally walk him through his own feelings, labeling them for him. "You were mad at your brother when he stopped pulling your wagon," "You were mad and sad when Mommy and Daddy went out to dinner," "You were afraid when you heard the bulldozer coming." Your two-year-old will rarely use words rather than actions, but if he's had his feelings labeled at age two, your three-year-old will begin to express them in words.

There are a number of phrases you can use to help your child grow in wisdom:

- "I can't let you" means you are really in charge. If you set the limits, he knows he can push hard but that you won't let him go too far.
- "You can do it." "You are a good. . . ." Just as he has begun to recognize his image in the mirror, your view of him is the reflection of his growing self-image. Let him know his strengths and capabilities in words he can understand so he sees himself as a good block builder, trike rider, or furniture polisher.

- "I like the way you. . . ." By praising his actions you are further defining his positive self-image.
- "I know you'll be able to . . . when you are older." By giving him the feeling that he'll grow in capability you give him the hope that he'll gain control over his actions. It will be a self-fulfilling prophecy.

Choices are often hard for two-year-olds. His efforts to define himself by being definite about everything cause him to move back and forth, unable to choose between vanilla or chocolate. Sometimes you have to choose for him, as the language of your two-year-old is punctuated by "Nos." His "Nos" are so constant that he forgets and says "No" when you offer him the choice of vanilla or chocolate ice cream. Remember his "Nos" are a way of saying "I am me; I have power" and help him when he overdoes it. You will want to say "No" as infrequently as you can. You will have heard it enough from him! You will have to oppose him at many a juncture, for his self-centered demands are often impossible. When you set a limit for two- or three-year-olds try to walk them through the possible; for example, "I can't let you take the baby's cracker, but you can get one from the box." Your "No" is like pulling the rug out from under him, but your positive suggestion may channel his energies in another direction. Encourage him to use words:

- "I want" or "I need." Once he can recognize his own needs and put them into words he will begin to recognize other people's wants and needs too.
- "I like" or "I don't like." Ask him his opinion of things, give him choices on the days when he can handle choices.
- The names of many things and people in his world. He will say simple two- or three-word sentences. When he names things incorrectly, calling the horse a "doggie," you can help him extend his vocabulary by saying, "You're right, that looks like a dog but that's a horse. It's bigger than a dog." In this way you can lead him to a larger vocabulary without making him afraid of using words because they might be wrong.

Observing your child's growth of language is like having a window to his mind. Listen to his words and enjoy his growing perceptions.

Four- and Five-Year-Olds: Your Child Begins to Order His World

Four- and five-year-olds are venturing out into the neighborhood and the community more and more. Their experiences with other people in different settings gives them a new view of themselves and their effects on other people. With their exposure to new people in new settings they are beginning to notice some of the exceptions to the rules they learned as two- or three-year-olds. In Tommy's house you can wipe peanut butter fingers on your jeans, but at Grandma's house you use fancy linen napkins. In Betsy's house you can watch television whenever you want but in Jane's house you must ask first. With each experience your child will be cataloguing feelings and relationships. Your child is not yet

ready to walk in another's shoes, but he is noticing the many ways of feeling and reacting to situations.

PEOPLE

Being a parent makes you constantly reassess your own feelings. You know that your four- or five-year-old has you under a magnifying glass and is observing your reactions to people and events. He notices the shudder you try to hide as the spider crawls by. He senses the anger behind your smile when the car pool is late for school in the morning. Don't let this awesome responsibility get you down; trying to mask feelings won't work for either of you. Honesty is generally the best policy. Four- and five-year-olds already have some notion that parents aren't perfect, so your confessions won't shake him. It may also help him to understand that it is alright to have feelings and fears.

Four- and five-year-olds need rules and boundaries, but not too many. Keep your prohibition list short and primarily based on safety if you want it to work. You will determine your child's limits based on your personality and his and on your mutual environment. Matches are forbidden for all, but street crossing would depend on the setting. Four-year-olds are cocky and confident and often attempt something beyond their abilities. Their bravado makes them hard to live with if you take them too seriously. They need a little elbow room to flex the muscles of their personality. Endure or ignore misdemeanors, bathroom words, and back talk when you can. Head-on confrontations only make matters worse with a four-year-old. Take your stand on a few positions firmly and then take a tip from experienced nursery-school teachers of four-year-olds and manage your child in more effective ways with a joke, a new word, or a new idea. Five-year-olds are compliant. If they have been allowed to spread their wings a bit and assert themselves at four, they are now able to abide by the rules of home, school, and society most of the time. Dealing with authority takes all of the childhood years. There are times of accepting authority and times of defying authority. The process of adapting one's own needs and feelings to the needs and feelings of others takes time. Don't feel that this all has to be squared away in the preschool years.

Gradually your child will learn that feelings and thoughts and the deeds he does are two different matters. At four and five years fantasy life is so vivid and rich that it is often frightening. As he grows bigger his feelings grow stronger. He experiences the warmth of sexual feelings and the fears and guilt that often accompany these feelings. Four years old is the age of Freud's famous Oedipus and Electra complexes. Little boys wish to marry their mothers and do away with their fathers. Little girls want to marry their fathers and regard their mothers as the chief impediment to this blissful future. The feelings are neither a joke nor a nightmare; they are just part of growing up. Little boys and girls learn to give up the romance but keep tender feelings for Mom and Dad. They learn to identify with and imitate the parent of their own sex. Treating your child's feelings with dignity will help him reveal them and grow through them. You too must remember that his words are not deeds, understand how he feels, and let him know that he can express his feelings in words but that you won't let him *do* anything he will regret.

Brothers and sisters are a pain and a pleasure. It is fun to have a live-in playmate when no one else is around, yet when a friend is over, little brother is a tag-along or third wheel. It's nice to show off a new baby sister all plump and pink. The emphasis is on "Look what belongs to me," but when the baby gets presents and he doesn't, it's a pain. Absence makes the heart grow fonder for siblings. Separation can work wonders. Spanking, yelling, and threats have little effect on family feuds and leave everyone feeling exhausted and guilty. A few minutes or hours of isolated play recharge everyone's batteries, and your children will embrace each other after the confinement. Too much togetherness can cause friction in any group of people. So plan your children's day with a few islands of time and space alone. All siblings have tangles as a part of normal growing up. Your child's rivalry with his siblings will give him skills in handling other people, his siblings, and his friends. Often the rivalry is at its fiercest in front of parents in order to win their attention. Out of sight the siblings may solve their own conflicts. The distance you can put between you and your children depends on the age and the match of the combatants.

Separation is a big help in preserving sanity, but in calmer times your children also need some help in understanding and handling the behavior of siblings. An eight-year-old can begin to understand that different ages are capable of different things and can admire a four-year-old's drawing for what it is, and not compare it to one he could do. A four-year-old can begin to understand that toddlers are easily distracted and that it's better to point a brother in another direction than to say "No, No" all the time. You may feel like a psychology professor conducting group sessions but your guidance will help your children handle their feelings and relationships more effectively. Dealing with the natural daily upheavals between brothers and sisters prepares your child for his relationship with others in the future.

Avoid one of the major pitfalls in being a parent: don't try to treat your children exactly the same. If you think you are and say you are, your children will find some measurable way to prove you wrong! One mother we know with boys who looked alike and who were close in age always gave her sons identical gifts, trying to be fair and hoping to reduce sibling rivalry. This approach proved disastrous because inevitably there was a tear on page five of one of the "identical" coloring books, leaving one boy yelling "unfair." Treat each child as an individual. Buy your animal lover a book on horses and your vehicle lover a book on cars, and if one complains that his book is shorter, say, "But you like. . . . " If there is a wide age gap between siblings you can expect your older child to be more understanding and responsible if he is treated slightly differently, with the privilege of an extra half-hour at bedtime, or a talking session during baby's nap time about his upcoming Halloween costume. This helps your four- or five-year-old feel big. If your four- or five-year-old is the youngest in a family, this individual approach works just as well. By having certain guidelines for each child and each age you are telling your four- or five-year-old that you expect different things of different ages and he need not exhaust or frustrate himself trying to keep up with his eight-year-old brother. You like him for what he is and what he can do now.

Friends are special to four- and five-year-olds. Their conversations are filled with "My friend . . . this" and "My friend . . . that." Hugs, holding hands, or sitting side by side cement the relationship. "Friends" love to wear matching boots or bows and have matching sandwiches and drinks. Your four- or five-year-old will learn a great deal from children his own age. He will learn to whistle and to swear, but the good outweighs the bad. Your child will learn the give and take of friendship and the joy of togetherness. He will share many a giggle and tussle in his new relationship. He will learn what works and what doesn't work when playing with a friend or a group of friends. You may have selected his playmates for his first years of life, but once he is out in the neighborhood or in school he will select his own friends. His friend may be the classroom "cut-up" or a quiet little dumpling of a girl, but your child has made the choice.

Some four- and five-year-olds are adept at socializing, others need more help in learning how to be a friend. You can help your child by:

- Timing—knowing when you should step in to offer a suggestion, a prop, a snack, or a change of pace
- Being sensitive to his special style of socializing. Children have preferences for one friend alone or a group all at once just as some adults like an intimate dinner and others a cocktail party crowd.
- Observing the leader and follower roles he assumes. Be sure your child has a chance to both direct the action and follow another's lead. A steady diet of either is not healthy for social and emotional growth.
- Acting as "hostess" to his group of playmates and building bridges between children just as you would when you have a group of adults to dinner. With children you need to be very concrete, "Jim, you and Joe both have new wagons. I'll bet he'd like to see yours," or "Sally, you and Sue both have baby sisters. Tell Sue the funny thing your baby did."

- Telling him about other people's feelings. "Johnny was happy when you let him play with your truck. Look, Susie is sad because she wants a turn." Explaining feelings of others to your child is not the same as asking him, "How would you feel if . . . ?" Your words are the labeling of the concepts "sad" or "angry" so that your child will recognize these feelings in others as well as in himself. A four- or five-year-old has no idea how he would "feel if. . . ." He can only manage a real, not a hypothetical, situation. Piaget believes this is not possible until a child is beyond the egocentric pre-operational period at about age seven. It's at the same age that your child can manage to take the perspective of a person sitting opposite him and imagine what that person sees. Before age seven he can only envision and describe his own point of view.
- Making sure the other child is on the same level of play in order to en-sure some success. A four- or five-year-old can tolerate a two-year-old for a short period of play because he knows that two-year-olds are "babies" and doesn't expect too much; but a four- or five-year-old expects certain things of his peers. For this age group grabbing toys and pummeling playmates are out, sharing and talking are in. If playmates don't abide by the same rules you have to stay close until they work some out.

Four- and five-year-olds love to do things for others. They are not altruistic, they just love secrets and surprises. The joy of giving rather than receiving develops slowly. Accept your child's motivation and en-courage his interest:

- Helping you plan the family birthday parties. Like Perle Mesta your child will think endlessly about the motif, food, and decoration.
- Making greeting cards and wrapping gifts for holiday giving. Any grand-parent or doting aunt would rather receive a handmade or hand-wrapped treasure anyway.
- Baking brownies for Daddy or big brother in celebration of a Friday or a soccer victory. Your baker is willing as long as the finished product doesn't leave the house and he gets a piece too!
- Painting a picture for baby brother. If the baby is still at the looking, not touching, stage, so much the better. A four- or five-year-old wants an ap-preciative audience for his work, not someone who will taste it or tear it to shreds.

BODY

The sense of self develops as body skills grow. Adults don't know which of their friends can skip, "skin-the-cat," or ride a bike, but four- and five-year-olds do. The leaders in nursery school and kindergarten groups are often the children who can run the fastest or climb the highest. Fortunately for the less athletically inclined among us, this standard changes a bit in grade school, and although physical prowess is admired, so are "school skills" and "social skills."

Four-year-olds are often frustrated in their efforts to master the physical feats in the world. A stuck jacket zipper or a twisted pair of pants that won't come down on the way to the bathroom will produce shrieks and wails. Five-year-olds seem calm and confident by comparison. They can manage their bodies most of the time in play, eating, and dressing, and they seem to sit back and enjoy their successes for a bit before they move on to new challenges.

Progress in a child's development means moving from dependence to independence. A child moves in the general direction of independence, but there are many peaks and valleys along the way. An earache or fight with a friend at school may be enough to cause a temporary pause in progress. An occasional lapse in behavior or performance is a good thing; it keeps both you and your child flexible. If you understand your child's needs and tie your five-year-old's shoe on a day when he is "all thumbs" he may understand when you say you are too tired to fix his broken toy.

Your child will respond to stress in his own way. He is generally able to cope more and more but responds physically to many feelings as part of normal growth. Your four- or five-year-old may do any or all of the following:

- Speed up his motor activity, running in circles, giggling loudly, or using silly talk
- Need to urinate when he is upset or excited
- Get stomach pains
- Have nightmares
- Bite his nails
- Pick his nose
- Blink his eyes

Both four- and five-year-olds have fears of vomiting or bathroom accidents, especially in public places. They feel grown-up and hate these signs of lost control. They need adult reassurance that the situation is temporary.

CLOTHING

One nursery school teacher we know was approached by a frazzled young mother seeking advice about a "serious problem." She and her strong-willed daughter were at loggerheads at the start of each day. The budding female at four would wear only skirts or dresses, while the mother insisted upon pants. From our experience, had this same mother insisted on dresses, her daughter would have yelled for pants. This very real problem, which seems trivial from afar, was ruining each day for this family. Clothes for four-year-olds or fourteen-year-olds can become heated issues if you let them. Compromises are possible. Slacks under a skirt or a shirt at the dinner table let parent and child feel reasonably happy without losing face. When compromises fail it's time to review the situation and check your priorities. To babies "on the move" clothes are a nuisance. To two- and three-year-olds, clothes are a sign of independence, "I can do it." "It" may refer to wearing "big boy" underpants or pulling up a zipper. To four- and five-year olds clothes are an extension of their bodies, an extension of themselves. Wearing clothes that say "I am me" becomes very important. Your child's fragile ego needs support more than you need him to look as if he just stepped out of the fashion pages. When your tastes match, clothes don't seem much of an issue, but when your four-year-old son wants to wear a tie and you favor plaid shirts for dressy occasions or your five-year-old daughter wants to wear sneakers with her party dress, the issue looms large. Swallow your pride and lower your standards.

Allow your four- or five-year-old some choices in the color, texture, or style of his clothing and think how remarkable it is that he knows blue from green, smooth from fuzzy, and long from short. Honoring his preferences will nourish his growing identity and independence. A child who is allowed to express his feelings and personality in clothing is easy to spot in a group. He might be sporting a belt around overalls, a sailor's hat indoors and out, or matching wristbands. As with adult fashion setters, this individual is often admired by his peers and "belts over overalls" may become a nursery school fad for a while. Some four- and five-year-olds are so tied into "clothes are me" that they cannot bear to wear communal paint smocks in school or a friend's sweater on a suddenly chilly day.

Hand-me-downs from siblings and friends instead of expensive and quickly outgrown clothing are becoming more and more a way of life. Some children like wearing "Mikey's pants." If they like "Mikey," it's no problem. But others feel like "secondhand Rose." If your child seems less than enthusiastic at the prospect of wearing a hand-me-down, individualize it for him. Four- and five-year-olds love "gingerbread" and "frills" on clothing—the more buttons, embroidery, iron-on patches, or lace the better.

Marriages and friendships would be short-lived if one adult said to another, "That shirt looks terrible with those pants" or "Those colors sure do clash." Children are as sensitive as adults and are devastated when you shudder at their selection and send them back to change. The joy of choosing suddenly disappears. Treat your four- or five-year-old like your best friend or spouse. Spare his feelings, ignore what's hard to ignore, and comment on the successes. If you say "I like the way you combined that striped shirt with those green pants" you will see that same outfit again and again. For some reason it's easier to have our ideas criticized than our taste.

TOYS AND ACTIVITIES

Two-year-olds "play" side by side, noting each other but each doing his own thing. Three-year-olds can play with another child for a short period of time and can share a bit. Four-year-olds really enjoy the company of friends and the spirit of cooperative play. They like toys that take two—a wagon, seesaw, big paper, and big blocks to share together. It may be a boisterous sort of play with lots of stops and starts, but the emphasis is definitely on "togetherness." Four-year-olds like play with more than one friend too. A small group of three or four children can enjoy games and projects like building forts and playing store with a minimum of adult supervision. A four-year-old in a larger group needs the help of a "social director" to channel the play. The large group size may be overwhelming and overstimulating. Birthday parties and preschool programs without a skilled adult to direct the action are doomed to failure. Five-year-olds with a year of small-group experience behind them enjoy larger and larger groups. They can organize groups for play, set up "rules," and handle most of the difficulties themselves. Kindergarten classes usually have a group identity, a sense of "our class" which is not found before this age.

The preschool years are years for doing and creating, and four- and five-year-olds are at the peak. They have enough physical, mental, social, and verbal skills to put their ideas and feelings into action. Dramatic play, with costumes, dolls, or puppets encourages your child to try new roles. Your child visits the dentist one day and the next day every available doll and animal are lined up for oral inspection. Art and music are ways to express feelings and thoughts before your child is old enough to symbolize them in written language. Four-year-olds' artwork is spontaneous and individual, free of the predictable square houses and flowers in neat rows found in five-year-olds' drawings. Four-year-olds create their own songs and dances as they play and enjoy them just as much as someone else's. Five-year-olds prefer to learn traditional folk songs and singing games. Miniature sets of people, buildings, trees, and vehicles appeal to both four- and five-year-olds. They can manage the intricacies of the details and like to re-create the environments they've seen. The arranging and rearranging of scenes make your child feel big and powerful. He has control over a small world. Four- and five-year-olds are proud of all their creative efforts. A two- or three-year-old may not even remember that he painted the picture dutifully carried home from nursery school, but four- and five-year-olds remember their creations and notice how you react to them. A comment to your child about "the pretty green you used" or the "nice arrangement of lines" is more effective than a gushy response about the wonderful "artist" he is. Children sense sincerity. A thoughtful remark about a particular aspect of the work says to your child "I'm paying close attention. I'm interested in what you do." A general remark about the spectacular artist or builder and not the work smacks of insincerity and inattentiveness. It's a fine line to walk; the right amount of response produces more wonderful creations. Too much praise or involvement produces nothing more. The child is afraid he cannot produce another "masterpiece"; he doesn't even know how he did the first one. Display your child's creations thoughtfully. Have your refrigerator-front art gallery change weekly or daily as need be, wear a bead-stringing creation to a meeting, tiptoe carefully around a special block tower for a day or two, have the carpentry project as a centerpiece for a while.

Your child experiences the sights, sounds, colors, shapes, textures, numbers, and speeds of the world and then re-creates them in his imaginative work with block, art, music, and dramatic play. The ability to re-create, fantasize, and imagine means the ability to abstract and conceptualize. "Pretending" is remembering, thinking, and creating all wrapped up in one. In play your four- or five-year-old is trying to sort out reality from fantasy. From time to time he will have some difficulty distinguishing one from the other. For this reason, television often confuses a young child as he attempts to sort out the world. On film action is fast, situations are created and resolved with a minimum of effort. Feelings are often ignored and physical violence is emphasized. Four- and five-year-olds need to be in real situations as participants not observers. They need the opportunity to use their minds and bodies to express themselves and solve problems. With friends and activities as an alternative, children rarely choose television. It is too passive and not social enough for four- and five-year-olds.

INDOORS AND OUTDOORS

Encouraging your child to participate fully in family life means a strong sense of self and a few glasses of spilt milk or pieces of chipped china. These "accidents" are necessary evils if your child is allowed the freedom to try and to learn. You will have to be the lenient forgiving one if your four- or five-year-old spills or drops. A young child's sense of justice is rather rigid and he will be as hard on himself as he is on others. If you are accused of a crime, hope that your jury will not be composed of four- and five-year-olds, for there would be no justice tempered with mercy. Piaget's studies on the ethical understanding of young children shows that there is a natural progression of moral development, just as there is of cognitive development. Preschool children with their egocentric view of the world can only look at the results of the crime committed, the concrete act. They are incapable of thinking about motives and intentions. They cannot look at something from another's perspective. To a four- or five-year-old the severity of a crime is based on specifics: the number of apples eaten, the size of mess that was made. To them a big mess made by accident is worse than a small mess made intentionally! The result is what they judge. With time and experience in the years ahead your child will develop a more complex view of morality.

Throughout *Growing Wisdom, Growing Wonder* there is an emphasis on accepting and enjoying your child as an individual. Parenting would be dull indeed if all little Greggs or Knotts or Smiths or Jones were punched out with a rubber stamp. One of the special pleasures in being a parent is watching your child's particular reactions to the world. Each child is different, each situation is unique. Value the differences and show your appreciation in your response to each child's special interests. One of us had a kindly neighbor who loved to chat with one of our kindergarteners. He asked the neighbor many questions and she was as serious about finding him answers as he was in his asking. One day he asked her about a fungus on one of the trees. She knew nothing of fungi but she delighted in a little boy's questions and invited him to tea the next day with her friend from the museum who was an expert on molds and fungi. This child is now in the banking business, having left fungi far behind, but he still remembers having his special interest honored by adults. Whether your child shows passing curiosity about baseball or baking see that he has an adult to share his interest from time to time.

In each chapter there are suggestions for things to do and places to visit. The idea is not to trudge from spot to spot but to select the activities and trips that would especially interest your child. It is the way of childhood that interests will change from time to time. Some of your child's interests will follow yours and some of his interests may cause you to develop new ones.

LANGUAGE

It's important to exercise the language of feeling, for unless children have words to use they usually resort to pulls, pushes, shoves, and howls. You can label the feelings your child has so he will know what he is feeling and what the name of that feeling is. After a social disaster you can model the words he should have used: "You can tell him you're mad. . . . Tell him you need your truck. . . . Tell him you're sad when he runs off." Pretty soon you'll hear your child saying "I'm mad" and hear his friend reply "I'm mad too," and in a moment you may see them hand in hand skipping down the walk. An increase in the use of language will bring a decrease in physical action. Words begin to get things out. Words for feelings have a magic beyond the words for other concepts. You can point to a "tall" tree, a "soft" chair, or a "red" rose, but feelings need to be talked about. The language of touch speaks first, but as your child grows older he will need to tell other people when he cares, loves, is mad, or is afraid. The language of feelings becomes the language of relationship. Talk about feelings and control of feelings develop together. Control of feelings promotes trust and friendship. A child who knows how he feels himself is on his way to understanding other people's feelings. Friendships blossom with four- and five-year-olds' language ability as ideas and plans fly back and forth.

Words have a special power. If you ask your child to express the words for emotions he does not feel they lose some of their power. Asking your child to say he's "sorry" when he's not is breeding insincerity. It's better for you to say you're sorry that he did whatever you feel is wrong and wait until he shares your feeling than have him mouth something he doesn't feel. In the meantime you will control and limit his actions.

There are many ways to talk to four- and five-year-olds which make them feel good about themselves and in turn ready them to reach out to other people. Ask your child some questions:

- "What were the happy things you did today?" If he has a hard time thinking of things, you can remember some happy things your child did and remind him that he fed the dog and made the baby smile.
- "What is your favorite color, food, friend, letter, number, or name?" Having favorites is the fashion at four or five.
- "What do you think of this?" It is flattering to him to have you ask his view and it helps him learn to make judgments. When your child continually seeks your approval of his every action and product try to get him to evaluate his own drawings or buildings. "What do you think of it yourself?" He needs to learn to please himself and judge what he does best.
- "What do you think he is feeling?" Begin by looking at other people and when your child becomes a good reader of smiles, frowns, and worried looks ask him about expressions in books or magazine pictures.

Good talkers require good listeners; part of the time you need to be an attentive eyeball-to-eyeball listener. Listen to his tales of what went on during the day. You'll be amused that in his egocentric view he can't imagine what you need to know about what he saw or did. He will leave out essential details, assuming you know what he knows. Eager parents want to hear about their child's day. Two- and three-year-olds often can't remember anything beyond the flavor of the day's juice. Four- and five-year-olds sometimes remember but don't want to share the events of the day. At last they have a life of their own that you don't know about. Listen to his language. Sometime he'll mispronounce and misname. When he mispronounces you don't have to "correct" him, just pronounce it right yourself. When he misnames you can extend his thinking saying, "That was a good idea, you thought it was a horse. Zebras are like horses but they have stripes and we see them in zoos because they are animals from another country." You don't have to reject the good thoughts in his guess, you can expand his naming and classifying skills beginning with what he does know. Listen to his questions, and answer them as best you can. Remember the answers he seeks are in terms of his own understanding. Leave the chemical, physical, and astronomical explanation for his schoolteachers and answer questions in a practical way. He'll ask "What is that?" Answer with the name of the object and mention its use. He'll ask "Where is Brazil?" Answer in terms of places and distances he has experienced, for example, "Faraway like our trip to New York." He'll ask "When?" Answer in terms of time he can comprehend, for example, "The day after your school play." Don't answer "In a week." He'll ask "Why are clouds?" Answer in terms of functions he can understand, for example, "To water the ground." Don't answer, "Clouds are collections of particles of moisture." He'll ask "How do robins sing?" Answer in terms of actions he understands, not in abstract scientific explanations, for example, "With parts of their bodies just as we talk with parts of ours." Don't answer "Their tracheas do this and that." Ask him sometimes what he thinks the answers are to his questions of what, where, when, why, and how? You will have some surprising peeks into his ways of looking at the world. As you share your child's world you too will grow in wisdom and in wonder.

Chapter 16

How to Use This Book with the Exceptional Child: Handicapped, Gifted, or Talented

*W*E KNOW PEOPLE with severe handicaps who are competent and confident adults achieving and contributing to the world. We know bright and talented people without known handicaps who never achieve or contribute anything that satisfies them. What makes the difference? The child or adult with an "I can do it" attitude is a winner, a source of pride to himself and his family. The new federal access laws as well as the education and recreation programs that are burgeoning acknowledge the capabilities of our handicapped, gifted, and talented populations.

In *Growing Wisdom, Growing Wonder* we have shown the framework of all children's learning, the exceptional child included. All children learn by progressing through stages:

- Starting with doing and moving to thinking
- Starting with the concrete and moving to the abstract
- Starting with the simple and moving to the complex
- Starting with one single plaything and moving to combinations of playthings
- Starting with solitary play and moving to play in a group
- Starting with dependence and moving to independence

The parent of a handicapped, gifted, or talented child often feels overwhelmed, not knowing where to begin, or how a child's exceptionality may affect his learning. A good beginning, we feel, is knowing what and how all children learn and in seeing the many ways there are to learn the same concept. This approach gives parents a sense of what they can do to provide the experiences a child might miss because of his handicap or need because of his gifts and talents. *Growing Wisdom, Growing Wonder* describes many opportunities to turn the day's routines such as eating, bathing, dressing, and housekeeping into learning experiences for children. This approach should be especially welcome to parents of children whose handicaps require extra family time and money.

Every person, handicapped or not, has preferred channels for learning. By watching your child, you can discover his stronger channels to emphasize when you provide him with learning experiences. Everyone has strengths, weaknesses, and uneven development. A physically handicapped child may be far ahead in language development. A deaf child may be a star athlete.

If your child is physically handicapped you can use *Growing Wisdom, Growing Wonder* to become aware of those experiences he needs. If he cannot go out into the world to explore you can bring objects to him or take him to those experiences he cannot reach alone. Since your child will be less able to get into a variety of positions in space, you will have to adapt the activities in that chapter to his capabilities.

The parents of a visually impaired or blind child can use the activities throughout the book to entice their child to interact with his environment. By being aware of the activities that vision would lead other children to explore, you can use his senses of touch, sound, taste, and smell to lead him into discovery of the world around him. Note that an infant's memory span is short and that touch or sound must be continuous, not intermittent, to hold his attention. See the section on infants in Chapter 4 describing how objects are "out of sight, out of mind" and adapt to "out of hearing, out of mind," or "out of touch, out of mind." Blind children learn color words as one of the label words of the sighted world even though they don't experience color.

The parents of a hearing-impaired child can use the activities in the book in conjunction with the communication of body language and pantomime. The toys and activities sections in each chapter will show you how children re-create what they have seen in the world by using blocks, dolls, trucks, cars, crayons, play dough, and role play. You may want to encourage your child to communicate his day in play and pantomime. These activities will help your child move from the concrete to a level of symbolic representation, a step toward the symbolization of language. The language sections in each chapter describe how words are best learned in conjunction with the object, action, or quality expressed.

The parents of a retarded child will find the sequence of activities especially useful. You can begin at your child's level of accomplishment in each area, whatever his age, and introduce him to new challenges when he is ready. Retarded children often learn best if concepts are presented in simple, concrete ways, one at a time, and the text of *Growing Wisdom, Growing Wonder* does just that. Your child may enjoy a good deal of repetition before he moves on to another area of learning.

The parents of an emotionally disturbed child can use the sequence of activities in the book to reduce their child's frustration. You can lead your child toward activities that are simple enough to ensure his success. It will be helpful if you simplify his stimulation, being sure that he has sound, shape, texture, and other experiences one at a time, not in confusion.

The parents of a child with a language handicap can use the sequence in the sound chapter for understanding the communication that precedes language. Through the language activities in every chapter you can enrich your child's receptive vocabulary even though he may have difficulty expressing himself.

A child's learning disabilities often go undetected until he is of school age. Your child's rich and varied experience in early childhood gives him the opportunity to develop every sensory area. If your child is diagnosed as having a visual learning disability you may have already noticed he learns best by listening rather than watching. If he has an auditory problem you can concentrate on the looking and doing activities. If your child has motor coordination problems you can choose appropriate activities from a younger age level.

The parents of an intellectually gifted child can enrich their child's learning by a broad variety of experiences drawn from every chapter. Gifted children progress through the same stages but often move from the concrete to the abstract at an earlier age. The more abstract language games in each section will be especially appropriate for gifted children.

If your child is talented in any one area such as music, art, movement, dance, or leadership, you will want to select more activities in his area of interest. In the chapter on sound you will find many suggestions for a musical child. An artistic child will enjoy the texture and color experiences. A child talented in movement or dance will pursue most of the activities in the chapter on position in space. A child who has special leadership ability may move through the stages in the feelings and relationship chapter at a more rapid rate.

The many areas of exceptionality require specialized resources, medical advice, and educational programs; but day by day you can enrich your child's life giving him a chance to experience whatever is within his capabilities. If the daily emphasis is on discovering the "Can dos," your child will prosper. The Bureau of the Handicapped of the U.S. Department of Education can suggest resources to develop detailed programs for either handicapped, gifted, or talented children. *Growing Wisdom, Growing Wonder* can give you a start in looking at your child's special learning style.

Reference Section: Words for the Basic Concepts Children Need to Know

MOST OF THESE WORDS are not absolute concepts but relative ones. See the many experiences in the chapters which children must have in order to learn these concepts. Real mastery takes all of the preschool years. These words are not of equal difficulty in learning or of equal importance to know. Some concepts take years to master, others take weeks. Some are not fully mastered in the preschool years. But taken all together, in this list appear the concepts that will help a child make sense of his world.

above	begin	cool
across	behind	corner
afraid	below	crooked
after	beside	cube
afternoon	between	curved
all	big	dark
almost	bitter	day
apart	black	diamond
around	blue	double
at the bottom of	both	down
at the same time	bottom	dry
away from	brown	dull
back	by	easy
backward	circle	edge
bad	close to	eight
balance	cold	empty
before	cone	end

equal	less	oval
far	light	over
far from	like	pair
fast	little	part
fat	long	pink
few	loud	purple
finish	love	quick
firm	low	quiet
first	mad	rectangle
five	many	red
flat	melt	right
float	middle	right side up
forward	mine	rough
four	more	round
freeze	morning	sad
friend	most	salty
from	my	second
front	narrow	seven
full	near	several
funny	nearly	share
go	need	sharp
good	next	short
green	next to	shut
gray	night	side
half	nine	sink
happy	noisy	six
hard	none	slanted
heavy	not equal	slick
here	not now	slow
high	nothing	small
hot	now	smooth
in	off	soft
in back of	on	some
in front of	on top of	sour
indoors	one	spicy
inside	open	square
into	orange	start
large	out	stiff
last	out of	stop
later	outdoors	straight
left	outside	sweet

tall	together	want
ten	tomorrow	warm
then	top	wet
there	toward	white
thick	triangle	whole
thin	turns	wide
third	two	wish
three	under	yellow
through	until	yesterday
to	up	zero
today	upside down	

Index

Index